# ANCIENT HIGH TECH

"Based on extensive research including the latest findings, Frank Joseph delivers in this book a comprehensive overview of our ancient ancestors' remarkable achievements, much of them lost to the sands of time. Frank Joseph once again shows why he is a leading expert on ancient civilizations with this impressive book backed up by plenty of evidence. Who would have thought that many of the modern conveniences we take for granted were also enjoyed by our ancient ancestors?!"

DAVID P. JONES, EDITOR AND DIRECTOR OF *NEW DAWN* MAGAZINE

"Frank Joseph is an utterly brilliant, fearless explorer of our ancient hidden past. His books are peerless, mind-bending trips of discovery into the scientific genius of civilizations that once ruled the planet. His dedication to revealing our true history—kept hidden from us by orthodox, grant-fueled 'science' and those who control our world—is unfailingly inspiring. In this, his newest work, he once again guides us on a breathtaking, dazzling journey into the reality of the advanced science and incredible technologies our forebears discovered and used to make their civilizations thrive."

JEFF RENSE, HOST OF THE *JEFF RENSE PROGRAM*

"Impeccably researched, *Ancient High Tech* transports the reader back through history to the remarkable technological achievements of various ancient civilizations around the globe. From the earliest attempts at aviation to refined structural engineering to sophisticated healing therapies, Frank Joseph's comprehensive investigation illustrates that early cultures were much more advanced than generally believed. Each of the progressive societies mastered various forms of technologies and each suffered a similar fate: they collapsed. Perhaps *Ancient High Tech* is a compelling reminder and warning that technology does not make a civilization superior."

BRIT ELDERS, CEO AT SHIRLEYMACLAINE.COM

"Frank Joseph's new book on the amazing technology and early break-throughs of ancient civilizations is a wonder to behold. It includes mind-blowing tangible proof in pictures of physical artifacts that depict everything from ancient heat rays to Byzantium-era hand grenades and early creations for human flight. When the world entered the dark ages of collapsing civilization in both the West and the East, so much of the scientific, technological, and early medical knowledge of the ancients was lost. Frank helps locate the missing pieces for us. Explore this amazing book and its fascinating author at your earliest convenience."

VON BRASCHLER, AUTHOR OF *SEVEN SECRETS OF TIME TRAVEL*

"Frank Joseph is an author of incredible talent and research ability. He is able to find information about topics that no one else can. His writing style is so engrossing, entertaining, and just enjoyable—an excellent way to present research to the general public. I strongly recommend *Ancient High Tech* and any of his other books. Frank Joseph is one of my favorite authors, and I always look forward to a new book of his."

JOHN DESALVO, PH.D., DIRECTOR OF THE GREAT PYRAMID OF GIZA
RESEARCH ASSOCIATION AND AUTHOR OF
*THE LOST ART OF ENOCHIAN MAGIC*

"With *Ancient High Tech,* Frank Joseph has once again created an exceptionally interesting and informative story of our highly advanced ancient ancestors. This book adds significantly to the evidence for advanced sophistication of our ancient ancestors. A master of in-depth research and fact gathering, he's helping us see our ancient past in a new light one book at a time."

ANDRÉE L. CUENOD, AUTHOR OF
*AWAKENING: A JOURNEY OF ENLIGHTENMENT*

"Frank Joseph can be controversial, but he is never anything less than thought-provoking. Written with a discerning eye and a global perspective, when he delves into a topic—be it an Aztec death whistle or the electromagnetic properties of Egyptian pyramids—you are guaranteed a fascinating journey into the past."

DAVID GOUDSWARD, AUTHOR OF
*THE WESTFORD KNIGHT AND HENRY SINCLAIR*

# ANCIENT
# HIGH TECH

## The Astonishing
## Scientific Achievements
## of Early Civilizations

# FRANK JOSEPH

Bear & Company
Rochester, Vermont

Bear & Company
One Park Street
Rochester, Vermont 05767
www.BearandCompanyBooks.com

SUSTAINABLE FORESTRY INITIATIVE    Certified Sourcing
www.sfiprogram.org
SFI-00854

Text stock is SFI certified

Bear & Company is a division of Inner Traditions International

Cataloging-in-Publication Data for this title is available from the Library of Congress

ISBN 978-1-59143-382-8 (print)
ISBN 978-1-59143-383-5 (ebook)

Printed and bound in the United States by Lake Book Manufacturing, Inc.
The text stock is SFI certified. The Sustainable Forestry Initiative® program
promotes sustainable forest management.

10  9  8  7  6  5  4  3  2  1

Text design and layout by Debbie Glogover
This book was typeset in Garamond Premier Pro with Agnostic, Gill Sans MT Pro,
and TT Supermolot Condensed used as display typefaces

Selected material excerpted from *Opening the Ark of the Covenant* © 2007 by
Frank Joseph and Laura Beaudoin used with permission from New Page Books, an
imprint of Red Wheel Weiser, LLC, Newburyport, MA, www.redwheelweiser.com.

To send correspondence to the author of this book, mail a first-class letter to the
author c/o Inner Traditions • Bear & Company, One Park Street, Rochester, VT
05767, and we will forward the communication, or contact the author directly at
**www.ancientamerican.com**.

# Contents

INTRODUCTION    *Ahead of Their Time . . . and Ours*    1

1   *Automation*    7

2   *Human Flight*    19

3   *Ancient Aviation*    28

4   *Preventive Medicine*    37

5   *Surgical Wonders*    45

6   *Therapeutic Achievements*    56

7   *Optics*    68

8   *Modern Marvels from Long Ago*    81

9   *Weapons of Mass Destruction*    97

10   *Wonder Weapons*    109

11   *Children of the Sun*    129

12  **Stone into Glass**                     137

13  **Electric Power**                        148

14  **Organized Lightning**                   163

15  **Inner and Outer Enlightenment**         174

16  **Mega Structures**                       186

17  **Ancient Engineering**                   203

18  **Subterranean Cities**                   221

19  **Tunneling into Antiquity**              232

20  **The Great High-Tech Mystery**           249

21  **Pyramid Power**                         263

AFTERWORD  **Antiquity Reborn**               275

⫷ ⫸

**Notes**                                     277

**Bibliography**                              292

**Index**                                     304

# Ahead of Their Time . . . and Ours

*History, then, should be written in that spirit, with truthfulness and an eye to future expectations, rather than with adulation and a view to the pleasure of present praise. There is your rule and standard for impartial history! If there will be some to use this standard, it will be well, and I have written to some purpose.*

LUCIAN OF SAMOSATA,
*THE WORKS OF LUCIAN OF SAMOSATA,* 170 CE*

The first modern, self-igniting match was invented in 1805 by Jean Chancel, a Parisian chemist. Yet, identical sulfuric matches were in common use among Babylonians thirty-six hundred years before.[1]

The flat surface of an ancient temple wall is sculpted in relief with the roughly twenty-inch-high image of a man in Hindu garb seated on a bicycle. Clearly depicted are standard handlebars, saddle,

---

*Although many readers prefer the use of BC (before Christ) and AD (*anno Domini,* "in the year of our Lord"), the house style of Inner Traditions is to use BCE to mean Before the Common Era (which corresponds to BC) and CE to mean the Common Era (which corresponds to AD).

wheels, spokes, and frame, with a pedal mostly obscured by the rider's left foot. No text accompanies the relief (fig. I.1). The carving appears in Panchavarnaswamy Temple, located in southeastern India, which is cited by name in the *Thevaram,* a seventh-century text written in the ancient Tamil language. Far earlier, the Greek traveler and geographer Claudius Ptolemy personally visited Panchavarnaswamy in about 150 CE, although its construction could be much older.

In any case, the relief sculpture is not a modern addition. Only normal repairs, no renovations or new artwork, were undertaken at the temple in recorded history, according to Indian researcher Praveen Mohar. He also points out that the anomalous bike rider could only have been carved when the stone on which he appears was horizontal, before subsequently being installed to its present vertical position when Panchavarnaswamy was being built millennia ago.[2] Baron Karl von Drais, a civil servant in Baden, Germany, was supposed to have built the first bicycle in 1817. Yet his invention was preceded by nineteen hundred years or more in ancient India.

Figure I.1. The Panchavarnaswamy Temple bicycle.
Photo by Bongan.

In 1999 archaeologists excavating a newly opened Aztec burial site in Mexico City uncovered the remains of a decapitated twenty-year-old sacrificial victim clutching baked-clay objects, one in either hand. Dated to circa 1450 CE, they were small whistles of a kind never before encountered anywhere. When blown, their loud sound was indistinguishable from a man screaming in terrible agony. Since their discovery, many similar so-called death whistles have come to light across Central America (fig. I.2, p. 4). Remarkably, no two are identical. They generate the realistic shrieks of men, women, or children; each one is unique, as though re-creating the voices of particular individuals. Other Mesoamerican whistles reproduce the sounds of jaguars, birds, and a variety of jungle animals with uncanny accuracy.

Scientific laboratory research into these wind instruments reveals their subtle, interior construction, but precisely how the little sound chambers are capable of making such loud, lifelike human- and animal-like cries has not been determined.

"A couple of these instruments we found were broken," archaeologist Paul Healy told the Associated Press, "which was great, because we could actually see the construction of them, the actual technology of building a sound chamber out of paper-thin clay. Still, [the source production of] their exact sounds will likely remain a mystery." Originally, the whistles may have "emitted terrifying sounds to fend off enemies, much like high-tech crowd-control devices available today."[3]

They may have been used as psychological weapons when blown simultaneously by hundreds or even thousands of warriors prior to an attack, some researchers speculate.[4] Spanish conquistadors fighting the Aztecs did recount the occasional sound of enemy whistles, but never in large numbers. Given that the whistles were found with a sacrificial victim who had been decapitated, the whistles could have been used in religious ceremonies. However they were employed, the six-hundred-year-old death whistles reproduce natural sounds with an exactness not equaled until the advent of modern recording technology.

Figure I.2. An Aztec death whistle.
Photo by Tim Evanson.

Another ancient American innovation dates back some twelve thousand years before Asian migrations crossed the Barents Sea land bridge from Siberia into Alaska. Among the hazards presented by their new home in the Arctic was snow blindness, a visual condition caused by relentlessly bright sunlight reflecting off seemingly limitless fields of snow and ice. To protect themselves from this environmental hazard, countless generations of resident Inuit inhabitants resorted to the world's first snow goggles. These were made of driftwood, antler, or bone to completely cover the eyes save for thin, horizontal slits through which the wearer could see sufficiently to travel through the polar landscape without jeopardizing their sight.[5]

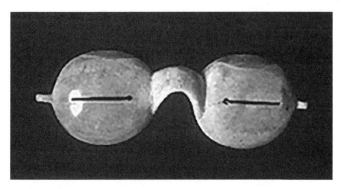

Figure I.3. Inuit goggles protect the eyes
from glare reflected from ice and snow by the sun.

In 2018 a rare specimen of forty-thousand-year-old jewelry was discovered in eastern Russia (see plate 1 for examples). *Atlantis Rising* magazine reported that an artificial hole in the Siberian chlorite bracelet "required a high-speed drill" to create, using "a tool thirty thousand years ahead of its time."[6] Such a find contradicts mainstream archaeological opinion that denies that ancient man experienced anything more than the most rudimentary material culture. But the Ice Age bangle is only among the most recent examples of surprisingly sophisticated technology invented centuries, even millennia, before the advent of our so-called Modern Age.

The many marvels of technology being uncovered around the globe, the better and the lesser well known, naturally sort themselves into two fundamental categories: those that were ahead of *their* time and those, incredibly, that were ahead of *our* time. Typical specimens of the former category, technology more advanced than even twenty-first-century applied science, include seventh-century Hindu bicycles, an Ice Age bracelet made with a power tool, and Babylon's phosphorus matches from the second millennium BCE, all cited above.

Forthcoming examples of the ancient world's superior technology include Roman concrete, the Incas' earthquake-proof architecture, Egyptian cancer cures, Imperial China's efficient and free public health care, fifth-century India's rust-free iron pillar, history's longest floating bridge built by Persian engineers, Turkey's underground cities for tens of thousands of residents, Persian refrigerators, Peruvian aquifers, and a Chinese reservoir. All are still in service after more than a thousand years of continuous use. They represent just a few of the past achievements modern civilization has yet to duplicate.

# 1
# Automation

Artificial intelligence is the iconic controversy of our times. Yet complex, even sophisticated robotics is not unique to early twenty-first-century technology. Original, surprisingly ingenious examples were actually built and operated by long-lost civilizations many thousands of years ago. Some android specimens were perhaps more advanced than current levels of applied science, as documented by a pair of Roman-era texts that describe hundreds of different kinds of machines capable of independent movement.

Sometime before 70 CE, *Pneumatica* and *Automata* were authored by Heron of Alexandria, a teacher at the city's museum, adjacent to the famous library, where most of his surviving writings appear as lecture notes for courses in mathematics, mechanics, physics, and pneumatics.[1] Although the field was not formalized until this past century, Heron's devices formed the first formal research into cybernetics.

For example, self-driving vehicles are at the cutting edge of contemporary technology, but Heron built a programmable, self-propelled cart powered by a falling weight nearly two thousand years ago. Its "program" consisted of strings wrapped around the drive axle. Heron also invented many automated props and devices for the Greek theater, including a mechanical play. His three-wheeled special-effects platform carried other robots onto to the stage, where they performed in front of audiences.

The contraption was powered by a binary-like system of ropes and knots and operated by a rotating, cylindrical cogwheel, while dropping mechanically timed metal balls onto a hidden drum to replicate the sound of thunder. A falling weight pulled a rope wrapped around the moving platform's two independent axles. Varying the length of the rope that was wound around each axle enabled Heron to program different routines for the performing robots before each show. Noel Sharkey, a computer scientist at Britain's University of Sheffield, relates this control system to modern-day binary programming.[2]

Regarded today as the outstanding researcher of antiquity, Heron was not, however, the earliest genius of his kind. He was preceded by another Greek, the father of robotics, Ctesibius. Inventor of the pipe organ in the third century BCE, Ctesibius went on to construct a cam-operated automaton resembling a god that alternatively stood up and sat down during public processions. Oxford University physicist Asim Qureshi states that "later ancient engineers used his [Ctesibius's] techniques on hydraulic systems."[3]

Between 806 and 820 CE, the Japanese inventor Han Zhile moved to China, where he was employed by the imperial court to create "mechanical birds, phoenixes, cranes, crows, and magpies," according to medical researchers Ashok Kumar Hemal and Mani Meno. "Though built of wood, some of the ornithological prototypes could be made to pretend to eat, drink, chirp, and warble like real birds. He is reported to have installed mechanical devices inside some of the birds to drive their wings to make them fly. He also created a mechanical cat."[4]

Chinese cybernetics was known as *khwai-shuh* from at least the first century. In the words of Andrew Tomas (1906–2001), a well-known Russian-born investigator into ancient technology, it was an art "by means of which a statue was brought to life to serve its maker."[5] An early example was a wooden humanoid atop a robotic cart, developed by Zhang Heng (78–139 CE), that pounded a drum when the self-propelled vehicle had traveled ten *li* (3.7 miles) and struck a bell at the one-hundred-li mark.[6]

Another humanoid was fashioned into the likeness of a Buddhist monk by an early Tang Dynasty craftsman circa 620 CE. Yang Wulian's creation begged for alms, which were deposited in a copper bowl. When the bowl was full, the animated figure bowed humbly, then deposited the offerings into a treasure chest.[7]

According to Hemal and Meno, Yin Wenliang, a late fifth-century mechanical engineer from Luozhou "created a wooden man and dressed him with an outfit made of colorful worsted silk. At every banquet, the small wooden man would propose a toast to each guest in order. Yin Wenliang also made a wooden woman. She could play the sheng [an ancient Chinese pipe with thirteen reeds] and sing, and she did them in perfect rhythm. If a guest did not finish the wine in his cup, the wooden man wouldn't refill the cup. If a guest did not drink enough wine, the wooden singing girl would play the sheng and sing for him to urge him to drink more."[8]

Yin Wenliang's contemporary Dafeng Ma was a skilled designer and constructed an automated dresser for the empress. Whenever the empress opened a full-length mirror, a robotic female brought washing paraphernalia and towels. When the towel was removed from the artificial servant's arm, it automatically triggered the machine to back away into a closet and deactivate itself.[9] Another mechanical domestic was commissioned by Ta-chouan, whose wife was overly impressed by the well-endowed male figure who was programmed to erotically service her when the emperor was away on state business. He eventually learned of the empress's bionic infidelity, destroyed the cuckolding automaton, and had its inventor beheaded.[10] Hers was not the first sex robot, however.

More than six hundred years earlier, Nabis, Sparta's monarch from 207 to 192 BCE, invented a lifelike reproduction of his famously beautiful wife after her death, concealing it from public knowledge by making it a state secret. Dressed in regal robes, the replica was a mirror image of the deceased Apega, controlled from a concealed nearby location by the king himself "through hidden devices."[11] Whenever a delinquent debtor was summoned to the palace, the deadbeat borrower was lavished with enough wine to inebriate his critical faculties, which might have otherwise detected any artificiality, then ushered into what the tipsy victim imagined was a private audience with the living Apega. Her automated likeness seductively welcomed the unwary defaulter with open arms. But as soon as he entered her, they sprang shut and pressed him ever tighter against her steel torso, studded with iron nails, from which there was no escape. Only when the tortured creditor loudly swore to pay up was his android queen's excruciating embrace released. This effective government revenue collection agent was described by Polybius, a no-nonsense historian of early Roman history and a contemporary of Nabis himself. The Spartan ruler's automaton "was one of the advancements in technology of the ancient Greco-Roman world," according to his Wikipedia entry.[12]

A thousand years before, during the Trojan War on the Aegean coast of what is now Turkey, the widowed Laodamia "made a bronze likeness of her [deceased] husband, Protesilaus, put it in her room under pretense of sacred rites, and devoted herself to it," according to Gaius Julius Hyginus, a Latin author and superintendent of the Palatine library under Caesar Augustus. A servant looked through a crack in the door and "saw her holding the simulacrum of Protesilaus in her embrace and kissing it. Thinking she had a lover, he told her father, Acastus. When he came and burst into the room, he saw the likeness

Figure 1.1. The profile of King Nabis appears on an early second-century Greek coin. Nabis created an automaton to seduce debtors and torture them until they paid everything they owed to the king.

of Protesilaus. To put an end to her torture, he had it and the sacred offerings burned on a pyre he had made, but Laodamia, not enduring her grief, threw herself on it and was burned to death."[13]

Ling Zhao's mid-sixth-century robots were likewise remarkable for their lifelike appearance, especially their skin and hair texture. Court historian Ming Xin told of how the Qi Dynasty monk from northern China dug a "pleasure pool" at the base of a mountain on the orders of Emperor Wu Cheng. "After the pool was finished, Ling Zhao built a miniature boat with exquisite details and put it in the water. When the miniature boat flowed before the emperor, he took a wine cup from it, and the boat would stop automatically. Then the small wooden man on the boat would clap its hands, and the boat would start to play music. When Emperor Wu Cheng finished drinking and put down the wine cup, the small wooden man would take the cup back to the boat. If Emperor Wu Cheng did not finish drinking the wine in the cup, the boat would stay there and would not leave."[14]

Ling Zhao's earlier colleague Lan Ling fashioned "a robot that could dance." As related by a mid-sixth-century text, the *Chao Ye Qian Zai*: "When the king wanted to offer a drink to a man, the robot would turn to that man and bow to the man with the drink in his hand."[15]

Lan Ling's lifelike wine servant was long preceded by the works of the Greek Philon of Byzantium (from the third century BCE), known as Mechanicus because of his impressive engineering accomplishments. These inventions included an automaton "in the form of a life-size woman. In her right hand, she held a wine jug. When a cup was placed in the palm of her left hand, she automatically poured wine first and then water to achieve the right mix. Both the wine and water were stored in metal jugs suspended in her chest."[16] Detailed in Philon's large treatise, *Mechanike syntaxis* (*Compendium of Mechanics*), the automaton's precise replica appeared in 2017 at an exhibition called *Amazing Inventions of the Ancient Greeks,* featured by the Herakleidon Museum annex on Apostolou Pavlou Street in central Athens. Like Heron of Alexandria mentioned above, Philon created an automated theater that dramatized the plots of popular myths with moving images, sound effects, and animated visuals. Interestingly, Lan Ling's automaton "looked like a man of a non-Chinese ethnic group," suggesting its foreign origins, which may have gone back very far indeed.[17]

## ATLANTEAN ORIGINS OF AUTOMATION

While many examples of automation have been found in Rome and China, some may have been lost in the sea. Chapter 7 of the Old Testament repeats an ancient Egyptian myth of possible predynastic provenance describing the younger brother of Osiris, Rocail, who lived before a great flood had obliterated early civilization: "Rocail erected an enormous sepulcher adorned with statues of various metals, made by talismanic art, which moved and spake, and acted like living men."[18]

The apparently Atlantean implications of Rocail's advanced technology having been overwhelmed by a predynastic deluge are not confined to biblical origins. Theosophical researcher David Reigle writes:

In an account of the sinking of Atlantis, taken from a secret commentary and given by H. P. Blavatsky in *The Secret Doctrine,* a kind of robot is mentioned (S.D. vol. 2, pp. 427–428). It is there called a "speaking animal" or "speaking beast." In a footnote, Blavatsky reports that, according to the accounts, these were artificially made beasts, mechanical animals. In another footnote, Blavatsky reports that, according to Brahmachari Bawa [a late nineteenth-century Hindu scholar], extensive Sanskrit treatises on such subjects once existed but are now lost.

There is an existing Pali text, *Loka-paññatti,* "Description of the World," that is largely based on lost Sanskrit texts [*La Lokapaññatti et les idées cosmologiques du bouddhisme ancien,* by Eugène Denis, 2 volumes, 1977. For the story of the robots, see the Pali text, pp. 157–59, and the French translation, pp. 141–43.]. It refers to such a robot in the words *bhūta-vāhana-yanta* (Sanskrit:

*bhūta-vāhana-yantra*), literally, "elemental vehicle machine." These elemental-driven machines in the account given in the *Loka-paññatti* are used to protect the relics of the Buddha.[19]

## ROBOTIC WARRIORS

If artificial intelligence did originate in Atlantis, something of its antediluvian roots may echo in the oldest mythic reference of Western Europe's Classical epoch. Talos, a robotic guard, appears in the *Argonautica,* an epic poem describing Jason's quest for the Golden Fleece (see plate 3). When he and his Argonaut followers approached the island of Crete by boat, they were bombarded by boulders hurled at them by a bronze warrior programmed to protect the Aegean island from all outsiders by patrolling its shores three times daily. The Argonauts nonetheless made landfall and overcame their giant opponent when Jason's soon-to-be-betrayed fiancée, Medea, pulled a bronze nail out of the defending automaton's heel. From it gushed a fluid known as *ichor,* draining this vital "blood of the gods" from Talos until he collapsed into a heap of broken, lifeless metal.

"In modern terms," observes *Popular Electronics'* reporter William Tenn, "that single vein could have been his main power cable and the pin, his fuse." He describes Talos as "a weapons-alert system and guided missile in one package."[20] *How Stuff Works* writer Robert Lamb concurs.

> Talos is far more than a mere curio amid other tales of gods and heroes. While myths can reveal much about history and culture, this episode also concerns the nature of technology. In its towering stature, we see the elite nature of bronze craftsmanship at the time, as well as the military prowess of bronze weaponry. It was an age of peak bronze technology. Talos is something special, even to modern humans. He's the embodiment of technological achievement and divine power intertwined in a single mythic being. . . . Talos is remarkably futuristic, anticipating the scientific possibilities of the

present age, and, even then, belonging more with the bizarre imaginings of the new mythology of science fiction than with the mechanisms created and used in real life. This killer robot stares back at us from the mists of ancient human civilization, reflecting the attitudes of its time, but also challenging us to consider the ramifications of artistic and technological creation. What are the limits of the modern Talos' might? Despite the never-ending onslaught of sci-fi killer robots, these questions remain as enthralling as ever.[21]

Such timelessness applies as much to their modern significance as to their origins. Although Classical scholars have dated composition of the *Argonautica* from 283 to 221 BCE, the basic story was "already well known to Hellenistic audiences, which enabled Apollonius [Apollonius Rhodius] to go beyond a simple narrative, giving it a scholarly emphasis suitable to the times," writes Robert Lamb. It was the age of the great Library of Alexandria, when Heron of Alexandria was himself at work on his robotic creations. "On one hand," states Lamb, "Talos stands as a potential metaphor for the might of bronze technology during the Greek Bronze Age, stretching from 3200 to 1200 BCE"[22]

In fact, some versions of Talos portray him as the last survivor of an ancient race of bronze-era men, or rather the last survivors of the Late Bronze Age. In Linear B, the ancient Cretan language, Talos was synonymous for "the Sun," and the Minoans worshipped Zeus as Zeus Tallaios. Tallaia is the Linear B name (perhaps derived from the older, still untranslatable Minoan Linear A) for a spur of the Ida mountain range where the Zeus cult was centered high up Mount Ida inside his cathedral-like cave, known as the Ideon Antron, or Navel of the World. Detailed representations of Talos preceded the *Argonautica* by at least 150 years on Greek vase paintings and Etruscan mirrors. His depiction on a Cretan coin from Phaistos is particularly significant because it was from the ruins of this large city that a baked-clay disc impressed with the earliest known example of movable type was retrieved. Dated to the Middle Minoan Bronze Age, it is two thousand years ahead of the same process reinvented by Johannes Gutenberg circa 1450.

Considering his associations with Crete, Talos may be regarded within the context of similarly advanced examples of ancient technology discovered there, an observation tending to affirm his actual existence during antiquity. Indeed, innovations such as a flush toilet found at Knossos, the centerpiece of Crete's pre-Classical urban center, and the Antikythera astronomical computer found nineteen nautical miles northwest of Crete, establish the conception of Talos long before the *Argonautica* was composed and well into the Bronze Age, which he appears to have personified. He was originally perhaps a kind of technologically advanced device built for military purposes.

## MAN VS. MACHINE:
## A PERENNIAL CONFLICT

If weaponized robots are as much dreaded today as their application was in antiquity, another anxious concern regarding the immediate future of artificial intelligence is its forecast capability for determining, programming, and enforcing its own concept of world government. That function was also prefigured by ancient robotics as long ago as 1100 BCE, when "moving statues" were documented by New Kingdom priests of Amun during the late Twentieth Dynasty. This was a tumultuous period of mixed crisis and innovation, when Pharaoh Ramses III successfully defended the Nile delta from a massive invasion by the Atlantean-like Meshwesh, also known as Sea Peoples, followed by the construction of his stupendous Victory Temple at Medinet Habu in Lower Egypt.

After Pharaoh's assassination, the moving statues reportedly chose his successor, Amun-her-khepeshef (meaning "Amun [king of the gods] is with His Strong Arm"), from male members of the royal family, just as today's super computers engage in America's modern presidential election campaigns, predicting and, as some observers believe, helping to predetermine their outcome. Qureshi declares that "it is entirely possible that these [3,100-year-old] artifacts were built. . . . Ancient Egyptians had enough knowledge of mechanics to develop a non-digitized machine based on a system of ropes and pulleys."[23]

They certainly were interested in advanced possibilities for such artificial intelligence, envisioning (at least) our own modern concerns regarding automated soldiers. An early Egyptian story tells of Nubia's humanoid commando unit sent to abduct the pharaoh. After his return to Egypt, he dispatched his own robotic SWAT team to retaliate by kidnapping the Nubian king. During the course of their man-versus-android confrontations, futuristic flamethrowers and even plasma weapons were deployed. This story, "The Tale of Say-Ausar," resembles modern science fiction. But all good science fiction must be based, at least in part, on real science familiar to audiences, a point that begs the question: What generally recognizable science could ordinary Egyptians have taken for granted five thousand years ago that would have been necessary for making "The Tale of Say-Ausar" credible? If nothing else, its synthetic warriors reflect modern-day suspicions about civilization's growing dependence on artificial intelligence, particularly when militarized.

Similar angst also arose from Han Zhile's automated animals in about 800 CE. His robotic menagerie of lifelike birds made to amuse mid–Tang Dynasty Chinese royalty prompted a contemporaneous cautionary story rewritten by Hans Christian Andersen in an 1843 fairy tale, which in turn inspired Igor Stravinsky seventy-four years later to compose his symphonic poem, *Le chant du rossignol* ("The Song of the Nightingale"). It tells of a Chinese emperor who, from childhood, dearly loved his pet nightingale, which returned his deep affection. One day, a visiting sorcerer presented a remarkable gift to his majesty: a mechanical nightingale that sang, flapped its wings, strutted and danced, and even took food in its beak from the emperor's own hand. He was so taken with this miraculous invention that he forgot about the real bird who had been his closest companion for so many years. Eventually, the monarch realized with a shock that his living nightingale had disappeared. Days, weeks, and months passed, but it failed to return through the palace window that was always left open and at which plates of food and water were placed.

The emperor sickened with regret for his vanished friend and could no longer bear to look at its robotic replacement, so he gave it away. As summer merged into fall and he realized that his feathered friend would never return, the monarch fell ill with regret and took to his bed, where he constantly watched the open window. At length, he began to die of grief and was closing his eyes for a final sleep when, incredibly, he heard his nightingale singing from the windowsill. A moment later, the bird landed upon his breast, still singing. The emperor quickly recovered and, together with the nightingale, lived a long, happy life.

This ancient tale demonstrates the potential for dehumanization posed by our distraction with and growing reliance on not only artificial intelligence but also technology itself. The most famous dramatization of this inner conflict was Walt Disney's "The Sorcerer's Apprentice," an animated short scored by the symphonic poem *L'apprenti sorcier* by Paul Dukas, after "Der Zauberlehrling," Wolfgang von Goethe's 1797 poem, which was in turn based on an ancient story by Lucian. Whether the mid-second-century Roman satirist actually invented the tale or perpetuated an earlier version of it in his *Philopseudes* ("Lover of Lies") is unknown. More certainly, its perennial appeal, from at least as early as Rome's Imperial Period to Europe's Age of Enlightenment down to the present day, underscores the archetypal story's recurrent theme expressed in technology's innate propensity to over-control.

Inanimate objects, such as brooms, are infused with intelligent energies by arcane powers to carry out the hard physical labor the apprentice, now afforded leisure time, previously undertook, until they become unmanageable and generate a destructive flood that is stopped by the sorcerer before it engulfs the world. The implication is clear: technology is a useful servant but a dangerous master. Man's alternating fascination for and ambivalence toward applied science has preoccupied him since the advent of his very first technical achievement, which set him apart from all other animals and gave him dominion over them.

This immemorial conflict of conscience continues to resound in perhaps the oldest surviving oral tradition, going back nearly half a million years to the earliest controlled use of fire by our *Homo erectus* ancestors. In Greek myth, Prometheus stole fire from heaven, giving it to humans, who suffered in cold and darkness. For this sympathetic act, he was severely punished because Zeus had ordained that only gods were wise enough to use fire. In the hands of flawed, selfish men, it would cause death and destruction not only among themselves but also to the natural world itself. In all art, nowhere is this fierce dichotomy more powerfully pronounced than in another symphonic poem, *Prometheus* by Franz Liszt. Since the allegorical tale's first telling, we still debate whether the compassionate Prometheus or the prophetic Zeus was correct.

Today, both might agree that while our modern world is relearning some of the old secrets of Philon of Byzantium or Ling Zhao, we might do better to first understand how and why their civilizations were lost. All these robotic creations vanished with the fifth-century collapse of Greco-Roman civilization, followed some four hundred years later with the gradual onset of China's own dark ages.

# 2
# Human Flight

*In ancient days, two aviators procured to themselves wings. Daedalus flew safely through the middle air and was duly honored on his landing. Icarus soared upwards to the sun till the wax melted which bound his wings and his flight ended in fiasco. In weighing their achievements, there is something to be said for Icarus. The Classical authorities tell us that he was only "doing a stunt," but I prefer to think of him as the man who brought to light a serious constructional defect in the flying machines of his day.*

SIR ARTHUR STANLEY EDDINGTON,
*SPACE TIME AND GRAVITATION,* 1968

During the early 1970s, American author James Woodman became fascinated with the so-called Nazca Lines, the largest art gallery on Earth. This collection of outsized designs—some geometric or linear, others portraying a variety of animals or unrecognizable images—was created in the Peruvian Desert by removing dark-gray cover soil to reveal faint yellow sand. Uncertainly dated within the parameters of the third century BCE and fifth century CE, the colossal geoglyphs are scattered across South America's western coastal arid plains. But the bizarre images were not discovered until the early 1930s by accident, when a local pilot happened to fly over the figures. All are superbly executed in perfect proportion—some several miles in length—demonstrating an exceptionally high degree of skill in surveying techniques, social cooperation necessary for executing the works on such a gargantuan scale, and the ability to accurately transfer artwork from normal-size sketches to gigantic illustrations on the arid plain.

To Woodman, the ancient geoglyphs appeared to have been made specifically for appreciation from an aerial perspective. Mainstream scholars insisted instead that they were sacrificial offerings only, not intended to be seen by their creators but meant for viewing exclusively by imaginary deities who dwelled in the sky. Despite this prevailing scientific opinion, Woodman wondered if South Americans had somehow achieved manned flight, the only means by which they could observe their enormous art tableau spread across the Peruvian Desert. It did not make sense to him that they should have gone to the trouble of creating such a huge collection only to deny themselves any opportunity of ever seeing it, no matter how deep their devotion to heaven. The very notion seemed contrary to fundamental human nature, regardless of cultural and temporal differences separating our time from the prehistoric Nazca.

During his research into the Nazca enigma, Woodman was surprised to learn that several tribes in Brazil and Peru were skilled in the manufacture of five-foot-tall envelopes of paper that could fly. Filled with smoke rising from small clay pots of smoldering cane suspended underneath a single opening, the contraptions actually rose into the air of their own accord. To the indigenous people, the little hot-air balloons belong to a legacy from their most ancient ancestors and were originally set forth into the sky for religious purposes to bring small offerings to the sky gods. At least two indigenous tribes, today in residence near the Honduran border and in the Peruvian highlands, still make these ceremonial aerostats or free-floating hot-air balloons.

The Incas, Woodman further discovered, honored a legendary figure they referred to as Orichan, who could fly to heaven and back in

Figure 2.1. During the early twentieth century, the British Army used kites, like this 1908 "Cody war kite" developed by Samuel Franklin "Wild Bill" Cody (better remembered for his traveling Wild West shows), to haul human lookouts into the air for observation purposes.
Photo by a Royal Air Force photographer.

a vessel of golden flames—imagery implying a gondola equipped with its firepot suspended beneath a hot-air balloon. Even more suggestive was the ancient Andean hero Antarqui, the boy-god who reconnoitered for Incan armies by flying high over battlefields and then returned to the emperor with intelligence about enemy dispositions.

The myth of Antarqui lends credence to the possibility that Andean lads—because of their light weight—were used to fly military observation balloons.*

The first such aerial reconnaissance had been invented around 400 BCE by Archytas of Tarentum, a philosopher, mathematician, astronomer, statesman, and strategist. It is possible, then, that similar contemporaneous advances in human flight were undertaken by pre-Columbian South Americans. Better known than Antarqui was Kon-Tiki-Viracocha, the Incas' red-bearded, light-complexioned, fair-eyed founding father, who fled as a flood survivor from some natural catastrophe. "Sea Foam"—a reference to his white skin and oceanic origins—allegedly shared the high wisdom of his lost homeland with native peoples to create Andean civilization. Among the cultural gifts he bequeathed them was the aerostat. A standard image in Nazca art may be a direct reference to and, in fact, a symbol of this gift. The likeness of a sea eagle, or frigate bird, appears as the single most reproduced animal on pottery shards found throughout the Pacific coast of Peru. The bird is remarkable for inflating its gullet to a grotesque size in mid-air, resembling a flying balloon.

Most Nazca drawings depict birds, likewise suggesting flight. Of these, the most cogent to our investigation is a half-human image, the so-called Owl Man. Regarded as one of the oldest bioglyphs, it portrays a standing, ninety-eight-foot-long anthropomorphic figure with the head of an owl incised into the sloping face of a cliff. Like its companions, the ground drawing may be properly appreciated only from the perspective of several hundred feet of altitude. It gestures with its right hand lifted toward heaven, while its left points to the earth. It is as though the figure were indicating something integrally important concerning all the Nazca Lines: "If you want to see us properly, you have got to go up into the sky!"

---

*Boys actually did serve as military observers for Greek armies in the field while strapped to large leather kites some two hundred years prior to the official advent of Nazca civilization twelve centuries before the Incas.

Figure 2.2. Aerial photograph of Nazca lines in the shape of a condor.
Photo by Diego Delso.

Owl "Man" is a misconceived name, however, because it appears to have been originally associated with a sorceress similarly portrayed on Nazca pottery and still revered by mountain tribes. Often shown holding a San Pedro cactus in her left hand, she was and still is worshipped as a supernatural guardian of the highland lagoons, where the plant grows. This hallucinogenic cactus, when ingested, makes possible the well-known "flight of the shaman," an out-of-body experience non-Christian priests use to soar up to the gods for healing and wisdom. Containing mescaline, the San Pedro cactus does indeed produce convincing sensations of flight in anyone who ingests it. Whether drug-induced astral projection or balloon flight, an aerial experience related to the geoglyphs seems suggested.

Even non-avian depictions point to connection with the heavens. The dog and fox, both portrayed on the Nazca plain, were symbolic messengers between divine spirits in the sky and human worshippers on the ground. Woodman was especially surprised to find that Quechua, the language spoken by the Incas, actually contains a premodern word for "balloon maker." Moreover, some surviving examples of pottery recovered from the vicinity of the Nazca geoglyphs portray objects resembling balloons flying across the sky, trailing ropes or streamers. Nazca tapestries housed at Lima's National Museum of Anthropology and Archaeology unquestionably depict humans in flight, either through the agency of hallucinogenic pathogens or via balloons. At the Nazca Lines themselves, broad patches of scorched earth may still be observed at the intersections of drawings or atop nearby low rises. They are the results of intensely hot fires that burned when the Nazca civilization flourished in the area. Woodman speculated that these fires were originally ignited by pre-Columbian aviators to inflate their balloons with hot air.

## A TWENTIETH CENTURY RE-CREATION

Putting his suppositions to the test, Woodman and his colleagues—fellow professional aeronauts from the United States—built a hot-air balloon designed to resemble the deltoid miniatures still flown by Honduran and Andean natives. The American scientists restricted their experiment to materials known to have been used by pre-Inca peoples. Nothing belonging to modern times was included in the undertaking. As a feature article in *Time* magazine reported later, Woodman's 88-foot-high replica "was made from fabric that closely resembles materials recovered from Nazca gravesites. The balloon's lines and fastenings were made from native fibers, the boat-shaped gondola was woven from totora reeds picked by Indians from Peru's 2.4-mile-high Lake Titicaca."[1] Even the ground fires for providing hot air were stoked only with desert kindling close at hand. Nazca pottery images appeared to illustrate prehistoric balloon makers stitching together large, four-sided, triangular envelopes—the same configuration chosen for the modern re-creation.

At dawn on November 25, 1975, after being inflated with eighty-thousand cubic feet of smoke, *Condor I* was released, ascending quickly at eighteen feet per second and bearing Woodman and William Spohrer aloft to six hundred feet above the Nazca plain in thirty seconds (see plate 4). From that altitude, the awe-inspiring drawings of a vanished, prehistoric race came into perfect perspective and proportion. As Woodman later wrote, "The sun had just cleared the mountains and now flooded the fantastic scene below. . . . Surely, I thought, the men who created these lines had to have seen them like this, with the shadows of dawn etching their magnificent art. For those two minutes, we were alone with Nazca. We had flown back in time, as much as we had climbed into the sky."[2]

After the twentieth-century balloonists landed safely in the Peruvian Desert, Spohrer remarked, "Up there, just now, I had the feeling we weren't the first ever to have flown with the wind above Nazca."[3] Spohrer's colleague in the International Explorers Society, Michael DeBakey, stated that the experiment capably demonstrated that ancient Peruvians could have manufactured and flown a hot-air balloon. "We set out to prove that the Nazcans had the skill, the materials and the need for flight," he said. "I think we have succeeded."[4]

Indeed, *Condor I*'s completed mission, the model orthostats flown by native South Americans for unknown centuries prior to the Spanish Conquest, Andean traditions of human flight, the remains of ancient bonfires at the geoglyphs themselves, and the fact that the lines and images there may only be properly appreciated from several hundred feet above them, persuasively argue on behalf of Peruvian flight in antiquity. Although the fact that a people sophisticated enough to create Andean civilization should have possessed the ability to achieve human flight is still beyond the intellectual scope of conventional archaeologists, it appears to be true nonetheless.

The Nazca hot-air balloons were certainly the privilege of upper-class passengers, perhaps reserved exclusively for royalty or clergy. Flights were probably undertaken for religious purposes during important, sky-worshipping ceremonies, in view of the geoglyphs' apparent astro-spiritual significance. Such ventures may also have been regarded as an elite sport. Antarqui's myth likewise appears real enough, and we may believe that boys were indeed used for airborne military reconnaissance by the Nazcans, just as history records they were deployed by their nearly contemporaneous Greeks.

## EVIDENCE IN HISTORICAL RECORDS

Chinese scholars at the time appear to have known about the Peruvian balloonists. China's first geography, the *Shan Hai Jing* (*Classic of Regions Beyond the Seas: East*), relates that a foreign race on the other side of the Pacific Ocean referred to as the Chi-Kung "are able to construct flying carriages which can follow the wind and travel great distances. The skill of the Chi-Kung people is truly marvelous. By studying the winds, they created and built flying wheels [perhaps mistranslation of a word meant to describe a circular, balloon-like object], with which they can ride along the paths of the whirlwinds."[5] The Chi-Kung people may have been South America's Nazca. Chinese archaeologist Tang Jigen "points to similarities in iconography of Shang artifacts and those of the Chavin and the later Mochica, Nazca and Paracas cultures" as evidence of China's impact on pre-Columbian Peru.[6] Indeed, traces of Imperial Chinese influence at work throughout the Americas, centuries before the Spanish arrival, are as numerous as they are identifiable. Although mythological elements are self-evident, "the ancient Chinese treated the Classic as a record of geography" that recorded "scientific and technological achievements at that moment," among them perhaps the hot-air ballooning mastered by the overseas Chi-Kung/Nazca.[7]

Third-century BCE Asians may have done more than merely report on early Peruvian advances in manned balloon flight. "A great airship constructed about 1279 CE, by Ko-Shau-King, Chief Astronomer to Kublai ["Khan" of the Mongol empire]," according to the prolific alternative science writer Brad Steiger, "was used at the coronation of the Emperor Eo-Koen in 1306. Marco Polo records that he saw the Great Armillary Sphere at the Court of Cathy [in 1292, at the time of his marriage to Kublai Khan's daughter], and Father Vasson, a French missionary in Canton, states that he saw an account of the airship recorded in a letter dated September 5, 1694."[8]

Although Jacques-Étienne Montgolfier is today remembered as the first known human to have made a balloon ascent on October 15, 1783, ancient masters of the air preceeded him by hundreds, perhaps thousands, of years.

3

# Ancient Aviation

*All ancient Chinese texts were ordered destroyed in 212 B.C. by Emperor Chi Huang Ti, the builder of the famous Great Wall. Vast amounts of ancient texts—virtually everything pertaining to history, philosophy and science—were seized and burnt. Whole libraries, including the royal library, were destroyed . . . all books in the Byzantine Empire [during the mid-fifth century CE] were ordered destroyed, except for a newly edited version of the Bible that the Catholic Church was issuing. The library at Alexandria was destroyed at this time, and the great mathematician and philosopher, Hypatia, was dragged from her chariot by a mob and torn to pieces. The mob went on to burn the library. Thus, the suppression of science and knowledge, particularly of the ancient past, began in ernest.*

DAVID HATCHER CHILDRESS,
*TECHNOLOGY OF THE GODS,* 2000

While possibilities for lighter-than-air travel undertaken by premodern civilizations seem credible, ancient tales of heavier-than-air flight told in China, Greece, India, and the American Southwest might be dismissed as entirely mythical, except for some physical evidence from the Lower Nile valley that casts new light on such perennial stories. Although discovered during French excavation of a tomb for a court official named Pa-di-Imen near Sakkara's step pyramid in 1898, the small, unprepossessing artifact was promptly cataloged at the Museum of Egyptian Antiquities in Cairo. There, it languished in obscurity for the next seventy-one years until archaeologist and professor of anatomy for the medical arts at Helwan University, Dowoud Khalil Messiha, stumbled upon birdlike Item 33109, Special Register No. 6347 (see plate 5).

Its lack of period documentation has led to a variety of interpretations of what the artifact was intended to be: the toy for an elite child, a sort of boomerang, the figurehead on a sacred boat used during religious ceremonies, even a weathervane. Why anyone would have been buried with something as mundane and commonplace as a boomerang or weathervane seems illogical. As a longtime model airplane enthusiast and member of the Egyptian Aeromodelers Club, Messiha instantly recognized it instead as something with which he was very familiar, despite the Sakkara Bird's allegedly Ptolemaic provenance.

Alternative researcher Joseph Robert Jochmans writes:

Within the context of today's technological mindset, we can immediately see just by looking at it that it bears an uncanny resemblance to a glider craft of some type. . . . The only markings on it are faint eyes painted on the nose and two red lines under the wings, in a similar fashion that decorations appear on modern aircraft. The eye dots are actually the ends of a very small obsidian bar, which is fitted through the head and gives the craft an important balancing weight. The model's wings are straight and aerodynamically shaped, with a span of 18.3 centimeters, or about 7.2 inches. [The 0.5-ounce Sakkara Bird is made of very light sycamore wood.] Its pointed nose is 1.5 inches long. The body of the craft totals 5.6 inches, tapered, terminating in a vertical tail fin. Messiha found evidence for a tail-wing piece that very likely had once been attached to the vertical tail precisely like the back tail on a modern plane.[1]

[During an interview with the *London Times*, Messiha said that] "the tail is really the most interesting thing which distinguishes this model from all others that have been discovered. No bird can produce such a contortion at the rear of its body to assume anything that looks like the model. Furthermore, there is a groove under the fin for a tail-plane [crosspiece], which is missing."[2]

Jochmans, who was allowed to closely examine and even handle the Cairo Museum's Sakkara Bird for almost an hour, observed:

It is obvious another wood component that was once part of the original model extended out the back end from this point, and that it was subsequently broken off. The very first impression one gets when looking at the model is that it is no artist's expression of a bird. Unlike the other objects in the same display case in which the model is kept, there are no renditions of legs, feet, aviary-type wings-in-flight attitudes, pronounced beak, or artistic portrayal of feathers, drawn or carved.

Jochmans noticed how a bird's beak was suggeseted by the front end's prominent feature, which, in any case, seemed part of the artifact's aerfoil-like configuration.

No paint or change of coloration was made to accentuate a bird beak—instead it is an aerofoil feature that is an essential part of the fuselage. There are no prominent holes anywhere on the body of the model—certainly not for holding feathers, or feet, or even a pole to swivel on as some have claimed if the object was once used as a weathervane.

When I was handed the glider I carefully turned it over, because there are no published photographs showing its underside. I found no evidence of any holes where legs or feet were once attached, or any smaller holes into which feathers could have been inserted. The underbelly was relatively smooth, though worn with age. The only original significant indentation that I could see was in the center of the top of the wing, where the wing assemblage was attached to the main body. There is, to be sure, a prominent circular indentation in the artifact's underside, but there is very good evidence that this was added soon after it had arrived in the Cairo Museum, toward the beginning of the last century.

The artifact's only modern alteration is a small hole drilled into the underside by a museum restorer, allowing the figure to be mounted on a display stand. Jochmans continued:

Neither does the artifact have any artist's renderings of feathers. Skeptics have suggested that painted on feathers could have been worn off over time. But though I had the time to carefully examine practically every square millimeter of the model, I saw no images of feathers, or even flecks of paint indicating residue that would have been left behind had the model's surface been subjected to some kind of paint coating which was subsequently weathered away.

The only painted images I could detect were the simple outlines of eyes, two lines under the wing, the inscription near the tail, and a catalog number added in modern times. The ancient markings, as Messiha pointed out to me, may have been placed on the model as an afterthought, part of an effort to make it into a religious relic, to better fit within a tomb setting. Or, as other researchers have surmised, these may have mirrored actual designs seen by the artist on the original craft-part of the same type of decal decorations seen on modern planes today. In fact, it is the striking absence of any traditional sacred markings that takes the model out of the realm of being a religious object and puts it instead squarely in the context of a technological artifact.

Stangely, the object's wing's and tail are its most un-avian details.

These are inherently linked with its aerodynamic body which is certainly very bird-like yet radically different from any other ancient Egyptian statues of birds, particularly deified ones. One need only look at the bird figures exhibited in the same museum display case as the model to see the glaring differences. The figurine bodies were often slightly deformed to accentuate deific strength and power, while the wings were spread wide, feathers splayed, either in an attack or protective mode. And the tail was invariably fanned out horizontally when the figures were portrayed in flight. In contrast, the model's body is sleek yet aerodynamically true, the wings are tight and fixed to support airlift capacity, and the back tail is rigidly vertical. All these are distinctive features of a glider, not a bird.[3]

But Item 33109 was not unique. After its rediscovery in 1969, "Egypt's Minister for Culture, Mohammed Gamal El Din Moukhtar, commissioned a technical research group to put other 'birds' under the microscope," writes David Hatcher Childress.[4] Since then, replicas of the Sakkara Bird have been constructed to further research its possibilities.

"The majority of those model plane enthusiasts who have taken the time and effort to actually build and fly a replica of the Sakkara glider," Jochmans continues, "and have added the lost tail-wing in precisely the designated position, where one very likely existed, find that the craft works very well and perfectly sails through the air over an extended distance. The little model itself, even though over two thousand years old, will soar a short distance with only a slight jerk of the hand. As Messiha discovered, fully restored balsa replicas will travel even farther."[5]

The most scientifically sophisticated testing of the Sakkara Bird was initiated in 2007 by British champion glider pilot and aerodynamics expert Simon Sanderson. He used the University of Liverpool's advanced computer analysis system to create a 3-D structural profile of every physical nuance of the artifact so as to replicate a precise model five times the size of the original. The larger replica was taken to Manchester Aeronautics Research Institute for extensive wind-tunnel testing, including the introduction of smoke to help define the Sakkara Bird's aerodynamic properties, if any. Increasing the wind speed gradually while altering its *attitude,* meaning its orientation relative to the smoky wind, revealed definite flight characteristics that produced four times the object's weight in lift, more than sufficient to allow it to fly. Returned to the University of Liverpool, it was subjected to the same trials as a modern fighter-jet design.

As a History Channel documentary explained, "Using data obtained from the wind tunnel experiments, the ancient Sakkara Bird is to undergo the most rigorous scientific analysis that twenty-first century technology can deliver." Sanderson piloted it in a virtual reality flight simulator above the Giza Plateau. The re-created aircraft handled beautifully and with ease, climbing swift and high with the desert's rising thermals. The History Channel concluded that "over two thousand years after the Ancient Egyptians carved this mysterious 'bird,' modern technology has proved beyond doubt that it could have flown."[6]

But what was its real function in ancient Egypt? Messiha told Jochmans that

the model from the tomb was an artist's impression of something much larger that he had seen up close and in operation when he was alive. A full-scale version of the plane could have flown carrying heavy loads, but at low speeds, between forty-five and sixty-five miles per hour. . . .

Simply by using the rising heat currents off the Egyptian deserts on either side of the Nile, such a craft would have been able to stay in the air indefinitely with skilled maneuvering. The small wooden object, when it was in pristine condition, probably did not fly very well. But that had not been its purpose. Its purpose, as far as the artist had been concerned, was to make a simple diminutive replica of something worthy enough to be a tomb offering for the afterlife. . . .

The ancient Egyptians always built scale models of everything they were familiar with in their daily lives and placed them in their tombs—model temples, ships, chariots, servants, and animals. Now that we have found a model plane, Messiha wondered if perhaps somewhere under the desert sands along the Nile there may yet be unearthed the remains of life-sized gliders, after which the actual Sakkara sailplane was copied.[7]

Because the Sakkara Bird was found in Padi-Imen's third-century-BCE burial tomb, Egyptologists concluded that the object was no more than 2,200 years old. But as Jochmans points out:

The remains were part of the general excavation findings associated with the tomb of Queen Khuit, one of the wives of Pharaoh Teti of the Sixth Dynasty, from two millennia earlier. As was the common practice during the later Ptolemaic period, many of the tombs of former royal dignitaries were reused, which was the reason Padi-Imen's burial objects were part of the Old Kingdom artifacts brought to light. Also on the tail can faintly be seen a hieroglyph inscription which reads, "The gift of Amun," who was the Egyptian deity associated with the wind.[8]

More to the point, this simple statement thoroughly removes the object from the third century BCE, because the god was known only as Amun before 1650 BCE. Thereafter, he was forever hyphenated as Amun-Ra. Amun was chief immortal of the Sixth Dynasty, when the Sakkara Bird was most likely fashioned. It and its kind do not appear to have survived the end of the Old Kingdom, which was followed by a prolonged period of chaos in which many of early pharaonic civilization's highest achievements were lost. Were the Sakkara Bird and its thirteen similarly airworthy objects the emblematic artifacts of mummified aviators they were meant to identify in the next world? At the very least, the Cairo Museum's wooden model of a working glider shows that ancient inhabitants of the Nile valley grasped the fundamental principles of heavier-than-air flight. Perhaps such knowledge was the only legacy to survive from some former era, when those principles were applied on a broader scale than Egyptologists have been been willing to imagine.

Likewise, the source of construction designs consulted by Archytas of Tarentum—the ancient Greek kite-flyer cited in chapter 2—for assembling the first successful aerial drone "had been obtained from manuscripts which eventually made their way into the Library of Alexandria," according to Jochmans, "dating back to a period already considered ancient in his day."[9]

A self-propelled device from about 360 BCE, the *Pigeon,* was hollow, bird-shaped, made of light-weight wood, and propelled by a jet of

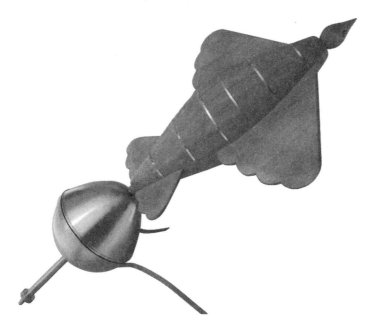

Figure 3.1. A re-creation of Archytas's *Pigeon.*
Compressed air was released, and the *Pigeon* would be separated
from its ignition ball. Image courtesy of the collection and archive of
the Kotsanas Museum of Ancient Greek Technology.

compressed air. When the air was released, the advance-programmed aircraft flew with astonishing accuracy more than 650 feet from one perch to another. Archytas's *Pigeon* at least suggests that other "Sakkara Bird" from Egypt.

About 520 years after Archytas's death, the Roman scholar Aulus Gellius described the flying vehicle in *Adversaria,* a compilation of unusual subjects he heard about in conversation or read in books. "Few details are given about the object," writes Tara MacIsaac of the Epoch Times, "which was said to have mystified and amused the citizens of Tarentum, according to educational materials developed by NASA. NASA described it as 'one of the first devices to successfully employ the principles essential to rocket flight.'"[10] For this and numerous other innovations, a crater on the moon, Archytas, is named in his honor.

4

# Preventive
# Medicine

*Medicine is essentially a learned profession. Its literature
is ancient, and connects it with the most learned periods
of antiquity; and its terminology continues to be Greek or
Latin. You cannot name a part of the body, and scarcely a
disease, without the use of a Classical term. Every structure
bears upon it the impress of learning, and is a silent appeal
to the student to cultivate an acquaintance with the sources
from which the nomenclature of his profession is derived.*

SIR WILLIAM WITHEY GULL,
*AN ORATION DELIVERED BEFORE
THE HUNTERIAN SOCIETY, FEB. 13, 1861*

The Dark Ages that emerged as a consequence of Western civilization's
collapse in 480 CE were characterized by equal measures of piety and
sickness. While sermonizing churchmen exercised uniform authority
over European society, pandemics recurrently ravaged their parishio-
ners and more died prematurely of wounds in battle, soaring infant
mortality was the norm, and average life span dropped to twenty-five
years of age. Prevailing religious dogma mandated mortification of the

flesh because the human body—together with all Nature—was deemed inherently sinful and irredeemably corrupt.

If immoral Romans had wallowed in the pagan practice of bathing regularly, devout Christians would demonstrate their faith by going unwashed. From such prevailing doctrines and unhygienic behavior naturally arose the ill health and early death of generations, relieved only centuries later by Renaissance scholars studying scraps of wisdom from the ancient world that had somehow survived the religious zealots who overthrew Classical civilization.

## HALTING INFECTION

From the birth of modern medicine with Swiss physician Paracelsus in the early 1500s to the present time, medical science continues to rediscover ancient procedures, pharmaceuticals, remedies, and disease prevention, some of which were superior to present-day methodologies or drugs. These past treatments and cures developed by our ancestors were many centuries, occasionally millennia, ahead of both their times and ours and need to be recognized and understood for the sake of future improvements. For example, a simple medical technique commonly employed by Spartan army field surgeons during the Peloponnesian Wars (431 to 404 BCE) was filling a sword cut with honey, then wrapping it with multilayered bandages. Honey not only soothed pain by sealing off raw flesh from exposure to open air and insects but also prevented infection. Moreover, honey enzymes initiated and contributed to the healing process itself.

"In the laboratory," writes Julie Edgar, a journalist specializing in health issues, "honey has been shown to hamper the growth of food-borne pathogens, such as E. coli and salmonella, and to fight certain bacteria, including *Staphylococcus aureus* and *Pseudomonas aeruginosa,* both of which are common in hospitals and doctors' offices." In 2007, the Food and Drug Administration approved honey "for use in treating wounds and skin ulcers. It works very well to stimulate healing, says wound care specialist Frank Bongiorno, MD, of Ann Arbor, Michigan."[1]

Seventeen centuries before Dutch microbiologist Antonie van Leeuwenhoek rediscovered bacteria in 1674, the Roman scholar Marcus Terentius Varro wrote how "there are bred certain minute creatures, which cannot be seen by the eyes, which float in the air and enter the body through the mouth and nose, and there cause serious diseases."[2] Accordingly, medics known as *immunites* (because they were excused all other duties in the Roman legions) were required to thoroughly wash their hands and clean surgical instruments in boiling water prior to making incisions, practices abandoned after the fall of Rome until revived by French physician Louis Pasteur less than 150 years ago.

Twenty centuries before Varro, Egyptian physicians not only identified infectious micro-organisms but also used "antibiotics contained in moldy bread to heal wounds by applying it as a poultice," as authors Peter James and Nick Thorpe describe.[3] A medical papyrus from the Eleventh Dynasty (which began in 2125 BCE) similarly mentions a specific fungus that flourishes in stagnant water and was prescribed for wounds and open sores. Later, by 450 BCE, the Greeks were effectively eradicating boils and carbuncles by applying soybean curd in warm soil, a combination with known antibiotic properties. Benzylpenicillin (Penicillin G), the modern world's first antibiotic substance, was only developed by Scottish pharmacologist Alexander Fleming in 1928.

The ancients were as successful at treating bacterial infection as they were at preventing it. In 2010, French researchers found that all classes of men, women, and children residing in the Nile valley during dynastic times commonly wore eye makeup with antibacterial properties that helped prevent optic infections (see fig. 4.1 and plate 2). Particles entering the eye during flood season caused diseases and inflammations. "Indeed," writes Christian Amatore at the École Normale Supérieure in Paris, "it is well recognized today that in most tropical marshy areas, such as was the Nile area during floods, several bacterial infections are transmitted to humans following any

When French navigator Samuel de Champlain first ventured into the Lake Ontario region in 1615, he observed resident Seneca mothers nursing their newborns with a primitive syringe. A bird quill was fastened to the bottom of a dried, oiled bear intestine, and this contraption was used to orally administer an infant formula of crushed nuts, reduced meats, and other nutrients in appropriately digestible pabulum. This indigenous modus operandi used by the Seneca for time out of mind was the earliest known form of a baby bottle, and it served as a pattern for its subsequent development in the West.[9]

## SEX ED

Ancient medical care during motherhood and child-birthing would not be matched until the twentieth century. Only during its first half did modern biophysicists identify the human *chorionic gonadotropin* (hCG), the hormone serving as a maternity marker found in the urine of pregnant women. Yet a fifth-century Greek pregnancy test mandated the placement of a needle into a woman's urine. If the needle rusted red or black, she was carrying a child. A variant mixed her urine with wine, its alcohol reacting with proteins found in a pregnant woman's urine. Both versions were remarkably effective, though less so than an Egyptian precursor that had a woman urinate into a jar containing barley and wheat grains. If, after seventy-two hours, they did not sprout, she was not pregnant. But increased estrogen levels produced during pregnancy caused the seeds to develop following a three-day period. Growing barley indicated that the woman was pregnant with a male child. Conversely, wheat germination signaled the birth of a female child.

This test is described by the *Brugsch,* or Greater Berlin Papyrus of the Nineteenth Dynasty (1292 to 1189 BCE). It appears much earlier in the Carlsberg Papyrus from Egypt's Classical age, which began in 2040 BCE. A laboratory experiment conducted more than four thousand years later, in 1963, showed that the urine of pregnant women caused the grains to sprout at least 70 percent of the time. Based on this revelation from the third millennium BCE, modern pregnancy testing was developed less than sixty years ago.

The same medical technology that gave dynastic Egyptian women an accurate pregnancy test likewise provided them with effective contraception remarkably similar to a modern intrauterine device used before sexual intercourse to prevent insemination. The ancient version was a mixture of crocodile dung, honey, and sodium carbonate combined in a highly acidic paste that formed an effective spermicidal to prevent fertilization. An alternative method called for the woman to squat low over boiling water filled with substances Egyptologists have so far not been able to identify. Steam rising with these medicines acted as a spermicidal.

The Greeks also had ways to prevent pregnancy. Prosthetic devices inserted into the vagina to support its internal structure injected the essences of pomegranates and other plants with high, natural levels of estrogen to prevent the pituitary gland from producing the hormone that stimulates ovulation. Such pessaries worked on the same principle as modern contraceptive pills. Brad Steiger explained how "it was only in very recent years that it was learned that acacia spikes contain a gum that is deadly to sperm. When the gum is dissolved in a fluid, its active constituent is lactic acid, a familiar ingredient in many modern contraceptive jellies."[10] No such contraceptive methods reappeared for another 3,180 years, in the late nineteenth century; an additional six decades of development were required before birth control became widely acceptable in the 1950s.

The Ebers Papyrus, a medical document from the Eighteenth, or Thutmosid Dynasty (1549/1550 to 1292 BCE)—the dynasty most famous for its boy-king, Tutankhamun—specifies a concoction of honey, an unspecified plant, dates, and finely ground acacia spikes for stopping pregnancy in the first, second, or third trimester.

Equally far ahead of their time were the Chimu, pre-Inca civilizers of Pacific Coastal South America. "A set of surgical instruments used to carry out abortions in ancient Peru" was described in a 1968 issue of the archaeological journal *Antiquity* (42:233). "The instruments found were scalpels, needles, forceps, and bandages in burial grounds dating from the Chimu period [450 to 750 CE]. . . . There are four dilators and five curettes, which closely resemble the modern instruments used to scrape a uterus in order to produce or complete an abortion."[11] Not only were these specialized surgical instruments far beyond anything known in contemporaneous Dark Age Europe, but nothing resembling them would be seen again for another 1,170 to 1,470 years, until the early twentieth century.

Another set of medical instruments from the ancient Old World compelled a similar comparison to modern counterparts when they came to light after 1,821 years during excavations at Pompeii—the Imperial Roman-era city made infamous for its destruction by the eruption of Mount Vesuvius in 79 CE. As a writer for *Scientific American* magazine declared:

> Gynecology was a science flourishing in its perfection long before that date. . . . In every instance the instruments are almost in their minutest particulars exact duplicates of those in use by the most approved modern science of today. . . . The workmanship is as fine as anything to be produced in this line in the twentieth century. The instruments are hand-wrought, the screws as thread-like and capable of delicate manipulation, as anything to be found in today's achievements.

Their excellence proved that the founding of modern gynecology in the late 1800s was but a "reinvention in the world of surgery."[12]

Surviving Roman surgical instruments were no less sophisticated. Imperial-era doctor bags held hemostatic tourniquets; arterial clamps to stop blood loss; and modern plunger forceps used in operations for removal of growths, hemorrhoids, organs, or parts causing trouble. These ancient medical utensils are virtually indistinguishable from twenty-first-century versions.

# 5

# Surgical Wonders

*Foolish the doctor who despises the knowledge acquired by the ancients.*

HIPPOCRATES, *ANCIENT MEDICINE,* 400 BCE

Nineteen miles south of Cairo, near the Sakkara pyramid complex, lies the tomb of Skar, the chief physician to a Fifth Dynasty ruler. In 2001, some thirty bronze medical implements were found inside. They confirmed the high surgical skill level achieved in Egypt's Old Kingdom, circa 2630 BCE. Several of Skar's needle instruments were lancets for pushing a clouded lens backward into the vitreous body of the eye. This delicate procedure required a sharp instrument to push the milky white lens to the bottom of the eye. Couching, or *lens depression,* dislodged the cataract away from the pupil, a technique that stood for the next 4,378 years, until the French ophthalmologist Jacques Daviel performed the first extra capsular cataract extraction in 1748.

Dating to Egypt's Second Intermediate Period (circa 1650 to 1550 BCE), a manual of military surgery is history's oldest known surgical treatise on physical trauma. The 3,600-year-old document describes forty-eight cases of injuries, fractures, wounds, dislocations, and tumors, together with their effective treatment. Doubtless, its encyclopedic scope was not the original invention of some lone Seventeenth Dynasty genius but rather the accumulation of medical experience and development long preceding its compilation circa 1600 BCE. Lost with the collapse of Classical civilization, nothing equivalent to the Edwin Smith Papyrus would be known for another fifteen centuries. In describing the plastic repair of a broken nose, the papyrus likewise reveals that ancient Egyptian physicians were history's first plastic surgeons.[1]

Based on their success, cosmetic surgery was later performed in Rome beginning in the early first century BCE, when damaged ears were skillfully repaired. These pioneering efforts in plastic surgery were discarded during the Dark Ages until reintroduced from India into Europe in 1815. Throughout the subcontinent, the practice was still common during the sixth century BCE, when medical doctor Sushruta was a master of *rhinoplasty,* the reconstruction of the nose. His *Sushruta Samhita* is divided into eight categories, featuring 121 different types of surgical instruments and 300 surgical procedures, such as reconstructing ear lobes with cheek flaps.[2] The tome comprises 184 chapters covering 1,120 illnesses, as well as several hundred types of drugs made from animals, plants, and minerals. The *Sushruta Samhita*'s vast assortment of restorative knowledge seems extraordinary for a 2,600-year-old text, but it nonetheless documents the high levels of medical science attained by ancient-world physicians.

## BRAIN SURGERY

Native brain surgeons in South America attained extraordinary levels of success long before the Spaniards arrived. "They seemed to know the cranial anatomy, avoiding areas that bled more," said David S. Kushner of the Incas and their predecessors. A professor of medicine at the University of Miami Miller School of Medicine, in 2018 he examined more than eight hundred skulls operated on by Incan practitioners between 400 BCE and 1500 CE, concluding that they understood how "survival was dependent on avoiding infection, and their changing techniques reflect this." The Andean method was known as *trepanation,* a procedure in which a hole is drilled into the skull. "We do not know how the ancient Peruvians prevented infections," said Kushner, "but they were very good in that field."[3]

So good, in fact, that their patients enjoyed an 85 to 92 percent rate of recovery, contrasted with surgical trepanation conducted in 1786 at the Paris Hotel Dieu, where such operations were virtually fatal.[4] Seventy-five years later, death rates from cranial operations during the American Civil War varied from 46 to 56 percent. "The survival rate for the procedure could be determined from any healing observed in the subjects' skulls," notes J. Douglas Kenyon. "If there was no healing, then it was clear the patient had not survived the operation."[5]

Kushner's findings were preceded by Fernando Cabajeis, professor of neurosurgery at the National University of San Marcos in Peru, where he collected and examined ten thousand trepanned Andean skulls predating the Spanish Conquest. He determined that their operations evidenced thirty different neurosurgical instruments made of bronze and used to treat a number of symptoms, including migraines, seizures, trauma, and mental illness. But what kind of highly advanced neurosurgical instrument made a one-inch-diameter, perfectly circular hole at the back of a two-thousand-year-old skull trepanned in what is now Detroit, Michigan, baffles modern medical investigators. The specimen was removed around the turn of the nineteenth century from perhaps the largest earthen structure that ever existed in North America, the eight-hundred-foot-long Grand Mound, built by construction engineers of the Adena culture, which flourished throughout the Midwest from 1000 to 200 BCE.

On the other side of the world, in 2011, archaeologists from Istanbul University excavated five trepanned skulls dated to circa 3000 BCE at Ikztepe, a village on the Black Sea. "Researchers have also found razor-sharp cutting tools made from volcanic glass" responsible for the skulls' "clean, rectangular incisions. . . . Such trepanning was used to treat hemorrhages, brain cancer, head trauma, or mental illness," Kenyon writes. "In some cases, new bone growth has been found around the incisions,

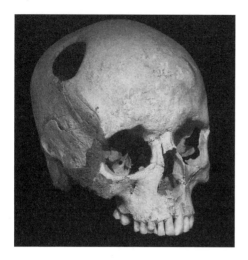

Figure 5.1. Healing ridges evident in a trepanned skull of a fifty-four-year-old New Stone Age Central European man indicate that he survived the earlier surgical operation to live a normal, healthy life. Photo by Rama.

indicating post-operative healing," which was greatly facilitated by the liberal use of soap in Mesopotamia by the earliest known civilizers.[6]

A simple item needed for all surgery and to prevent infection, soap was invented by the Sumerians by boiling oil and alkalis together in great vats. Among their more than thirty thousand surviving cuneiform tablets, about one thousand of them deal with medicine and medical practices, including pediatrics, gynecology, and neurology. They also describe treatment for convulsive disorders, skin diseases, and fevers, with descriptions of accurately observed symptoms.

## DENTISTRY

In the ancient world, such sophisticated surgery was on a par with dentistry. A case in point was the discovery in 1997 of a human jaw-bone from Colorado's Rio Blanco County. Still in place, a canine tooth had been neatly bored to remove decay by an obsidian drill that, under microscopic scrutiny, left discernable striations on the surface enamel. Dated to before 1200 CE, the tooth had been treated by a form of dentistry centuries ahead of its time. At least 1,400 years earlier, Mayan dentists likewise treated tooth cavities with iron fillings, as described in *Science* magazine on July 26, 1929: "Two teeth containing circular holes filled with iron pyrites were found by the Marshall Field Expedition to Honduras"; both are still on display at Chicago's Field Museum of Natural History.[7] Mayan dentists were self-evidently knowledgeable about tooth anatomy, because they knew how to drill into teeth without contacting the pulp inside.

Among Adena skeletal remains entombed inside the C. L. Lewis Stone Mound near the town of St. Paul in south-central Indiana, archaeologists from the Indiana Historical Society removed a human skull on the Flatrock River exhibiting dental bridgework: "A small, copper object was found which was originally associated with an upper incisor, fitted over the bottom to form a sheath-like covering."[8]

Dentistry's oldest known example was discovered in 2001. According to the April 19 issue of *New Scientist,* the well-preserved eight-thousand-year-old skull of an adult human male belonged to a highly advanced, if unidentifiable, culture in Pakistan, earlier even than the Indus valley civilization circa 3100 BCE. "A molar still firmly fixed in the jawbone," writes encyclopedist William Corliss, "shows a tiny, perfectly round hole, which, under the microscope, shows concentric grooves left by a drill. The top of the hole is rounded by chewing, indicating that the patient survived."[9]

"Sites in Pakistan have revealed dental practices involving curing tooth related disorders with bow drills operated perhaps by skilled bead craftsmen," according to April Holloway in *Ancient Pages.* "Reconstruction of this ancient form of dentistry showed that the methods used were reliable and effective."[10] The oldest known dental filling was found in a southern Slovenian cave during 2012, when a sixty-five-hundred-year-old jawbone with a cavity deep enough to impact the dentin layer of the tooth had been packed with beeswax for reducing pain, sensitivity, and swelling from a vertical crack in the enamel.[11] This Neolithic procedure was literally millennia ahead of its times and not equaled until Hesi-Re, history's first official dentist, who served under the still-famous Third Dynasty pharaoh Djoser from 2687 to 2668 BCE. The Old Kingdom discoverer of periodontal disease, or gum disease, was honored as Chief of Dentists and Physicians and Doctor of the Tooth.

Nearly a thousand years after Hesi-Re, the anonymous author or authors of the Ebers Papyrus described eleven cures for various oral issues, including four for loose teeth.[12] The compound specified is similar to modern-day composite filling: ground barley mixed with honey in a liquid matrix, plus an antiseptic agent of yellow ocher. Oral hygiene for people in ancient Egypt included brushing with frayed twigs and "a type of dentifrice like sodium bicarbonate or natron for cleaning their teeth," according to the 2019 University of Alberta study of a Nile valley woman who lived circa 2180 BCE. "Use of natron or other natural salt could even have had the secondary effect of an analgesic" for treating toothache.[13]

Examples of Egyptian, Pakistani, Mayan, and Anasazi dentistry are extraordinary, because none of them was carried out in a crude or primitive fashion and instead demonstrated forms of applied technique unmatched until the late nineteenth century. In other words, they showed that earlier civilizations achieved levels of technological sophistication lost with their downfall and independently reinvented only centuries later. For example, dental prosthesis for the tooth of a Peruvian skull from about 1300 CE was so skillfully crafted, it was not only far in advance of any contemporaneous parallels but also compares favorably with some of the best modern work in the field.[14] Far earlier still, there were Etruscan partial dentures of false teeth set in a three-to-five-millimeter band of gold dated to circa 700 BCE.[15] The Etruscans were a highly civilized people who dominated western Italy prior to the rise of Rome. Their rivals for domination of the Mediterranean Sea were the Phoenicians, who also practiced advanced dentistry. One Phoenician was found still wearing gold-wire bridgework on his teeth in a tomb from the sixth century BCE at the ancient port city of Sidon, the most powerful city-state of ancient Phoenicia in what is today Lebanon, about twenty-five miles south of Beirut.[16]

During the Dark Ages that superseded Classical civilization, dentistry was reduced to nothing more than primitive extraction at the unwashed hands of barbers. Not until 1723—when a French surgeon, Pierre Fauchard, became the father of modern dentistry after publishing his comprehensive system of caring for and treating the teeth—did the profession begin to approach its former levels of excellence achieved thousands of years earlier.

## PAIN KILLERS

While ancient Egyptian physicians have long been recognized for their advanced skill, how they anesthetized patients against excruciating pain arising from surgery was not understood until the late twentieth century. During mid-1991, curators at the Cairo Museum began noticing trace elements of cocaine in virtually all the numerous mummies of their collection, from the first to last dynasties, among literally thousands of male and female specimens, including persons of all classes and ages.[17] The narcotic was present even among many mummified dogs, cats, and horses. Egyptologists concluded that the missing anesthetic of pharaonic times had finally been discovered. Unfortunately for conventional scholars, whose denial of any connections between the ancient Old World and pre-Columbian America is academic dogma, coca never grew in North Africa; its growth was restricted instead to Argentina, Bolivia, Peru, Ecuador, and Colombia. Defying this irrevocable fact, innumerable Cairo Museum mummies nonetheless contain traces of cocaine. Today cocaine hydrochloride topical solution is used as a local anesthetic before medical procedures to numb pain in certain areas of the body such as the mouth, nose, and throat. Offensive as the prospect may be to mainstream opinion, an abundance of physical evidence clearly establishes that transatlantic mariners from the Nile valley were in contact with their South American suppliers of cocaine, which quite literally made Egyptian surgery possible.

They likewise sailed far to obtain another natural substance no less vital for public health: olibanum, a dried resin better known as frankincense from the genus *Boswellia;* specifically, *Boswellia sacra* and *Boswellia carterii*. Although these trees were found in Oman and Yemen, they grew in greater profusion around the Horn of Africa, requiring an eight-thousand-mile round trip from the Nile delta. Until as recently as 2010, archaeologists long wondered why something as insignificant as incense could have occasioned such a major expedition. Scientists then noticed that frankincense prevented the spread of cancer and caused cancerous cells to close themselves down, according to a 2010 BBC News report.[18]

M. Z. Siddiqui, at the Indian Institute of Natural Resins and Gums, tells how olibanum's "medicinal properties are also widely recognized, mainly for the treatment of inflammatory conditions, as well as in some cancerous diseases."[19] Its ancient efficacy was borne out the following year, when "researchers analyzed hundreds of Egyptian mummies and discovered that cancer was extremely rare, contrasting sharply with conditions today, where cancer accounts for almost a third of all deaths," observes Kenyon. "Professor Rosalie David, a bio-medical Egyptologist at the University of Manchester, and her colleague, Professor Michael Zimmerman, examined mummies dating back three millennia. They identified only five tumor cases, and most of those were benign."[20]

Frankincense was burned in great quantities at every sacred temple and shrine throughout the Nile valley, allowing its entire population— beginning with about one million inhabitants during the First Dynasty and reaching five million by the Roman era—to regularly inhale its cancer-preventive properties. As investigative scientists are only just now beginning to recognize, this miraculous resin possesses additional medicinal qualities applied by Egyptian physicians. "They found that frankincense had antiseptic, anti-inflammatory, and analgesic properties," writes Wu Mingren for Ancient Origins, "and therefore prescribed it as a cure for a variety of ailments, including indigestion, cough, and halitosis (bad breath)."[21]

Important frankincense components are monoterpenes, or organic compounds, such as alpha- and beta-pinene, which help eliminate toxins from the liver and kidneys. Frankincense also stimulates antimicrobial activity and aids wound healing. "Another research team found that an extract of *Boswellia serrata* resin produced sedative and analgesic outcomes in rats," states Siddiqui, asserting that frankincense "definitely has anti-anxiety and anti-inflammatory effects [in mice]. It may also be an anti-depressant."[22]

In addition to these purely medical results, according to Joseph Robert Jochmans, olibanum "was said to have the unusual effects of bringing peace of mind, relaxation and a heightened sense of spiritual experience." Jochmans explains:

> In early 2008, Arieh Moussayeff, a pharmacologist from the Hebrew University in Jerusalem, led a team of Israeli and American scientists in successfully isolating from *bowellia* tree resin a compound they named incensole acetate. By injecting mice with this substance, they discovered the subjects had significantly reduced levels of stress and anxiety. The new chemical helps to regulate the flow of ions in and out of neurons in a similar way that modern anti-depressant drugs work today. The experimenters concluded that their findings will one day aid not only in developing a new class of chemicals that will shed light on the molecular workings of the brain, but will also facilitate in creating a general calming effect that promotes a healing mental state.[23]

Mingren agrees that "analysis of this precious substance using modern chemistry could lead to the discovery of new ways in which frankincense may be used for medicinal purposes."[24] No wonder the ancient Egyptians went to such great lengths to obtain frankincense!

Another resin they similarly valued on behalf of good health was amber. "Geologically speaking," explains the Al-Kemi website, "amber is the fossilized resin of a number of different conifer trees, all now extinct. When injured or broken, these trees would exude a sap to seal the wound and protect the inner wood, sometimes to a depth of two feet all around the tree. This resin fossilized over the millennia."[25] The originally gluey plant substance dripped from the trees to be trapped in rocky fissures or on the seashore, where it was rolled back and forth by wave action. Over time (about forty-five million years), fragments hardened into translucent yellow-orange stonelike pieces handily collected from the beach. Relatively soft, they can be carved into beads and other forms that, when skillfully cut and highly polished, result in fine jewelry and precious ornaments.

It was not primarily for baubles, bangles, or beads, however, that ancient Egyptians traveled far to obtain large quantities of amber. They were convinced that this organic gemstone was vital for health and guaranteed protection against infectious disease. The late fourteenth-century-BCE tomb of Tutankhamun contained a solid silver breast ornament studded with large roundels of amber. About 1210 BCE, Merenptah, the fourth pharaoh of the Nineteenth Dynasty, sent a man-size amber statue of his personal deity—Ptah, the god of life—to an allied Syrian ruler suffering from some unspecified illness. An Eighteenth Dynasty tomb inscription, circa 1450 BCE, tells how "an embassy through the Haunebu [ancestors of today's Lithuanians, Latvians, and Estonians], from the northern lands by the end of the world [the Baltic Sea coast], brought with them four and one half tons of amber."[26] This statement not only reveals the prodigious quantities of organic gemstone that arrived in ancient Egypt but also specifies the long-distance travel necessary for their importation.

Mark Cartwright writes on the Ancient History Encyclopedia website that "tests have revealed that amber found at sites across the Levant and Near East came from the Baltic."[27] But why, when amber could have been far more easily obtained from relatively nearby Greece? "Baltic amber contains three percent to eight percent of succinic acid," according to gemologist Svajunas Petreikis. The name for succinic acid comes from *succinum*, Latin for "amber," and it is also a crystalline acid occurring in living tissue. Petreikis defines it as "a scientifically examined medical substance used in contemporary medicine. The highest content of the acid is found in the amber cortex, the external layer of the stone. When Baltic amber is in contact for periods of time against the skin, it actually increases the strength of the immune system, eases pain, and reduces stress."[28]

John Snyder, M.D., assistant professor of pediatrics at Tufts University School of Medicine and a practicing pediatrician at Amherst Pediatrics in Amherst, Massachusetts, explains how "Baltic amber beads, when warmed by body heat, release tiny amounts of succinic acid, which passes trans-dermally [through direct contact with the skin surface] into the blood stream, where it acts as an analgesic."[29]

# 6

# Therapeutic Achievements

*The first physician who is known to have counted the pulse,*
*Herophilos of Alexandria [born 300 BCE], lived in Egypt.*

JAMES HENRY BREASTED,
*THE EDWIN SMITH SURGICAL PAPYRUS*

The ancients were clearly adept at preventing infection, disease, and pregnancy. And they developed the instruments and anesthetics necessary to make surgical procedures and recovery possible. But they were also advanced in the art of managing chronic health issues and rehabilitation.

## ELECTROMAGNETIC THERAPIES

Discussed in the previous chapter for its use in easing pain, amber's healing qualities have been only very recently recognized by scholars, who for the previous sixteen centuries scoffed at dynastic Egyptians for their unfounded belief in its medicinal effects. The English word *electricity* derives from *elektron,* the Greek word for "amber," and not without cause.[1] This unique gem actually has electrical properties that make it able to pick up small items, like straw, as well as create sparks when rubbed against silk, wool, or fur, demonstrating that magnetism and electricity are manifestations of the same force Egyptian physicians used to interface with a patient's own bioelectrical fields for magnetizing and withdrawing certain illnesses. The average human at rest produces 97.2 watts of power. The world record holder for farthest distance biked in one hour, Ondrej Sonsenka, generated an average of 430 watts during his ride of about thirty miles.[2] Our brain alone at rest generates almost 20 watts.

Dynastic Eygptian physicians believed that human bioelectrical fields can be made to resonate with amber's static electrical and electromagnetic frequencies for metabolic stability as the basis for a wide range of therapy, particularly regarding brain tumors. This view has been dismissed as fallacious by medical doctors for the past several centuries, "but now it turns out that a new therapy for brain tumors involves intentionally bombarding the brain with electric fields from a cap of electrodes," reported Kenyon. "A team of researchers from a biotech firm in Israel has begun a clinical test for the new therapy. For eight hundred patients in an eighteen-month trial, a lightweight, battery-powered device which generates 200-kHz fields through a series of electrodes was attached to the skull for twenty-four hours a day. In some of the patients, the tumors stopped growing, and the survival time on average was increased from twenty-nine to sixty-two weeks."[3]

Ancient Egyptian medical practitioners supplemented their reliance on amber with a more readily available rock mineral, one of the main iron ores: magnetite, the most magnetic of all naturally occurring minerals on Earth. Capable of attracting small pieces of iron, it is also attracted to magnets and can be magnetized to become a permanent magnet itself. Ancient Egyptian insistence on the efficacy of electromagnetism in healing, like amber, was long derided by modern-era medical doctors as base superstition.

As recently as 2017, however, researchers have apparently discovered a new way to treat the often fatal condition of sepsis, also known as blood poisoning. Kenyon writes:

> In the treatment, antibodies that bind to dangerous sepsis-causing bacteria are coated with iron particles. Then later, after the solution has picked up the sepsis, it is run through a dialysis machine where magnets literally pull the iron-coated antibodies and attached bacteria, right out of the solution, leaving it sepsis-free. Right now, the treatment can only be used on one type of bacteria, but researchers think they are on the path to much broader applications. Considering the alarming growth of antibiotic resistance everywhere, magnetic therapy of this type, they think, could be a powerful new weapon in the doctors' arsenal.[4]

While it may seem new to contemporary medical scientists, magnetic therapy of this type was common practice among Nile valley physicians three thousand years and more ago.

In 2011 the cancer-curing promise of biomagnetism was described by *Science Magazine*'s Tim Wogan, who explained that cancer cells can be killed at temperatures above 43°C. "One promising idea, known as magnetic hyperthermia, involves injecting minuscule 'nanoparticles,' basically microscopic lumps of iron oxide or other compounds, into tumors to make them magnetic." Tumors have been eliminated in mice using this procedure, and modern researchers are exploring the concept for human treatment.

> The patient is put into a magnetic field that reverses direction thousands of times every second. The magnetic nanoparticles are excited by the applied field and begin to get hot, heating and potentially destroying the surrounding cancer tissue. Because healthy tissue is not altered by the magnetic field, it does not heat up and is not damaged.

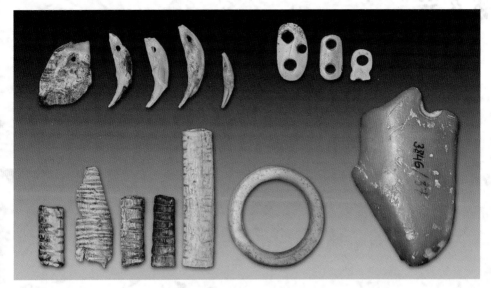

**Plate 1.** These perfectly perforated artifacts from Siberia's Denisova Cave are contemporaneous with a power-drilled Old Stone Age bracelet found nearby. Photo by Thilo Parg.

**Plate 2.** Displayed at the Paris Louvre, this Nineteenth Dynasty female figure forms the handle of a 4,000-year-old Egyptian applicator for medicinal cosmetics created to effectively prevent eye infection. Photo by Guillaume Blanchard.

MEDEIA AND TALVS

**Plate 3.** Talos at the feet of Medea.
1920 illustration by Sybil Tawse.

**Plate 4.** Rising over the Peruvian Desert, *Condor I* re-creates the flight of its Nazca precursors after some two thousand years. Photo by Julian Nott, who died March 2019 doing what he did best and loved most: ballooning.

**Plate 5.** The Sakkara Bird: Dynastic toy, or ancient Egyptian model of an operational aircraft? Photo by Dawoud Khalil Messiha.

**Plate 6.** A Viking sunstone of the kind used by Norse seafarers for transatlantic voyages to America more than five centuries before Columbus. Photo by Arni Ein.

**Plate 7.** Military history's first trench mortar was developed for Roman legions by the Greek inventor Heron of Alexandria around 50 CE. Spring loaded, it hurled super-heated, three-inch stone balls with accuracy not to be seen again until the First World War. Modern re-creation displayed at Wisconsin's Castlerock Museum in Alma. Author's photograph.

**Plate 8.** Florentine Renaissance architect Giulio Parigi's late sixteenth-century painting of Archimedes's heat ray in action against the Roman navy's invasion of Syracuse.

**Plate 9.** A human skull inlaid with turquoise and other semi-precious stone fragments in the likeness of Tezcatlipoca, the Aztec god of war. Both eyes are reflective obsidian, signifying mirrors. Photo by Z-m-k.

**Plate 10.** A specimen of Tula's plumbate ware. Innovative Toltec artisans created pottery through the unknown process of vitrification, turning sand into glass. Photo by HJPD.

**Plate 11.** Three of the four atlantean columns at the Toltec capital city of Tula. Each of the thousand-year-old figures grasps in its right hand a pistol-like specimen of surprisingly high technology. Photo by SERFEDCONMAT.

**Plate 12.** Artist's conception of the Pharos Lighthouse.
Image by Emad Victor Shenouda.

**Plate 13.** Undersea discovery of the fallen Pharos Lighthouse.
Photo by Roland Unger.

**Plate 14.** The ancient Egyptian Temple of Dendera, where artificial electric light shows dramatized religious spectacles. Photo by Bernard Gagnon.

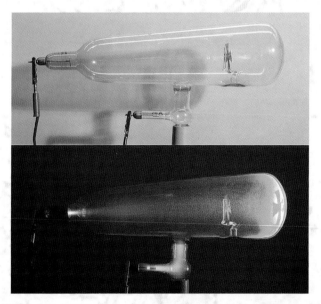

**Plate 15.** A Crookes tube at rest (above) and electrified. They compare with ancient Egyptian versions illustrated on the temple walls of Dendera (see page 177). Photo by D-Kuru.

**Plate 16.** The massive pillars of India's Hoysaleswara temple bear witness to their creation via a lathe technology beyond modern comprehension. Photo by Ankush Manuja.

**Plate 17.** The mirror-like sheen of Hoysaleswara's stone bull could only have been achieved by a rotary power tool at least eight centuries before its modern reinvention. Photo by Sarah Welch.

**Plate 18.** Sigiriya, or Lion Rock, in Sri Lanka, is topped by ancient mind-boggling mega-construction. Photo by AndyWFUK.

**Plate 19.** Machu Picchu, engineered to resist earthquakes, as partially afforded by these trapezoidal windows, still stands after centuries of seismic activity. Photo by Martin St-Aman.

**Plate 20.** Incan suspension bridges were the greatest structures of their kind and spanned longer distances than anywhere else on Earth.
Photo by Rutahsa Adventures.

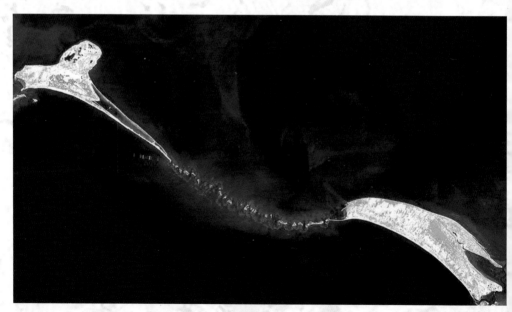

**Plate 21.** A subset of Landsat 5 TM true color composite showing India's Rama's Bridge. Original image acquired on February 6, 1988, at 4:42:00 GMT.
Photo by USGS and NASA.

**Plate 22.** Rolling stone doorway at Turkey's ancient subterranean metropolis near Derinkuyu. Photo by Nevit Dilmen.

**Plate 23.** Turkey's ancient underground cities were well-organized urban centers. Photo by Nevit Dilmen.

**Plate 24.** Ancient Egypt's Serapeum: A mortuary for sacred bulls or a source of electrical power? Photo by Happa.

**Plate 25.** One of the Serapeum's huge stone boxes: Bovine sarcophagi or electric storage cells? Photo by Ovedc.

**Plate 26.** The pre-Incan Nazca's ingenious *puquio*. Wind trapped in the spiral design draws water up to the surface. Photo by Diego Delso.

**Plate 27.** What can explain the Grand Gallery's remarkable acoustic properties inside Egypt's Great Pyramid? Photo by Peter Prevos.

**Plate 28.** Egypt's Great Pyramid may have ceased to function as a monumental power plant when its King's Chamber crystal was lost during serious political upheavals of the nineteenth Dynasty, circa 1200 BCE. Photo by L-BBE.

**Plate 29.** Artist's rendition of Egypt's Giza Plateau as a pyramid power complex.

. . . Nanoscientist Jinwoo Cheon of Yonsei University, in Seoul, and colleagues set out to create a nanoparticle that would get hotter than traditional nanoparticles so that not as many would need to be injected into the body. . . . The team tested its technique on three mice whose abdomens had been grafted with cells from human brain cancer. The researchers injected the tumors with core-shell nanoparticles and placed the mice inside a coil of wire. They turned on an alternating current in the coil, creating an alternating magnetic field.

After ten minutes, the team removed the mice from the coil and monitored the tumors for the next four weeks. All traces of cancer disappeared from the mice with no apparent side effects. . . . For comparison, another group of mice was treated instead with a single dose of doxorubicin, a traditional anticancer drug. Although it initially shrunk some of the tumors, they grew back to four times their original size by the end of the trial.[5]

Nanoengineer Naomi Halas of Rice University in Houston, Texas, exclaimed, "I am so happy that more of these types of nanoparticle-based hypothermal therapies are being developed to increase the arsenal of weapons against cancer."[6] Four or five millennia ago, electromagnetic weapons were already in the medical arsenal of Egyptian medical specialists, as their understanding and successful application of amber and magnetite prove.

## HERBAL REMEDIES

Other natural substances the ancient Egyptians understood and applied, which modern science has only recently rediscovered, included a gum derived from the acacia tree, successfully used for gastrointestinal and urinary tract diseases. Mixed with boiling water to form a mucilage, acacia coated the digestive tract to treat cases of gastritis, diarrhea, and ulcers. Nile valley physicians exploited *kuzbarah,* their name for the coriander plant, for the relief of headaches, arthritis, and rheumatism. They rubbed its essential oil on the body to effectively relieve inflammatory conditions, muscular aches, pains and stiffness; remove toxins; and stimulate circulation. Coriander seeds were used as a paste for mouth ulceration and a poultice for other ulcers.

Yet even these advanced medicinal applications were immensely predated by a prehuman species, as brought to light by a Columbia University faculty member and archaeologist best known for his excavation of a Neanderthal site in northern Iraq. In 1960, Ralph Stefan Solecki and his team members unearthed the remains of a thirty-five-to-forty-five-year-old male about fifty feet from the mouth of Shanidar Cave 4, where the man had been intentionally buried in a shallow grave about sixty thousand years ago.[7] His body, configured into a fetal position, was placed on a bed of woven wood horsetail, a plant with a hollow jointed stem bearing whorls of narrow leaves and producing spores in cones at the tips of the shoots.

Surrounding him was the pollen of medicinal plants used by modern herbalists, including yarrow, cornflower, ragwort, groundsel, grape hyacinth, St. Barnaby's thistle, joint pine, and hollyhock. All of them have long-known curative powers as diuretics, stimulants, and astringents, as well as anti-inflammatory properties. While early-twenty-first-century archaeologists believe the presence of these herbs are actually much later extrusions brought into the burial site by a gerbil-like rodent known as the Persian jird, their conclusion is contradicted by the wood horsetail bed on which the Neanderthal man had been placed in a position suggesting rebirth, together with the therapeutic character of his accompanying plants.

Other herbal marvels have jumped over many centuries from the moment of their ancient discovery into our time. A hooked herb, a root extract, and a dash of bark are three compounds that have been traditionally used in China to treat various diseases, such as Parkinson's and irritable bowel syndrome, that have so far foiled Western doctors. Wendy Zukerman reported in *New Scientist* magazine that for over two thousand years Chinese doctors have treated Parkinson's disease with *gou teng,* an herb with hook-like branches. Earlier this year [2011], one hundred fifteen people with Parkinson's were given a combination of traditional Chinese medical herbs, including *gou teng,* or a placebo, for thirteen weeks. At the end of the study, volunteers who had taken the herbs slept better and had more fluent speech than those taking the placebo. . . .

Meanwhile, Zhaoxiang Bian, also at Hong Kong Baptist University, is developing a drug called JCM-16021 for irritable bowel syndrome (IBS) using seven herbal plants and based on a Chinese formulation called tong xie yao fang, used to treat IBS since the 1300s. . . . In 2007, Bian gave eighty people with IBS either JCM-16021 with Holopon—a drug that interrupts nerve impulses in the parasympathetic nervous system responsible for digestion—or Holopon alone.

After eight weeks, fifty-two per cent of those given JCM-16021 with Holopon reported reduced IBS symptoms, compared with thirty-two per cent of those given Holopon alone.[8]

Modern medicine is finding its way back to its ancient roots.

Perhaps the most mysterious, certainly the most popular, mendicant of antiquity went by the appropriately exotic name of *silphium.* Used by early dynastic Egyptians, who gave the herb its own glyph, silphium's popularity spread to Crete. There it was likewise identified by a Minoan hieroglyph and survived the collapse of Bronze Age civilization to become the rage of Hellenic Greece, where it was revered as a gift from Apollo, the god of healing. Later the Romans sang its praises in poems and songs as "worth its weight in *denarii* [silver coins]," or even gold.[9] About 50 BCE, Julius Caesar went so far as to store a fifteen-hundred-pound cache of silphium in the capital's official treasury. Long before then, a great North African city near the present-day Mediterranean town of Shahhat had become so wealthy from its monopoly on the manufacture and exportation of the resin—

Figure 6.1. Silphium shown on an ancient coin.
Photo by CNG Coin.

the plant's valuable product—that Cyrene emblazoned its coins with the image of silphium.

It flourished only at Cyrenaica within a narrow coastal area of northeastern Libya, about 125 miles east to west by 35 miles north to south. All attempts at growing the herb elsewhere invariably failed. Its intoxicating fragrance went into a variety of perfumes coaxed from the flower's delicate blooms and was highly regarded as an aphrodisiac, while also functioning as a contraceptive and an abortifacient, a drug that causes abortion. In various forms of application—including liquids, salves, and creams—it was used to treat coughs, sore throat, fevers, indigestion, bites inflicted by feral dogs, aches and pains, warts, and other maladies. About 390 BCE, Hippocrates advised, "When the gut protrudes and will not remain in its place, scrape the finest and most compact *silphium* into small pieces and apply as a poultice."[10]

Yet for all its vast regard, the precise identity of this miracle herb and the cause of its extinction were lost. Numerous contemporaneous illustrations of silphium still exist on pottery and murals, and Theophrastus—the fourth-to-third-century-BCE father of botany—described it as being about nineteen inches long and having thick roots covered in black bark, a hollow stalk similar to fennel, and golden leaves like celery.[11] But nothing more is known. Similarly mystifying is why silphium died out so thoroughly—never to be seen again—by the mid-first century. The Roman naturalist Gaius Plinius Secundus (better remembered as Pliny the Elder) writes that only a single stalk—the last known specimen—was discovered during his lifetime, plucked, and sent to Emperor Nero "as a curiosity" sometime between 54 and 68 CE.[12]

Scholars today guess that over-grazing, -farming, or -harvesting at Cyrene; excessive popular demand for its contraceptive use; climate change; desertification; and similar speculations were perhaps responsible. Zaria Gorvett, a science writer for the BBC, wonders if silphium was a hybrid, "which often results in very desired traits in the first generation, but [the] second generation can yield very unpredictable outcomes. This could have resulted in plants without fruits, when planted from seeds, instead asexually reproducing through their roots."[13] If so, then the panacea plant may have been bioengineered. But by whom? Egyptians were using it as early as the First Dynasty but had to import the resin from Libya, which they neither occupied nor controlled.

Perhaps the anonymous, if redoubtable, construction engineers of prehistoric Libya achieved levels of bioengineering in the form of silphium to match their impressive megalithic center. Five millennia before the earliest pharaoh, a populous megalithic culture filled Libya's Terrgurt valley with "dolmens and circles like Stonehenge, cairns [stone mounds built as memorials or landmarks, often aligned with celestial targets], underground cells excavated in rock, barrows topped with huge slabs, and step-pyramid-like mounds. Most remarkable are the trilithons, some still standing, some fallen, which occur isolated or in rows, and consist of two squared uprights standing on a common pedestal that supports a huge, transverse beam," observed the late nineteenth-century British archaeologist H. S. Cowper.[14]

"There had been originally no less than eighteen or twenty megalithic trilithons in a line," Cowper continued, "each with its massive altar placed before it."[15]

## PROSTHETIC INNOVATIONS

More certain were the ancients' surprisingly sophisticated orthopedics—surgery and treatment of the musculoskeletal system including degenerative conditions, trauma, sports injuries, tumors, and congenital issues. In 1995 forensic investigators probing the left leg of an Egyptian mummy donated to California's Rosicrucian Museum more than two decades before were astonished to find "a nine-inch metal orthopedic pin that had been inserted with such advanced bio-mechanical principles, that initially scientists could not distinguish it from a modern-day procedure," according to Prakesh. He writes that also discovered "were traces of ancient organic resin, similar to modern bone cement, as well as traces of ancient fats and textiles still held firmly in place." The mummified man dated to the Twenty-Sixth, or Saite, Dynasty, a late resurgent period of Egypt's cultural greatness. Team members "were astounded that the pin had been created with the same designs used today to create bone stabilization," Prakesh continues.[16]

Dr. Richard T. Jackson, an orthopedic surgeon at Brigham Young University (BYU), tells how he and his colleagues "are amazed at the ability to create a pin with bio-mechanical principles that we still use today—rigid fixation of the bone, for example. It is beyond anything we anticipated for that time." He explains that the pin "tapers into a corkscrew, as it enters the femur, or thigh bone, similar to bio-mechanical methods currently used. The other end of the pin, which is positioned in the tibia, or shin bone, has three flanges extending outward from the core of the pin that prevent rotation of the pin inside the bone." BYU professor Charles Wilfred Griggs remarked that "this is the first case of a metal orthopedic implant. I assumed at the time that the pin was modern. The story tells us how sophisticated ancient people really were."[17] The advanced procedure dated to approximately the turn of the sixth century BCE.

Dynastic Egyptian medical practitioners were no less adept in the development of prosthetics, as demonstrated by the artificial phalanx

Figure 6.2. An ancient prosthetic toe,
the so-called Greville Chester Great Toe.
Photo by Jon Bodsworth.

attached to a woman's right foot that is housed at Cairo's Egyptian Museum. Dated to the Twenty-First, or Tanite, Dynasty of Pharaoh Amenemope, from 1001 to 992 BCE, the so-called Greville Chester Great Toe was discovered in a plundered tomb that had been carved into an older burial chamber known as Sheikh Abd el-Qurna at an acropolis just west of Waset, which was a capital city called Thebes by the Greeks found in today's Luxor.

Researchers determined that the lifelike dactyl had been refitted several times to match the exact shape and fit of its owner, the daughter of a priest. "The artisan or artisans who made the device must've been very familiar with human physiology," writes George Dvorsky for the Gizmodo website. "The technical know-how can be seen particularly well in the mobility of the prosthetic extension," he quotes one of the forensic investigators, "and the robust structure of the belt strap. The fact that the prosthesis was made in such a laborious and meticulous manner indicates that the owner valued a natural look, aesthetics, and wearing comfort, and that she was able to count on highly qualified specialists to provide this."[18]

## ADVANCED HEALTH CARE SYSTEMS AND FACILITIES

The ancient world's greatest medical achievement surpassed anything comparable today. Roman authorities of each town and city in the empire collected from their citizens a moderate tax—variable according to local population size—that enabled free health care at clinics and hospitals built with public funds and staffed with physicians munificently paid by the state for their expertise and supplies. No one was charged for treatment, not even visiting foreigners or noncitizens, because refusing to medically assist indigent sufferers was deemed shamefully unethical. Private physicians noted for their exceptional skills were available to wealthy patrons able to afford them, but average persons were not denied state-of-the-art help. The Romans also cared for their soldiers far better than the American Veterans' Administration treats its military personnel.

"The Romans built military hospitals in many of their forts constructed during the expansion of their empire," as described by science writers Peter Thorpe and Nick James. "At the base of Neuss, on the Rhine, archaeologists found more than one hundred medical and pharmaceutical implements in one site. The hospital wards were well drained and lit and were in the quietest part of the fort. The military hospital included casualty reception centers and space for administration, including staff facilities. In many cases, the courtyard was used to grow healing plants, and legionaries would rest in the surrounding corridor during convalescence. Roman doctors set up clinics and nursing homes in all their cities."[19]

Roman health care progressively evolved over subsequent centuries, culminating in a large hospital "founded in Byzantium by Emperor John II (1118 to 1143 A.D.)," according to Thorpe and James. "Men and women were housed in separate buildings, each containing ten wards of fifty beds, with one ward reserved for surgical cases and another for long-term patients." Thorpe and James go on to tell that there was a full staff of male physicians plus one female physician and one female surgeon, qualified assistants, and pathologists. Vegetarian meals were available, a dispensary provided medication, and a school in which the sons of the entire medical staff were trained as doctors was next door.[20] Although Classical civilization perished in the late fifth century, a lone remnant of Roman medical care at Emperor John's city survived another thousand years on the European side of the Bosporus Strait, in what is now Turkey.

"The Chinese, too, had a system of publicly financed doctors," Thorpe and James continue, "paid for—unlike the Romans—by the central government. Set up in the second century B.C., it was originally confined to the major cities, but was extended in the first century A.D. to cover all of China. This national medical coverage was unique to China until modern times. The Chinese backed up their state medical service with systematic training. There were professors of medicine in the Imperial University at L-yang by A.D. 493. About a century later, the Imperial Medical College was established at Ch'ang-an, together with medical colleges in chief provincial cities, all of which had the authority to award degrees."[21]

Clearly, we have much to learn from the deep past.

## 7

# Optics

*Sometimes, our cultural arrogance gets in the way of our being able to appreciate how people from other cultures and times were able to also think and act in quite amazing ways.*

PROFESSOR CHARLES WILFRED GRIGGS,
"BYU PROFESSOR FINDS EVIDENCE OF ADVANCED
SURGERY IN ANCIENT MUMMY"

That Vikings sailed round-trip expeditions from Scandinavia to North America five centuries or more before Christopher Columbus landed in the New World is today accepted fact. But the means by which they achieved their extraordinarily difficult voyages is still debated. How medieval mariners steered a true course over thousands of miles of open water, beyond sight of land and at least three hundred years prior to the introduction in Europe of the magnetic compass, remains controversial among mainstream scholars. Even such an otherwise invaluable navigation instrument becomes useless when traveling within the general vicinity of the magnetic pole. Yet there is no excuse for academic bewilderment, because the answer was plainly spelled out by the Northmen themselves, as long ago as 1275 CE.

*Hrafnkel's Saga* recounts a perilous voyage in which "the weather was thick and stormy. . . . The king looked about and saw no blue sky. . . . Then the king took the sun-stone and held it up, and then he saw where the Sun beamed from the stone."[1] Additional source materials from this period describe sunstones as effective navigational aids in common use throughout the Viking Age (see plate 6). Norse navigational genius was inadvertently duplicated after nearly a thousand years, during the late 1940s, when research technicians at the U.S. National Bureau of Standards developed a sky compass based on the same principle of polarization so successfully employed by Viking mariners. The device was a twilight compass invented by A. H. Pfund of Johns Hopkins University. "The principal advantage of the sky compass is during twilight," reported a 1949 NBS paper, "and when the Sun is several degrees below the horizon, as well as when the region of the sky containing the sun is overcast, so long as there is a clear patch of sky overhead. The sky compass is thus of particular value when the sextant is not usable. Since the extent of polarization of the sky's light is greatest at right angles to the incident beam of sunlight, the compass is most accurate in the polar regions, where it is also most useful, because of the long duration of twilight."[2]

U.S. Navy and Air Force researchers conducted experiments with the sky compass throughout the early 1950s. Thereafter, it was used by pilots of Scandinavian Air Service (SAS) for several years on polar flights, following in the technological travels of their Viking forefathers. Even so, modern skeptics dismissed all medieval references to Norse sunstones as entirely legendary until Danish archaeologist Thorkild Ramskov postulated in 1967 that such objects were not flights of skaldic fancy. They were actually cordierite, "a kind of natural crystal with birefringent and dichroic properties which change color and brightness when rotated in front of polarized light, allowing for precise location of the Sun's position on an overcast day," according to *Ancient American* magazine writer Earl Koenig. "Birefringence, or double refraction, is the splitting of a light-wave into two different components: an ordinary and an extraordinary ray otherwise invisible to the naked eye. The color of cordierite will change from blue to light yellow when pointed in the Sun's direction. To back up his conclusion, Ramskov pointed out that cordierite pebbles are found in large numbers along the coast of Norway."[3]

Optical calcite, or Iceland spar, performs similarly well, playing an important role in the scientific discovery and study of polarization. Iceland was found and occupied by the Norse. Even today many high-performance polarizers use Iceland spar. Such stones could have performed even when the sun was several degrees below the horizon, when the atmosphere was still illuminated. Light fog and an overcast of thin clouds cannot eliminate light polarization, as revealed by optical calcite or cordierite crystal. Only under a thickly overcast sky would sunstones fail to operate. "At first," Koenig continues, "Ramskov's theory was well received and widely accepted by public and academics alike. Even ordinarily conservative *Scientific American* and *National Geographic* magazines published articles applauding his plausible research."[4] In time, however, conventional scholars caricatured all discussion of Viking sunstones as "comic book archaeology."

But in early 2007, Hungarian researchers testing cordierite used during the Viking Age (800 to 1200 CE) found that the crystals do in fact reveal the sun's position with a remarkable degree of accuracy, even in bad weather. "For more than a month," according to Koenig, "Gabor Horvath led a team of investigators from Budapest's Eotvos University recording polarization in the Arctic. They proved that the crystals located the Sun's position in foggy or cloudy conditions."[5] In the words of British author Robert Temple, "any number of armchair scholars can quibble, but there is no substitute for physical demonstration. . . . This [the sunstone] was the secret technology which enabled the Vikings to reach America."[6]

Temple is the foremost authority concerning optics in Classical and pre-Classical times. "I have been working on this problem for more than thirty years," he states, a claim attested by his detailed tome on the subject, *The Crystal Sun: Rediscovering a Lost Technology of the Ancient World.*[7] His uniquely thorough investigation relates that more than one hundred magnifying lenses crafted during the Middle Ages have been discovered across Scandinavia. Their profusion demonstrates that the Norse sunstones were not cultural exceptions among an otherwise barbaric society but rather part of broader skills in optics denoting a highly creative, inventive people who were masters of metallurgy and great poets, likewise capable of designing some of the most seaworthy vessels ever built.

The appearance of Norse magnifying glasses and sunstones from the late ninth to mid-eleventh centuries CE occupies a peculiar place in history between the termination of Classical-era lens production after 476 CE and the development of modern eyeglasses in thirteenth-century Italy. It reveals that a particular example of useful technology may be lost then independently reinvented later, possibly more than once and by different cultures, because in this instance at least, the Northmen knew virtually nothing about the long-dead Classical civilization with its flourishing optics manufacture. Nor did they share their own similar discoveries with Italians, who centuries later crafted what they imagined were the first magnifying lenses. But the Vikings were not the only premodern people in possession of advanced optics long before more recent developments.

During the late 1990s, the quartz crystal eyes of early dynastic statues were examined by Jay Enoch and Vasudevan Lakshminarayanan from the schools of optometry at, respectively, the University of California, Berkeley and the University of Missouri, St. Louis. Both were surprised by the intricacy of anatomical details found in the artificial eyes of a Fourth Dynasty representation of Prince Rahotep and a sculpted scribe from a Fifth Dynasty tomb at Sakkara (fig. 7.1, p. 72), which the scientists tried to reproduce with the latest optical technology. The ancient Egyptian lenses were found to be of a superior quality to the duplications. Enoch and Lakshminarayanan concluded that "because of the performance quality and design complexity, it is highly doubtful that the lenses used to re-create eye structures in ancient Egyptian statues were the first lenses created, despite the fact that they are four thousand six hundred years old."[8] Their research was complimented by a nearly thirty-year investigation published in 2001.

Figure 7.1. The anatomically intricate eyes of this Egyptian scribe statue from the Fifth Dynasty make it astonishingly lifelike. Photo by Rama.

Temple told Australia's *New Dawn* magazine that

the earliest actual lenses that I have located are crystal ones dating from the Fourth Dynasty of Old Kingdom Egypt from circa 2500 B.C. These are found in the Cairo Museum and two are in the Louvre in Paris. But archaeological evidence showing that they must have been around at least seven hundred years earlier has recently been excavated at Abydos in Upper Egypt. A tomb of a predynastic king there has yielded an ivory knife handle bearing a microscopic carving, which could only have been done under considerable magnification, and, of course, can only be seen with a strong magnifying glass today.[9]

Egyptian contemporaries in Asia Minor, what is modern Turkey, were likewise familiar with advanced optics according to Temple: "Ephesus and Troy were prominent centers of crystal lens manufacture, and excavations at Troy [by its late nineteenth century discoverer, Heinrich Schliemann] have yielded forty-nine specimens, whereas the number found at Ephesus now exceeds thirty. . . ." He writes of "the Ephesus lenses, which are concave rather than convex, and reduce images by seventy-five per cent, thus being good for myopic (short-sighted) people." Other Bronze Age locations for the discovery of magnifying glasses occur in Mycenaean Greece and at Phaistos—Minoan Crete's second most important city after Knossos—where a great number were found, "including the remains of a crystal lapidary workshop." This discovery was especially intriguing because, as described in chapter 6, it was here that the first example of movable type came to light, implying an urban center for technological advancement. Temple describes "masses of microscopic cuneiform texts written on Babylonian and Assyrian baked clay tablets and cylinder seals, and some ancient Greek coins contained secret inscriptions invisible to the eye, which could only be read through a lens."[10]

He concentrates on a particular Assyrian specimen dated to circa 620 BCE. It is known as the Layard lens, named after British archaeologist Austen Henry Layard. Layard found it during the course of his 1849 excavations at Kalhu, an ancient upper Mesopotamian city located on the outskirts of Mosul in modern-day northern Iraq. Laying in place, as it had been for the previous twenty-five centuries, amid ruins of the capital's northwest palace, the somewhat oval object was expertly carved from clear rock crystal then highly polished to an average 5.3 millimeters thick, with a maximum thickness of 6.2 millimeters at any point. It is 1.6 inches long and 1.4 inches wide, featuring a perfectly flat base, though the piece is damaged with "chippings, which appear to have been made downwards from the convex surface by someone who pried the lens out of a metal band, presumably of gold. If the band were a base metal, there would be no point in doing this."[11]

Figure 7.2. The Layard lens.
Photo by Geni.

Despite these imperfections, the lens has a general distortion-free magnification of 1.25X, but it may be increased to 2X if raised or tilted at a slight angle in much the same way modern bifocals are added near the bottom of less powerful reading glasses. Temple noticed that

> its shape and size suggest it was made to cover the orbital aperture (eye-socket, in ordinary English) fairly accurately, and its focus certainly suggests that it was deliberately designed to magnify some special kind of near work. . . . The Layard Lens was a carefully crafted monocle to correct for the astigmatic condition of a particular individual, possibly a king [given the circumstances of its find in the palace of Assyria's capital]. Astigmatism occurs when the eye does not focus light evenly on the retina, resulting in distorted or blurred vision at all distances. [The Assyrian sufferer could have been alternatively afflicted with common hyperopia, or far-sightedness, in which close objects appear blurry]. It was made to fit the eye-socket, was held up to it in a mounting by some means—perhaps something like a longnette [a lens held in front of a person's eye by a long handle at one side]. . . . It is thus probably one of the most remarkable technological artifacts to survive from antiquity.[12]

Magnifying glasses had improved so much by 55 BCE that the famed statesman Marcus Tullius Cicero told of how a parchment copy of Homer's epic poem *The Iliad* was enclosed in a nutshell—at 75,980 words, it was unreadable save through a strong lens.[13] Pliny explained that Roman-era optics were likewise capable of extraordinary microscopic feats: "Fame has been won in the making also of marble miniatures, namely by Myrmecides, whose Four-Horse Chariot and Driver were covered by the wings of a fly, and by Callicrates, whose ants have feet and other parts too small to be discerned."[14] The skill of these two artisans was still admired more than 120 years later when Claudius Aelian, a Roman teacher of rhetoric, added to Pliny's description by noting that "they inscribed an elegiac couplet in gold letters on a sesame pod."[15]

Some Roman-era gemstone carvings at Turkey's Bodrum Museum are so small that they must be displayed under bright lights behind powerful magnifying glasses because their images are otherwise invisible to the human eye—sufficient proof that they were originally cut almost twenty centuries ago with the invaluable aid of enlargement lenses, which were doubtlessly made likewise available to customers who purchased the jeweled artwork so as to see and appreciate it. Some of these minuscule masterpieces are incredibly complex and miraculously detailed, thereby validating Pliny's and Aelian's praise of the long-lost miniatures created by Myrmecides and Callicrates.

With the advent of modern optics capable of enlarging the appearance of objects, the development of microscopes and telescopes naturally went hand in hand, as exemplified by Zacharias Janssen, a Dutch spectacle maker who invented both the first optical telescope and the first truly compound microscope between 1590 and 1618. What was true for his time was no less valid during antiquity, when close-up glasses like the Layard lens naturally led to the consideration of possibilities for viewing distant objects as well.

Hoysaleswara Temple was carved from soapstone on the banks of a large man-made lake in the south of India 425 years before Zacharias Janssen's birth. A sculpted frieze there depicts a man peering through a skyward-facing tube, tapering from a slightly wider end to a more narrow termination at his eye. If the object is not a self-evident telescope,

Figure 7.3. India's Hoysaleswara Temple. Sculpted figure on the
far right peers through a tubular object resembling a handheld telescope.
Attired in military uniform, like his companions, the warrior's position
suggests that he is an advance guard, lookout, or point man, for whom
such an instrument would be especially useful. Photo by Ashwin Kumar.

misinterpretations of the figure or any alternative identification for it
do not spring to mind. Yet the appearance of such an instrument in
mid-twelfth-century India would have been entirely anomalous, because
nothing else resembling it occurred throughout the expansive Hoysala
empire responsible for building the temple.

Nor was the production of optical lenses ever associated with the
time or place concerned. The frieze in question does not, however, portray contemporaneous events or personages but illustrates instead a battle between the forces of nature, as personified in the benign Devas and
the demonic Asuras and described in the *Rig-Veda,* an ancient Indian
collection of Sanskrit hymns composed between the sixteenth and
twelfth centuries BCE. This reflects a period of cataclysmic meteor falls

in 1628 BCE and again in 1198 BCE, during which time telescopes would have been useful for tracking the comet that caused these global catastrophes. As such, the portrayed telescope belongs to a time memorializing the instrument's identification with the Devas and predating it by 2,360 years. The figure with telescope appearing in the frieze appears to be leading the Devas, not unlike eighteenth-century field commanders outfitted with a spyglass for reconnoitering enemy troop movements.

During the early fourteenth century, Hoysaleswara was twice sacked and plundered by Muslim armies, falling into a state of ruin and neglect when all memory of the telescope its frieze depicts was lost. Temple writes that abundant material evidence exists to suggest that telescopic devices were employed in monumental building construction as long ago as the New Stone Age. A case he cites is Britain's largest megalithic monument at Avebury, a Wiltshire village in southwest England, which consists of three stone circles laid out with great exactness some 4,200 years ago. The outer ring, with a diameter of 1,088 feet, is surrounded by a ditch and external bank 1,381 feet across and 4,430 feet in circumference, enclosing an area of 28.5 acres. The ditch alone was 69 feet wide and 36 deep.

Avebury originally comprised ninety-eight standing stones, varying in height from twelve to fourteen feet, some weighing more than forty tons. In other words, the Neolithic builders of Avebury moved and precisely oriented some 2,450 tons of stone, while additionally removing an estimated 1,000 tons of soil. The megalithic circles were built in several phases between 2850 BCE and 2200 BCE and then abandoned about one thousand years later. The site's original purpose is unknown, although it appears to have been a kind of outdoor temple or ceremonial arena for ritual activity, incorporating various celestial alignments.

"The two inner stone circles," observes Freddy Silva, author of *The Divine Blueprint,* "originally comprised of twenty-nine and twenty-seven stones, respectively; one represents the days in the synodic lunar month, the other the sidereal lunar month. These are enclosed within a massive, ninety-nine-stone circle with eight attendant stones, marking the calibration of lunar-solar calendars every eight years. So, aside from a temple, Avebury is a calendrical masterpiece marking the motions of the moon."[16]

Alexander Thom, a renowned Scottish engineer, found that Avebury featured a site-to-site alignment with a star called Deneb in the constellation Cygnus, known as the Swan, that also forms part of the Summer Triangle and is associated with mid-season. Professor Thom, writes Temple, "demonstrated in his survey that the site of Avebury was laid out with such precision that its accuracy was one part in a thousand. This is impossible without optical surveying techniques [especially in light of the location's gargantuan dimensions]. The very existence of Avebury thus constitutes evidence of the use of rudimentary telescopes in ancient Britain, for surveying purposes."[17]

If its Stone Age builders were not so equipped, then their immense achievement in southwest England is inexplicable. Yet possession of such surveying instruments may not have been as anomalous as it might seem. In 55 BCE, according to English medieval philosopher Roger Bacon, "Julius Caesar, when he wished to subdue England, is said to have erected very large mirrors, in order that he might see in advance from the shore of Gaul the arrangement of the cities and camps of England."[18]

Pliny the Elder similarly wrote of "stones whose body is stretched out, when on their backs in the same way as mirrors, do give back the images of things. In employing a mirror, if the thickness of the mirror has been polished and beaten out into a slightly convex shape, the size of the objects reflected is enormously magnified." He writes, too, how "the Emperor Nero [37 to 68 CE] used to look at the fights of gladiators in a smaragdus," which is a translucent precious stone of a bright-green color, perhaps some high-quality emerald, evidently capable of magnifying the appearance of distant targets.[19]

Eighty-two years later at Egypt's Great Library of Alexandria, a Greek cartographer named Agathodaemon drew up the earliest known world map, strictly based on the work of a fellow Alexandrian scholar, the geographer Claudius Ptolemy, circa 150 CE. Another map that may be associated with Agathodaemon was accidentally found in 1939, when a collection of ancient documents was being transferred from Armenia's Echmiadzin Matenadaran, meaning the city of Echmiadzin's depository for manuscripts, to the capital city at Yerevan.

Randomly going through some the depository's original source materials, a Soviet officer in charge of the project, Viktor Arutunyan, accidentally discovered an ancient "map of the Martian surface," according to Russian-born historian Paul Stonehill. "Moreover, a circumference was a small circle depicted in it was drawn around Mars. Obviously, this was a satellite of the planet. Of its origins, Stonehill claimed that "the text was in Latin, but it was apparently a translation from an Egyptian text," suggesting a second-century provenance at the Great Library of Alexandria. Arutunyan sent the nearly two-thousand-year-old map to the Armenian Academy of Sciences for examination and testing, though Stonehill believes it was returned shortly thereafter to the Yerevan Matenadaran, where to this day the diagrammatic representation of Mars remains unrecognized among the depository's two hundred thousand documents, most of them uncataloged.[20]

The story was first reported by Tatyana Samoilova for the Russian science journal *NLO* in January 2000. If true, as she and Stonehill believe given that it is supported by Soviet-era records, then the ancients may have turned their increasingly powerful lenses toward the heavens nearly twenty centuries ago. Whether or not they actually constructed a map of the Martian surface from direct observation of the Red Planet, nothing similar would come again until the independent reinvention of the telescope fourteen hundred years later. Contemporaneous evidence does, however, exist to suggest that that Greco-Roman surveillance of Mars belonged to similar optical investigations of the cosmos.

In *Moralia,* composed after the turn of the second century CE, Plutarch mentions how "the moon is very uneven and rugged," which, author Larry Brian Radka notes, "requires a telescope for detection." He also cites Democritus, generally regarded as the father of modern science for his formulation of atomic theory around 350 BCE, who "announced that the Milky Way is composed of vast multitudes of stars. . . . He could only have been led to form such an opinion from actual examination of the heavens with a telescope."[21] The very term was used by an early fourth-century Greek philosopher, Iamblichus, indicating that such an instrument was in use even during Pythagorean times, before 495 BCE: "Sight is made precise by the compass, the rule, and the telescope."[22]

Clearly our ancient ancestors' mastery of advanced optics extended their celestial as well as their magnified vision of existence millennia before the development of modern astronomy and microscopy.

# 8

# Modern Marvels from Long Ago

*Modesty teaches us to speak of the ancients with respect, especially when we are not very familiar with their works. Newton, who knew them practically by heart, had the greatest respect for them, and considered them to be men of genius and superior intelligence, who had carried their discoveries in every field much further than we today suspect, judging from what remains of their writings. More ancient writings have been lost than have been preserved, and perhaps our new discoveries are of less value than those that we have lost.*

EDWARD NEVILLE DA COSTA ANDRADE,
*HIGH TECHNOLOGY FROM NATURE*, JULY 1946

Twenty-first-century homes are typically equipped with common elements such as central heating, air-conditioning, plumbing, refrigerators, clocks, and telephones. However, these everyday features are relatively new additions to domestic life. Central heating was invented by 1830, but most public and private buildings went without it until after the turn of the next century.

## COOLING AND HEATING

U.S. physician John Gorrie built the earliest refrigerator in 1844. The first air conditioner began working in Buffalo, New York, on July 17, 1902, but air-conditioned theaters were still so rare fifty years later that they displayed public announcements proclaiming the fact. The first patent for a flushing toilet was issued to Alexander Cummings in 1775, though the device did not begin to achieve general usage for another one hundred years. Alexander Graham Bell gave us the telephone in 1876, but even in his day, clocks were luxury items not everyone could afford. Accordingly, the household standard of living to which we have been fully accustomed for the past generation or so only became generally available from the mid-twentieth century. For the previous 1,500 years, humans did without those technological services we take for granted today.

Yet all these and more were part of civilized life before it collapsed and everything was lost, only to be gradually, accidentally rediscovered within the past two hundred years. The first known example of central heating warmed the Greek temple of Ephesus in what is now western Turkey at about 550 BCE, although earlier lost versions undoubtedly existed. Later, Roman improvements provided warmth to the whole interior of a building from one area to multiple rooms through caliducts—pipes installed under the floors—while the hypocaust was a specialized system for heating walls. After the collapse of the Roman empire, overwhelmingly across Europe, heating reverted to more primitive fireplaces for almost a thousand years.[1]

The issue of *Chemical Engineering* magazine published on July 27, 1959, reported how a two-thousand-year-old valve "found in a Roman villa was used regularly until three years ago by the peasants whenever they required water for irrigation. In 1956, it was decided that the cost of the valve had been amortized [paid for itself], and it was replaced after twenty centuries of service."[2]

More than two thousand years ago, Romans excavated massive

refrigerators for cool storage from spring to at least mid-summer. Filled with snow topped by blocks of ice during winter, then covered with straw as insulation, the deep shafts perfectly preserved cheese, fish, meat, oysters, and other perishable goods in warm months. Several of these subterranean refrigerators, some fifteen feet deep, have been identified in Switzerland at a site known as Augusta Raurica about twelve miles from Basel. The underground shafts retained snow levels throughout June, while their ice blocks survived longer still, according to studies undertaken by archaeologists at the University of Basel.[3]

A far older, more complex, and completely different kind of refrigerator operated across the Persian empire from about 400 BCE. Resembling a rounded pyramid, examples sometimes stood as high as thirty feet over the deserts of what is today Iran and parts of Afghanistan. Still known as a *yakhchal,* meaning "ice pit," it covered a square-shaped basement entirely coated with *sarooj*—a mortar of mixed clay, sand, ash, goat hair, and lime that effectively waterproofed the walls and floor. The spiraling, dome-shaped tower was designed as an insulator to keep heat out while preserving lower interior tempera-tures generated by ice blocks brought from nearby mountains. Cold-water mountain streams entered an underground containment section through subterranean channels known as *qanats.*

Descending through a vertical shaft open at ground level just out-side the yakhchal, air currents traveled through the qanats, further cooling its incoming water with convection and evaporation and rising to create a cooler low-pressure zone over the bottom of the basement. At the apex of the open-ended yakhchal was a *badgir,* a mechanism that caught and diverted passing breezes down into the containment area to be cooled by ice and mixed together with the air brought inside by the qanat's running water, thereby simultaneously forcing warm air to rise up and out of the structure, facilitated by a process spiraling grooves.

These indented spirals were remarkable in themselves because they were nothing less than *rifling,* something that was reinvented in the West many centuries later. Rifling is a helical groove pattern machined

Figure 8.1. An Iranian yakhchal seventy-five miles north of Baghdad
still functions perfectly and stays cool inside after nearly two thousand years.
Photo by PasteGitaken.

into the internal surface of a gun barrel, exerting torque that makes
a bullet spin around its longitudinal axis and increase the projectile's
accuracy. Air entering through the top of the yakhchal was similarly
affected by grooves spiraling downward into its containment area. The
badgir was oriented to receive only colder breezes from the north and
blocked entry against southerly winds. In this, it was sometimes aided
by a high east-west wall standing outside the yakhchal to block these
often hot breezes.

The southward-facing side of the badgir was cunningly designed to
vent any warm air that happened to rise inside the dome while shut-
ting out higher temperatures. Basement water froze overnight, enabling
cold storage of fruit, dairy products, poultry, and a great variety of similarly perishable foods. So successful were these ancient ice pits that—
incredibly—several original specimens still operate today in remote
areas of the Middle East where electricity is scarce. By comparison,

how much of our twenty-first-century technology will be functioning 2,400 years into the future?

The Persian badgir may have been based on a much earlier Egyptian design, as found with the 1954 excavation of a boat pit at the base of the Great Pyramid. Inside, archaeologists found a perfectly preserved 143-foot-long cedar-wood ship conventionally dated circa 2500 BCE, but it was actually more than five hundred years older, as disclosed by several subsequent series of radiocarbon tests. It was found to be from about the First Dynasty, the beginning of pharaonic civilization. Despite its very early provenance, "Khufu's barge," as mainstream Egyptologists refer to it, features an air-conditioned cabin. Its low, partially opened attic featured a so-called fly roof. As the ship moved forward, air passing through the attic and over a tarp soaked in cold water was directed through vents into the passenger compartment.

Every Egyptian domicile, from the humblest home to the grandest palace, was installed with its own air-conditioning system. Some variants were simple designs, like that found on Khufu's barge, with a fly roof always oriented to take advantage of cooler breezes from the north. Others, for larger public temples or government buildings, were more sophisticated. "The architecture of these air conditioners is too complex that even the best ac contractor cannot understand it," declares a reporter for the Curious History website. "The ancient Egyptian roof air conditioner was an amazing concept of that time. Its action cooled down the entire brickwork of the buildings. This ancient Egyptian air-conditioning technique can be compared to modern evaporative coolers. Using water to decrease air pressure is an environmentally friendly cooling approach. The Egyptian air conditioners did not harm the environment, like modern air conditioners."[4]

## CLEANLINESS NEXT TO GODLINESS

In Europe the standard for modern sanitation was raised by the leaders of Minoan civilization when, four thousand years ago, private toilets with a central system of stone drains and ceramic pipes were common in the city of Knossos, Crete.[5]

One thousand years before, residents of the Indus valley high culture in Pakistan and India utilized similar receptacles. "The cities of Harappa and Mohenjo-Daro," according to hydrologists J. C. Rodda and Lucio Ubertini, "had a flush toilet in almost every house attached to a sophisticated sewage system." The flush toilet and the good hygiene it helped establish for more than three millennia were forgotten following the fall of the Greco-Roman world. Rodda and Ubertini continue: "It was only in the mid-nineteenth century, with growing levels of urbanization and industrial prosperity, that the flush toilet became a widely used and marketed invention."[6] Childress writes that "more than five thousand years ago, in the Tigris valley near Baghdad, Tell Asmar had homes and temples with elaborate arrangements for sanitation. One excavated temple had six toilets and five bathrooms."[7] Most of this plumbing equipment was, according to a July 1935 issue of *Scientific American* magazine, "connected to drains which discharged into a main sewer, one meter high and fifty meters long. . . . In tracing one drain, the investigators came upon a line of earthenware pipes. One end of each section was about eight inches in diameter, while the other end was reduced to seven inches, so that the pipes could be coupled into each other just as is done with drain pipes in the twentieth century."[8]

The earliest recorded use of toilet paper dated back to China's Tang Dynasty circa 851 CE.[9] But toilet paper only became commercially available in the Western world after Pennsylvania-born entrepreneur Joseph C. Gayetty reinvented it a thousand years later.

## COMMUNICATION

Alexander Graham Bell supposedly placed history's first telephone call in 1876, even though he was actually preceded more than a thousand years by an extinct people known as the Chimu. About 850 CE they founded the largest metropolis in pre-Columbian South America, Chan

Chan. At 7.7 square miles, with a population of one hundred thousand residents, it flourished another five hundred years until it was conquered by Incan imperialists.

While excavating the city's ruins in 1937, German archaeologist Wolfram von Schoeler discovered a pair of identically carved gourd tops, each 3.5 inches long and coated with resin. Their bases, covered with stretched hide, were connected by a long line of cotton twine. After returning to Germany, Schoeler's curious discovery found its way into Washington, D.C.'s National Museum of the American Indian, where curator Ramiro Matos identified it as a proto-telephone fundamentally similar to the string-attached tin cans with which children play, although far more effective at 750 feet. "This is unique," Matos told the Smithsonian Institution. "Only one was ever discovered."[10] Today the ancient Peruvian device is preserved in a temperature-controlled environment as the first specimen of its kind.

Figure 8.2. Entrance to the pre-Incan city of Chan Chan.
Photo by Marrovi.

## HIGH-TECH GADGETS AND GIZMOS

Among the everyday appliances we associate exclusively with our modern world was the earliest known alarm clock, conceived twenty-four hundred years ago by none other than the Greek philosopher Plato. His invention differed from today's version, with its bell or buzzer, as explained by the Booksfact website: "Plato was not very happy with his students at the academy [who] kept oversleeping. So, he added a tube to the filling vessel, so it formed a siphon. When the water got high enough to fill the tube and start spilling over, all of it at once was siphoned off into yet another vessel. This last vessel was mostly enclosed, but it had thin openings, making it whistle like a teakettle when it filled up quickly. Plato's invention was successful and people who used his alarm clock woke up on time."[11]

It appears to have been an elaboration of the water clocks long in use by the fifth century BCE. Already familiar by then to the Egyptians for more than one thousand years, their aquatic chronometer was a full tank that gradually drained through a small hole at its bottom. Reduced water levels were correctly correlated with the hours of the day. After the tank had emptied, it needed to be refilled by hand, a clumsy process remedied by a brilliant Greek mathematician in Alexandria.

At about 250 BCE, Ctesibius affixed an additional pair of containers to the standard water clock. A jar supplemented the original tank by keeping it full in a reciprocal exchange of water, the world's first automatic self-regulatory system. Because it prevented any drop in levels by which to measure time, water flowed from this second container to yet another featuring a float that rose or fell with the rising or falling water. Attached to the float was a pointer with notches, which turned a gear that moved the hand to indicate the correct time. The accuracy of his *clepsydra,* meaning "water thief," was unmatched until the advent of seventeenth-century wind-up clocks two thousand years later. Despite their individual accuracy, universally synchronizing these early time-keeping devices continued to be problematic. As an exasperated Seneca,

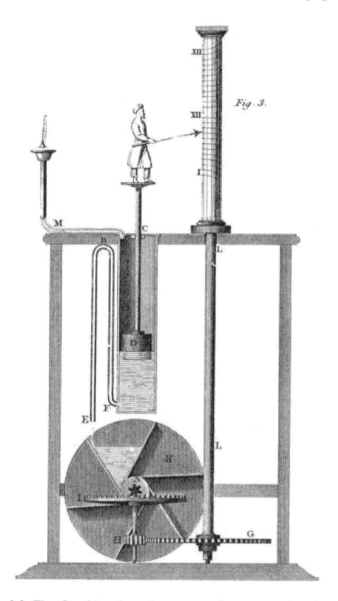

Figure 8.3. The Ctesibius clepsydra, accurately re-created in this early nineteenth-century illustration by British artist John Farey Jr. The water thief's hour indicator ascends as water flows in, while a series of gears ingeniously rotates a cylinder corresponding to the temporal hours.

the Roman rhetorician, exclaimed in 30 CE: "One can expect an agreement between philosophers sooner than between clocks."[12]

A Greek inventor residing in Alexandria, Heron fabricated a holy water dispenser circa 120 BCE. "A coin was dropped into a sealed vessel," writes Childress, that "made a small plunger pull up, which then allowed a measured quantity of fluid to be dispensed." Heron's device was an improvement on earlier vending machines installed in Egyptian shrines and at the Temple of Zeus in Athens. "The quantity of water which flowed from the tap," Childress goes on to explain, "was in direct relation to the weight of the coin thrown into the slot."[13]

Nor did the ancients do without computers, as Derek J. Solla Price learned when the true identity of an artifact he happened to be cleaning finally dawned on him. The curious object had lain in Athens' National Museum for half a century, after having been hauled up from 120 feet beneath the surface of the eastern Mediterranean Sea sometime around Easter in 1900. It had been found by Elias Stadiatos, a Greek sponge diver working off the coast of Antikythera, a small island near Crete, while he was salvaging the wreck of an ancient Roman freighter that included statues and other period materials dating to circa 80 BCE.

While examining the object on May 17, 1902, Greek archaeologist Valerios Stais noticed a gear wheel embedded in what appeared to be a piece of rock. It was actually a heavily encrusted, badly corroded mechanism in three main parts, comprising dozens of smaller components. The Antikythera Device, as he called it, remained an enigma for the next forty-nine years until Price, a professor of science history at Yale University, recognized it for what it really was: a mechanical analog computer, an instrument millennia ahead of its time. "It was like finding a turbo-jet in Tutankhamun's tomb," Price wrote in his June 1959 article for *Scientific American*, "An Ancient Greek Computer."[14]

He pointed out that the Antikythera Device uses a differential gear, not reinvented until the mid-1500s, for computing the motions of stars and planets, bringing it into the Space Age. A differential gear permits the simultaneous rotation of two shafts at different speeds, as used on the rear axle of automotive vehicles, allowing different rates of wheel rotation on curves. Associated dials show the Metonic cycle of

235 synodic months, approximately nineteen solar-years, used to predict eclipses. It formed the basis of the Greek calendar.

Made of bronze and originally mounted in a wooden frame, the Antikythera Device is 13 inches tall, 6.75 inches wide, but just 3.5 inches thin, and inscribed with more than two thousand characters. Although most of their text has been deciphered, its complete translation still awaits publication. The complex instrument is displayed in the Bronze Collection of the National Archaeological Museum of Athens, but an accurate reconstruction of this ancient analog apparatus is housed at the American Computer Museum in Bozeman, Montana.

The original served as an extremely useful navigational instrument that enabled the Roman freighter in which it was found to successfully complete transatlantic voyages to America more than fifteen centuries prior to Christopher Columbus. In fact, an abundance of physical evidence affirms ancient Roman influence on the Americas during pre-Columbian times. Doubtless, the Antikythera Device was not the first of its kind but rather the result of prolonged development stretching back long before it came to rest at the bottom of the Mediterranean Sea more than two thousand years ago.

The Roman statesman Cicero wrote that the consul Marcellus brought two mechanisms back to Rome from the ransacked city of Syracuse.[15] One contrivance mapped the sky on a sphere, and the other predicted the motions of the sun, moon, and planets. His description seems to match the Antikythera Device, interestingly enough, because Syracuse was the scene of Marcellus's victory over Greek enemies, aided by the inventive genius of Archimedes, as described in chapter 11. The Antikythera Device, or a previous original on which it was based, might very well have been created by one of history's greatest inventors.

Another highly advanced instrument developed in antiquity was the seismometer for measuring ground motion caused by earthquake or volcanic eruption. The first such device was believed to have been invented by Jean de Hautefeuille, a French physicist in 1703. Not until the mid-twentieth century, however, did sinologists discover that his apparatus was preceded in China by 1,571 years. Their translation of the fifth-century *Hou Hanshu (The Book of the Later Han)* revealed that Zhang Heng, an accomplished polymath, built an "instrument for measuring the movements of the Earth," in 132 CE.[16]

Born fifty-nine years earlier in Nanyang, he was a proficient astronomer, mathematician, engineer, geographer, cartographer, artist, poet, statesman, and literary scholar. His Houfeng Didong Yi was a six-foot-wide bronze vessel, around the sides of which were fastened the likenesses of eight downward-facing dragons, each one holding a bronze ball in its mouth. These figures aligned with the four cardinal directions and as many inter-cardinal points. When seismic activity occurred, the jaws of a particular dragon would open, allowing one ball to drop into the open maw of a bronze frog positioned beneath it at the base, thereby indicating the direction in which an earthquake was then taking place.

A loud, metallic clang made by a fallen ball and amplified by the hollow frog sounded the alert to geologic upheaval. As described by the *Hou Hanshu,* a central column inside the vessel—perhaps an inverted pendulum on the axis of the seismograph—moved along eight tracks corresponding to the cardinal and inter-cardinal directions and linked to a mechanism that would open only one dragon's mouth at a time. "When earthquake waves pass," theorized Sourcebook compiler William R. Corliss, "the internal pendulum sways, hitting and pushing outward one of the eight horizontal rods. The rod just nudged knocks a ball out of the mouth of one of the eight dragons mounted on the outside of the instrument. The dislodged ball is caught (hopefully) by one of the gaping frogs below, thereby indicating the direction opposite that of the quake epicenter."[17]

*The Book of the Later Han* goes on to mention that the first earthquake indicated by Zhang Heng's seismometer transpired "somewhere in the east" but was not believed by Emperor Shun to have actually occurred because he personally felt no tectonic movement. Days later, a rider arrived at the palace to report that tremors had indeed devastated an eastern province 310 miles away. Another event correctly indicated by a bronze dragon and that went otherwise unnoticed at Luoyang, the imperial capital, was the even more distant Gansu earthquake of 143 CE.

Zhang Heng went on to invent the world's first mechanically operated armillary sphere. He constructed this "sky globe" from rings and hoops representing the equator, tropics, and other celestial circles. Able to revolve on its axis, his water-powered version represented a major leap forward in geography and astronomical observation.

## THE PRINTED WORD

Although "paper" derives from *papyrus* (Greek for the original Egyptian word *djet*) and was invented at the Nile delta around the turn of the fourth millennium BCE, the ancient Chinese did more than write on it. They used it to print paper money 970 years ago. In the early Song Dynasty, merchants began presenting metal coins to royal officials, who issued paper bills for credit or exchange notes equal to the cash value of civilian deposits. Making these notes increasingly available stimulated commerce but was progressively more difficult to realize without being able to print them in quantity. The dilemma was already solved, however, almost two hundred years earlier when wood-block printing appeared during the Tang Dynasty. The procedure involved inking an engraved wood block, which was then impressed on a large sheet of blank paper, resulting in a hard-copy reverse image of the carved inscription.

Among the first productions of this primitive publishing method was *The Diamond Sutra,* an important Buddhist text, released in 868 CE and, according to the British Library, "the earliest, complete survival of a dated, printed book."[18] Although such a process was slow, just one wood block could produce about twenty thousand copies. As a needful improvement, Bì Shēng's introduction of movable-type printing during the mid-eleventh century finally enabled the issuance of printed script. The clever artisan carved individual characters on clay. These were fire-hardened pieces attached to an iron plate for printing a single page of text. Afterward, the clay pieces were broken up and reorganized to print another different page. While Bì Shēng predated Germany's more famous Johann Gutenberg, inventor of the first true printing press, by four hundred years, both men were anticipated by an anonymous inventor in Crete.

Investigating the Bronze Age ruins of Phaistos, the Minoan capital, Italian archaeologist Luigi Pernier found a peculiar object in 1908. The 5.9-inch-wide, 0.39-inch-thick item he excavated was covered on both sides with a spiral of forty-five symbols that had been impressed into its originally soft clay in a clockwise sequence, spiraling toward the center of the saucer-shaped artifact before it was fire hardened. Although an original function is still debated by scholars, it was most likely designed as a kind of zodiac, judging from the repetition of apparently astrological signs (the eagle for Aquila, a ram for Capricorn, etc.). The plate is perhaps a lone surviving specimen of numerous personalized horoscopes once produced by professional soothsayers in quantity between 1850 and 1600 BCE for their large, expanding cliental. To keep up with growing demands for celestial guidance, movable type became more necessary, as explained by a well-respected typesetter and linguist.

Herbert Brekle said of the Phaistos artifact, "we are really dealing with a 'printed' text, which fulfills all definitional criteria of the typographic principle. . . . The decisive factor is that the material 'types' are proven to be repeatedly instantiated on the clay disk."[19] He was seconded by archaeologist Benjamin Schwartz, who wrote in the prestigious *Journal of Near Eastern Studies* that the disk's identically repeated figures could only have been impressed with "the first movable type."[20]

Ancient Imperial China's exploitation of paper's multifarious potential did not end with Bì Shēng's press of 1048 CE. That same year also bore witness to the debut of the world's first menus on the tables of Chinese restaurants. About the same time, a technologically sophisticated people remembered as the Hohokam flourished throughout the American Southwest. Centered in what is today northern Arizona, they engineered a colossal irrigation network of cement canals that, if placed end to end, would have stretched from Phoenix to beyond the Canadian border. "But it was a small number of decorated marine shells, dated to about 1000 A.D.," writes Emil W. Haury, a foremost authority on the Hohokam, "that intrigued us most. We were baffled by the incredible fineness of the working of horned toads, snakes, and geometric forms that adorned them. Our study pointed to only one, plausible hypothesis: The shells were etched. We knew full well that this meant crediting the Hohokam with the first etched artifacts in history—hundreds of years before Renaissance armorers in Europe came upon the technique."

These ancient Americans first discovered, according to Haury, "the corrosive power of fermented cactus juice, which produces a weak, acetic acid. Shells soaked in the vinegar would be eaten away unless protected by a resistant substance, such as pitch. Hence, the procedure by simple reasoning: For a design of pitch on a shell, soak it in acid, scrape off the pitch, and the result is an etched design. . . . The invention of etching enabled the Hohokam to create some remarkable works of art."[21] They were also advanced metalsmiths. Small silver bells Haury excavated surprised his fellow archaeologists who until then assumed that Hohokam furnaces were incapable of reaching the 2,006 degrees Fahrenheit necessary to melt silver. They represent proof that such artifacts could only have originated with a highly advanced people, a conclusion reaffirmed by a small Chimu rattle currently at Germany's Ethnographical Museum of Gothenburg.

"To a one hundred fifty-mm copper handle," S. Linne writes in the *Anthropological Institute Journal* (X6, X7, 1957), "is affixed a slightly oblong, hollow head containing two five-mm copper pellets and made of two, bell-shaped halves of 0.5-mm copper sheeting. These two halves are expertly welded together in a virtually prefect joint, no seam whatever being visible in the metal itself, although the joint had opened along some thirty millimeters."[22]

Furnace technology required to attain the extraordinary temperatures for achieving such metalwork was not restricted to the American Southwest, according to Brad Steiger: "Although a temperature of over seventeen hundred eighty degrees is required to melt platinum, some pre-Incan peoples in Peru were making objects of the metal."[23]

How the ancients achieved such high melting points contradicts academic opinion, thereby affirming the as-yet-undiscovered high technology invented and used by our ancestors.

## 9

# Weapons of Mass Destruction

*Can a society in which thought and technique are scientific persist for a long period, as, for example, ancient Egypt persisted, or does it necessarily contain within itself forces which must bring either decay or explosion?*

BERTRAND RUSSELL,
*A HISTORY OF WESTERN PHILOSOPHY*

## CHEMICAL WARFARE

Fritz Haber is considered the father of chemical warfare for weaponizing chlorine and other poisonous gases during World War I.[1] But he was preceded three thousand years by the earliest recorded use of gas warfare, during the 429 BCE siege of Plataea in ancient Greece. The city had successfully resisted all attacks by Sparta's king Archidamus, who heaped up an enormous mound of firewood against its impregnable battlements. To this man-made hill were "added liberal quantities of pine-tree sap," writes Classical folkorist Adrienne Mayor, "and, in a bold innovation, sulfur."[2]

When the combined components ignited, they produced a toxic sulfur dioxide gas that killed some of the defenders and forced the rest to abandon their defensive positions at the wall. Thanks to the fortuitous intervention of a sudden thunderstorm, the fire was extinguished and Plataea's defeat postponed. Thereafter, poisonous gas was abandoned by Greco-Roman commanders as unreliable, although its use persisted in the East.

The Hindu *Arthashastra* (Science of Politics), composed circa 290 BCE by India's royal adviser Kautilya, contains literally hundreds of recipes for creating poisonous weapons, toxic smoke, and other chemical weapons. Less than one hundred years later, the Mohists—philosophical rivals of Confucius—urged the use of ox-hide bellows connected to furnaces to pump smoke from burning balls of toxic plants into tunnels dug by besieging armies. Among the vegetables specified was dried mustard, "anticipating the mustard gas of the trenches in the First World War," writes historian Robert Temple, "by twenty-three hundred years."[3]

In 178 CE, Chinese Imperial troops dispensed a "soul-hunting fog" laced with arsenic into the air, together with clouds of finely divided lime, to suppress a peasant revolt. The earliest archaeological evidence for gas warfare was found at Dura-Europos, a fortress-city built three hundred feet above the right bank of the Euphrates River near the village of Salhiyé in today's Syria. In 256 CE nineteen of its Roman occupiers died within two minutes after their Persian enemies ignited bitumen and sulfur crystals, filling the tunnels in which the legionnaires were burrowing with sulfur dioxide. Their remains were discovered in January 2009 by University of Leicester archaeologists, who found a lone Persian soldier among the bodies; he was probably the soldier responsible for releasing the gas before its fumes overcame him as well.

## BIOLOGICAL WARFARE

With the onset of the post-Classical Dark Ages, chemical warfare disappeared until its early twentieth-century comeback in World War I. Biological warfare is a salient feature of our times, but no less characterized the ancient world. Two thousand years ago, when besieging forces approached a Mayan city in the Guatemalan highlands, they were confronted by deliberately positioned manikins outfitted in the regalia of warriors, including cloaks, spears, and shields. As the foe came within close proximity of the effigies, war bonnets adorning the life-size dolls' heads—realistically adorned with ears, nose, and painted facial features—suddenly exploded, releasing swarms of angry hornets. They repeatedly stung the would-be attackers, driving them off. The manikin war bonnets were actually gourds, each in which an entire insect nest had been sealed. When the enemy came within range, the Mayas' most accurate hurlers broke the gourds with well-thrown rocks, releasing the infuriated yellow jackets and wasps.

In 72 BCE, Roman sappers burrowing tunnels under Persian strongholds at Amisus, on the Black Sea, were foiled when the enemy drilled holes into the tunnels, funneling down thick swarms of aggressive bees by means of blacksmith bellows. Stinging insects helped defeat the Romans again in 198 CE, when their legions were bug-bombed during the Second Parthian War. While besieged in the fortress city of Hatra, south of Mosul, Iraq, the defenders, according to the Syrian historian Herodian, threw clay pots filled with "poisonous insects," which Adrienne Mayor more specifically hypothesizes as scorpions.[4] Whatever the creatures' precise identity, they played their part in Hatra's successful defense.

"The insects fell into the Romans' eyes and the exposed parts of their bodies," Herodian reports. "Digging in before they were noticed, they bit and stung the soldiers, causing severe injuries."[5] About ten years before, Eumenes II, the ruler of a powerful kingdom dominating north coastal Asia Minor called Pergamon, was confident of victory at sea over Hannibal's numerically inferior naval units. As Eumenes II's flotilla came within catapult range of his opponents, volleys of earthenware jars crashed aboard the Pergamene vessels, scattering hundreds of venomous snakes across their decks. Taking advantage of the ensuing chaos, the innovative Carthaginian general won the battle.

Early in Alexander the Great's campaign against the Persians, they so badly outnumbered the Greek army that their triumph seemed far less likely than annihilation. To make his relatively meager forces appear larger than they actually were, he had branches tied to the tails of herding sheep, which stirred up immense billows of dust that the enemy mistook for many thousands of invading troops on the march. Thus deceived, the Persians hesitated to attack at a moment when decisive action could have obliterated the Greeks.

During 321 BCE, one of Ptolemy's surviving generals resorted to the same tactic when his cavalrymen, confronted by a greater number fielded on the Egyptian frontier, fastened branches to herds of pigs and cattle and stampeded them before the clash of opposing forces in the direction of Perdiccas. Horrified by the approaching cloudbank of rising dust he imagined must have been generated by an enormous contingent of horse soldiers, Alexander's successor turned and fled, incurring heavy losses.

As an attentive student of Classical history, General Erwin Rommel borrowed from antiquity shortly after he arrived on February 10, 1941, in Tripoli, Libya, with the first few units of the new German Afrika Korps. If detected by Allied reconnaissance, they would have been in serious jeopardy of destruction by overwhelming enemy forces. When a RAF spotter plane inevitably appeared overhead, Rommel ordered horse-drawn plows to drive through the desert in circles around his handful of armored vehicles. The artificial sandstorm thus raised by a few agricultural implements convinced the British pilot that Rommel's forces had landed in strength far too great for any counterattack. The fledgling Afrika Korps was saved by a military ruse conceived more than 2,200 years before by Alexander the Great.

### Elephants to the Front!

The ultimate in ancient biological warfare were history's first tanks: militarized elephants. They were totally unknown in Europe when the first weaponized versions routed all opposition from the field, even before they could be seen. Their mere scent was sufficient to panic the best cavalry horses beyond control, while combined trumpeting by dozens or hundreds of the beasts no less unnerved human foes. Terror engendered by the elephants' monstrous, unfamiliar appearance was magnified by their surprising speed. Massed formations of elephants charged at twenty miles per hour, faster than an armored infantryman could run. The creatures were themselves protected by impenetrable armor sheeting the trunk, flanks, head, neck, and legs.

Trained to grasp an enemy soldier with their trunk and dash him to the ground, they plowed into troop concentrations, trampling men beneath their huge feet. Special advance pachyderm squads swung custom-manufactured broadswords sporting six-foot-long blades to cut great swaths of casualties through enemy ranks or impaled them on tusks sheathed in pointed steel (fig. 9.1) while kicking them with iron anklets featuring two-foot-long spikes.

Backs of the largest war elephants carried an armored, towerlike cabin for the *mahout,* or driver, as well as archers and javelin throwers who rained death on opponents below. "Elephants were also used as siege weapons," according to author David Ison. "There are several accounts of elephants using their heads and tusks to batter fortifications until they faltered. . . . The animals were also used to ford rivers. They

Figure 9.1. This socketed spear from Carthage was
part of ancient war-elephant armament.

could be used as bridges or simply to block the current to allow troops to cross a rapid."[6]

They were additionally engaged in transport convoys, freighting heavy equipment and supplies over otherwise impassable terrain and long distances. Only males were combat operational, the females being smaller and less aggressive. Four types saw service: the forest elephant (*Loxodonta cyclotis*); the savannah or bush elephant (*Loxodonta Africana*), tallest of all at between ten and thirteen feet; its subspecies, the *Loxodonta pharaoensis;* and Asian or Indian elephant (*Elephas maximus*). It was in India that the Asian elephant was first domesticated about four thousand years ago. Only individual examples captured in the wild, however, received military training, beginning about 1100 BCE.

Europeans saw them for the first time in northern Iraq in October 1331 BCE. However, the Persians' fifteen specimens, exhausted from the previous day's long march to Gaugamela, were physically unable to participate in the battle, which was won by Alexander the Great. Five years later, after invading Punjab, he was more seriously confronted by upward of two hundred war elephants at India's Hydaspes River. Observing that Parvataha, or King Porus, had neglected to adequately protect his mahouts, the Greeks directed their arrows at them. Suddenly deprived of their drivers, the elephants were effectively deactivated.

The largest deployment of war elephants during a single engagement took place in what is now central Turkey, where five hundred to six hundred of them clashed at the Battle of Ipsus between the late Alexander's contesting successors. Among them, General Seleucus was victorious in 301 BCE, thanks to his superior tactical command of elephant battalions. An invasion of southern Italy in the next century was opposed by ten thousand more Roman defenders than Greek forces under Pyrrhus of Epirus. The outcome of 280 BCE's Battle of Heraclea tottered back and forth until Roman horse soldiers threatened a decisive charge. To counter it, Pyrrhus unleashed his twenty elephants. Aghast at the sight of these strange and brooding creatures, which none had

Figure 9.2. War elephants carry the day at Heraclea.

seen before, the horses galloped away and threw the Roman legion into rout. Pyrrhus then launched his Thessalian cavalry among the disorganized legions, which completed the Romans' defeat.[7]

They withdrew to devise various anti-elephant weapons, such as catapulted firepots and squads of ax men to hack away at the animals' feet. Some three hundred of these countermeasures were meant to compensate the previous year's debacle at Heraclea, but, once again, Greek elephant units prevailed in the Battle of Asculum. Writing for *The Guardian,* science reporter Philip Ball tells of how during the Second Punic War "the Carthaginian army made a move that no one expected. Their commander, Hannibal, marched his troops, including cavalry and African war elephants, across a high pass in the Alps to strike at Rome itself from the north of the Italian peninsula. It was one of the greatest military feats in history. The Romans had presumed that the Alps created a secure natural barrier against invasion of their homeland. They hadn't reckoned with Hannibal's boldness. In December [218 BCE], he smashed apart the Roman forces in the north, assisted by his awesome elephants, the tanks of Classical warfare."[8]

Hannibal was defeated sixteen years later in part by Roman naturalists, who discovered the war elephant's weakness. At the decisive Battle of Zama, just as the Carthaginians' pachyderm detachments were about to charge, Roman musicians stepped forth to play loud trumpet calls, which so distracted the elephants that the beasts became thoroughly unmanageable. Afterward, war elephants were raised and trained to ignore the irritating sounds, so new methods were brought to bear, including the deployment of pigs slathered with oil, set afire, and sent squealing in the elephants' direction. The elephants did indeed stampede, but the pigs were almost impossible to aim with precision of any kind.

Beginning about the turn of the first century CE, ivory hunting began to deplete pachyderm populations in Africa and India to an extent that the continued weaponization of elephants was no longer feasible. After the fall of Classical civilization and attendant loss of the applied traditions and military science that had made the creatures so successful—even decisive—on the battlefield, war elephants were relegated to India and Southeast Asia, increasingly among micro-monarchies, until the proliferation of gunpowder weapons after 1500 CE rendered the animals obsolete. In yet another example of the modern world resorting to ancient technology, Imperial Japanese Army commanders made extensive use of elephants to efficiently carry supplies through jungle terrain where no motorized vehicle could operate, thereby enabling them to take the Allies by surprise in a series of stunning victories during World War II. Their outstanding achievement was the capture of Singapore on February 15, 1942. Although, as Sir William Slim explained, "Britain had one hundred thousand troops to Japan's thirty thousand and twice as much artillery," the 25th Army led by Lieutenant General Tomoyuki Yamashita won the Battle of Malay, partially because "he made great use of elephants crashing through the bushes." Sir William Slim wrote of the elephants under his own command of the XIVth Army: "They built hundreds of bridges for us, they helped to build and launch more ships for us than Helen ever did for Greece. Without them, our retreat from

Burma would have been even more arduous, and our advance to its liberation slower and more difficult."[9] The last such recorded military operations occurred in 1987, when Iraqi army commanders hitched elephants to heavy weapons for transport to Kirkuk.

Plato states in his dialogue the *Kritias* that "there were a great number of elephants in the island" of Atlantis, although he does not mention if they were used in war.[10] "It is not impossible," writes Ignatius Donnelly, the father of modern Atlantology, "that even the invention of gunpowder may date back to Atlantis . . . we are not surprised in the legends of Greek mythology events described which are only explicable by supposing that the Atlanteans possessed the secret of this powerful explosive." He cites the War of the Titans, in which weapons "with force equal to the shock of an earthquake, as from a continuous blaze of thunderbolts, made the Earth catch fire. The rebels were partly hurled into deep chasms, with rocks and hills reeling after them." Donnelly wondered, "Do not these words picture the explosion of a mine?"[11] He speculated that they preserved the memory of actual prehistoric events, however dramatized in the service of mythic tradition, characterizing the effects of black powder bombs during Atlantean times.

## INCENDIARY MISSILES

Less hypothetically, a very real weapon—and a highly advanced one—in the arsenal of Imperial Rome may have originated from the sunken civilization. The *falarica* was an exceptionally long, heavy javelin, hand-thrown or modified as a machine-launched iron bolt and armed with an explosive warhead (fig. 9.3, p. 106). The leading half of its six-foot length was composed of a metal shaft containing unknown, if potent, inflammable materials—at least pitch and sulfur, which alone were sufficiently combustible to release large amounts of energy emitting strong destructive power. Silius Italicus, a Roman consul, witnessed the falarica in action: "When in flight it struck the side of a huge tower, it kindled a fire which burnt until all of the woodwork of the tower was utterly consumed."[12] The

Figure 9.3. In this modern reenactment of a Roman legion,
the legionnaires carry accurate reproductions of the falarica.
Photo by Sprachprofi.

incendiary projectile doubled as an excellent armor-piercing weapon and
was the first long-range ballistic missile when shot from spear-throwers or
siege engines to significantly increase its range and velocity.

Although its Latin name was derived from the Greek word *phalēròs,*
meaning "shining," the falarica was not a Greco-Roman invention.
Its earliest recorded use was among Iberians defending Spain from
Carthaginian invaders in 237 BCE, as verified by falarica fragments
identified in Spanish archaeological deposits from the mid-third century BCE. In Greek myth the Titan Iberus, after whom the entire
Spanish peninsula was known, is the brother of Atlas, the eponymous
founder of Atlantis, a name that means "daughter of Atlas." The city
was allegedly located near the base of his mountain, Mount Atlas. It is
hardly surprising then that the Romans referred to all Iberians as "the
children of Atlantis."[13]

None of these comparisons prove, only suggest, that the falarica's origins lie with the underwater ruins of Plato's lost civilization, while the javelin's combustible warhead may lend at least some credence to Donnelly's belief that an earlier culture employed similarly explosive weapons. They were more certainly conceived by Imperial Chinese inventors and actually used in combat for the first time by a Ming Dynasty general assigned to destroy pirate armadas plundering the southeast coast of China. In 1558 CE, Qi Jiguang won a decisive victory against the multinational privateers at Cen Harbor, due in part to his unprecedented deployment of rocket-propelled weapons.

Gunpowder was stuffed into twenty-eight-inch-long bamboo tubes armed with armor-piercing blades. The missiles were so erratic, however, that they could not be aimed directly at a target with much hope of hitting it. To compensate for this inherent inaccuracy, they were laid on racks in large rectangular boxes, their individual fuses braided together. When lit, large numbers of rockets simultaneously streamed helter-skelter across the sky, but, perhaps surprisingly, enough struck the enemy to help turn the tide of battle. Of the more than 2,000 rockets fired from ten Imperial Chinese Navy warships, plus the 4,760 launched by Chinese infantry and cavalry units, hundreds of them found their mark in the largest battle of its kind in history. Thus armed, the general went on to another victory in Taizhou prefecture, where missile-blasted pirates suffered more than five thousand casualties. When later reassigned to protect the Great Wall, Qi Jiguang covered part of its eastern section with forty carts carrying thousands of armed rockets in multiple batteries.

His mid-sixteenth-century military application of gunpowder may nevertheless have been preceded, as evidenced by a skull (belonging to an extinct species of large wild cow called an aurochs) on display at Moscow's Paleontological Museum. The remains were found west of Russia's Lena River, the easternmost of three great Siberian rivers that flow into the Arctic Ocean. Examining a small perforation in the forehead of the aurochs's cranium, museum curator Professor Constantine

Flerov noticed how the perfectly round hole had "a polished appearance," reports Childress, "without radial cracks, indicating the projectile entered the skull at a very high velocity. The aurochs survived the shot, as is evidenced by calcification around the hole."[14] It was identical to effects made on hard bone by a lead bullet or musket ball discharged from a firearm. In fact, no other cause appears likely, given the same pathological evidence the hole in the skull shares with typical gunshot victims today.

Aurochs lived during the early Pleistocene epoch, or most recent Ice Age, more than two million years ago; the last survivor died in Poland in 1627 CE. Their habitat ranged far from Siberia and included Lithuania, Moldavia, Transylvania, and East Prussia by the thirteenth century CE. The bullet hole in the anomalous skull at Moscow's Paleontological Museum had to have been made no more recently than two hundred years before the first recorded use of firearms in the Lena River region, about 1400, because the Siberian aurochs was hunted to extinction before 1200 CE. The actual shooting took place long before, however. In *Secrets of the Lost Race,* Rene Noorbergen states that Professor Flerov and colleagues determined that the aurochs skull in question was "several thousand years old"—circa 3000 BCE, when it was shot.[15]

# 10 ⧨

# Wonder Weapons

*The new science will be a manifestation of ancient technologies. It will come suddenly; humans will experience technological shock.*

TOBA BETA, *MY ANCESTOR WAS AN ASTRONAUT*

A far more extreme example of prehistoric firearms was unearthed during the early twentieth century, when team scientists were investigating a cave at Broken Hill, or Kabwe, in what was then known as Northern Rhodesia and is now the country of Zambia. They found remains of a Middle Stone Age hominid similarly shot in the head as was the aurochs from chapter 9. Rhodesian Man, or *Homo rhodesiensis* as he was initially known, is now mostly considered a synonym of the current binomial for *Homo heidelbergensis,* a subspecies of archaic humans that inhabited South Africa about seven hundred thousand to three hundred thousand years ago.

The initial discovery from 1921 is on public display at London's Museum of Natural History, where Noorbergen examined it and made his observations.

> On the left side of the skull is a hole, perfectly round. There are none of the radial cracks that would have resulted had the hole been caused by a weapon such as an arrow or a spear. Only a high-speed projectile

such as a bullet could have made such a hole. The skull directly opposite the hole is shattered, having been blown out from the inside. This
same feature is seen in victims of head wounds received from shots
from a high-powered rifle. No projectile moving at a slower speed
could have produced either the neat hole or the shattering effect. A
German forensic authority from Berlin has positively stated that the
cranial damage to Rhodesian Man's skull could not have been caused
by anything but a bullet. . . . Either the Rhodesian remains are not
as old as claimed, at most two or three centuries, and he was shot by
a European colonizer or explorer; or the bones are as old as they are
claimed to be, and he was shot by a hunter or a warrior belonging to
a very ancient, yet highly advanced culture. The second conclusion is
the more plausible of the two, especially since the Rhodesian skull was
found sixty feet beneath the surface. To assume that Nature could
have accumulated that much debris and soil over only two or three
hundred years would be ridiculous.[1]

That someone possessed firearms nearly a third of a million to
three-quarters of a million years ago thoroughly disorients our understanding of the past and challenges current anthropological parameters
in the light of hard, unfamiliar evidence. Yet not our preconceptions,
however self-assuring they may be, but the truth, regardless how discon-
certing it often is, must be served. Data should not be customized to
reinforce dominant theories or prevalent paradigms. Quite the opposite:
conclusions must be allowed to arise freely and logically of their own
accord from the facts. Only a theory formed within the context of reason by the evidence it attempts to explain, no matter if the result is
unpopular or contradicts fashion, is worth considering.

## THE POLYBOLOS

If a single-shot firearm appears wildly out of place in antiquity, how
much more so must seem a prehistoric machine gun. Yet such advanced

Figure 10.1. This modern re-creation of the polybolos demonstrates a firing rate at least three times faster than the Scorpion, the Roman army's standard light artillery piece. Photo by SBA73.

weaponry was invented during the third century BCE by Dionysius of Alexandria, an engineer working at the arsenal of Rhodes. His *polybolos* was personally inspected by fellow Greek writer on mechanics, Philo of Byzantium, whose military treatise details the redoubtable "multiple thrower" at some length. It could, according to his *Belopoeica,* simultaneously and repeatedly hurl numerous projectiles with high accuracy over a respectable range before it needed to be reloaded. Its operator, while turning a windlass attached to the rear prism, could lock the bolts, load, and shoot automatically—over and over again. Not unlike a modern machine gun, ammunition was fed into Dionysius's device via a magazine attached to a rotating tray, providing it a higher rate of fire than any other ancient artillery pieces.

The polybolos was used primarily against enemy personnel for its capability of locking onto a target. The faithful reconstruction of this proto–machine gun by German engineer Erwin Schramm (1856–1935) was so accurate that a second bolt discharged from the weapon was able to not only hit its target but also, in the process, split the preceding bolt. A single "multiple thrower" could completely break an enemy charge and was a lifesaver against surprise attack, while batteries of the weapon were capable of decimating whole units within a few minutes.

The Romans improved on the polybolos approximately 100 CE with a more accommodating sling, into which each replacement arrow dropped as the previous shaft shot off. With an impressive range of two hundred yards, the upgraded catapult's only drawback lay in its sighting, which could not be readjusted quickly enough for battlefield conditions. It took the Chinese another thousand years to solve this disadvantage by fastening a workable magazine of twenty bolts to each crossbow. Large, winched versions could deliver multiple darts almost simultaneously at 1,160 yards. When continuously firing in squads, they laid down a devastating barrage, especially against massed infantry. One hundred crossbowmen armed with handheld models were able to shoot two thousand shafts at five hundred yards within fifteen seconds. The effectiveness of these concentrated volleys was substantially augmented by tipping their warheads with lethal poison. Nothing equal to the rapid fire of a polybolos or its Roman and Chinese variants was seen on the battlefield again until Hiram Maxim reinvented it as the modern machine gun in 1884.

Imperial Rome's far-flung empire was made possible in large measure by highly advanced artillery. For example, a *ballista's* 550-yard range was

Figure 10.2. Modern ballista reconstruction.
Photo by Ron L. Toms.

not equaled for more than one thousand years, until after the weaponization of gunpowder in early twelfth-century China. Each Roman legion comprising five thousand men was equipped with fifty-five ballistae.

## THE BOEOTIAN FLAMETHROWER

The earliest operational flamethrower of modern times was a brainchild of Hungarian engineer Gábor Szakáts at the outset of World War I. However, his work was preceded by 2,338 years, after the Boeotians joined in the Peloponnesian War. To liberate the rest of their culturally rich kingdom in central Greece from Athenian conquest, they needed to retake the occupied city of Delium, which had been transformed by the enemy into an apparently impregnable fortress dominating a strategic location.

Lacking sufficient numbers for a lengthy siege, but with a genius for innovation, the Boeotians felled a thirty-foot-long oak tree, hollowed it out, and wrapped its exterior with iron plates. Through the length of the timber's interior they inserted an iron tube that curved down into a large metal cauldron suspended from the back of the modified log by chains (fig. 10.3, p. 114). Mounted on a prodigious cart, the device resembled a modern artillery piece as it was wheeled up to the very battlements of Delium. Once in position, an enormous pump patterned after a blacksmith's bellows was attached to the weapon's rear end, where, worked up and down by a team of operators, powerful blasts of air coursed through the tube. These sucked out a mix of hot coals, sulfur, pitch, and other unknown combustible materials from the steadily refilled cauldron, disgorging them in a continuous stream of immense, high-temperature fire. The strong fortifications collapsed in blazing ruin, and numerous Athenians were incinerated while fleeing their posts as Delium fell.

The Boeotian flamethrower was not only the first of its kind, but it is also among history's largest and most effective models ever built. They were still operational more than six hundred years later, about 140 CE, when Apollodorus of Damascus, a Greek engineer from Roman Syria,

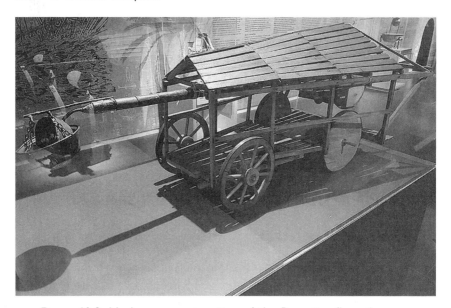

Figure 10.3. Modern reconstruction of the Boeotian flamethrower.
Photo by Gts-tg.

developed an improved type that destroyed stone walls by loading its cauldron of ammunition with correct proportions of vinegar.

From the end of Classical times until the present day, academics scoffed at Apollodorus as an alchemical fraud for his military claims on behalf of vinegar. In 1992, however, chemists—not archaeologists—demonstrated how acidic vinegar splashed in sufficiently large quantities on a stone heated to high temperatures will fracture it. "Further experiments with sour red wine (the source of vinegar in antiquity)," writes Mayor, "produced even more violent results, as the hot rocks sizzled and cracked apart. The scientists found that the chemical reaction worked best on limestone and marble, which happened to be the favorite building stone for ancient fortification walls."[2]

## GREEK FIRE

As ancient weapons technology progressed over time, flamethrowers less resembled heavy artillery than deck guns. Developments in pneumatics enabled far smaller, mobile, and more powerful siphons, syringes, and pumps capable of spraying larger quantities of flammable liquids at greater distances with concentrated accuracy. Downsizing enabled flamethrowers to be mounted on ships, radically transforming naval warfare. These steady improvements coalesced in the creation of Greek fire—likely a concoction of sulfur, saltpeter, gasoline, and pine and gum resin squirted through a nozzle at or even in the general direction of an opponent, invariably with horrific results.

Because it was oil-based, Greek fire floated, burning on the surface of the sea, consuming sailors who jumped to save themselves from their ships that were likewise set aflame from the waterline. Direct hits on a vessel incinerated sails and rigging along with decks and crewmen, who were unable to extinguish the flames except partially with inadequate buckets of sand. These awful scenes were replays from Rome's war against Hannibal 450 years before, when General Gnaeus Scipio's marines hurled the first Molotov cocktails at Carthaginian ships. In close-quarter fighting, clay jars filled with pitch and resin were set alight and thrown on enemy decks, where they shattered, spreading conflagration (see plate 7).

Greek fire was supposedly originated by Kallinikos, another engineer from Syria, but historian James Partington argues that it was more likely "invented by chemists in Constantinople, who had inherited the discoveries of the Alexandrian chemical school."[3] In any case, the new incendiary weapon made its spectacular debut in 673 CE, when it was decisive in breaking the Arab Muslims' seven-year siege of the city, repeating its first success forty-five years later by saving Constantinople yet again from another Arab fleet. Thereafter, the Byzantine empire prospered, more or less, for another two centuries before it entered a prolonged period of deepening political corruption and mostly unrelieved incompetence that allowed, even fostered, the steady degeneration and spreading decay of domestic life, culminating with the installment of a notorious prostitute on the patriarchal throne.

It was during this cultural end-time that the aphorism, "a fish rots from the head down"—analogous to a civilization in decline, beginning with failed leadership—was coined by Nicetas Choniates, a Greek Byzantine government official, whose history of the late Eastern Roman empire chronicled its ultimate demise. Choniates tells of how the military secret of Greek fire, having been sold off to the highest foreign bidders along with the technological know-how required to operate the hitherto invincible weapon, was not available to prevent the Crusader sack of Constantinople in 1204.[4]

## SUBMARINES

Among the most surprising but well-attested advancements in ancient military technology was the submarine, faint memories of which persisted into the Middle Ages, when such a craft was unthinkable. *La vrai histoire d'Alexandre* is a thirteenth-century French manuscript describing a voyage undertaken by Alexander the Great in a "glass barrel" that carried him from one Greek port to another, unnoticed beneath the keels of his fleet of warships in 332 BCE. He was said to have been so satisfied with the submarine's performance that he ordered its production for his navy. If *The True History of Alexander* was our only source for such a report, we might be inclined to dismiss it as a medieval fantasy, even though a submarine was far more inconceivable during the Middle Ages than it was in Classical Greece. His teacher, Aristotle, wrote of "submersible chambers" deployed in that same year by Greek sailors. They reportedly threaded the enemy blockade of Tiros, in coastal Greece, when their underwater craft emplaced sunken obstacles and moored subsurface weapons of some kind.[5]

During Xerxes I's invasion of Europe, a Greek officer surfaced the submarine at night to stealthily make his way undetected among the Persian fleet anchored offshore, cutting several warships loose from their moorings. After having set several enemy units adrift, Scyllis navigated his unseen craft nine miles back to Cape Artemisium, where he rejoined fellow Greeks, having successfully completed the earliest documented instance of submarine warfare. Additionally, his vessel featured a snorkel, a hollow breathing tube protruding just above the surface of the water. This apparatus would not be deployed again for another 2,224 years, when it equipped German U-boats, allowing them to operate submerged almost indefinitely during their North Atlantic attacks against Allied shipping during World War II.

Naval actions similar to the sortie undertaken by Scyllis were recounted by some of Classical civilization's foremost scholars, including Herodotus (460 BCE) and Pliny the Elder (77 CE).[6] Chinese chronicles cited the operation of a submarine carrying one man successfully to the bottom of the sea off Hailkou, in the Gulf of Tonkin, and back again circa 200 BCE. The vessel was, however, without any military application.[7]

## HIGH-TECH BLADES

Despite military innovations such as underwater warships, swords were still the preferred weapons of choice while engaging the enemy on both land and at sea. They were first made of hardened copper, but after 3200 BCE, the discovery of bronze so transformed the civilized world that the next two thousand years became rightfully known as the Bronze Age. Bronze became the metal that empowered the superpowers, separating the conquerors from the conquered. Its metallurgical miracle of combining copper, zinc, and tin gave a decisive advantage to any army facing an opponent less well armed. But bronze production in the ancient world varied widely, from rudimentary edged weapons to blades of specimens beyond anything comparable since, as the best metalsmiths mixed secret elements still unknown in proportions no less forgotten to create blades never equaled for their resilient strength, perfect balance, and keen edge.

The Classical epoch that gradually emerged from Europe was dominated by Sparta in the mid-seventh century BCE. That dynamic

Figure 10.4. Spartan steel

city-state's military ascendancy was in no small part due to its people's invention of steel, which combined the hardness of cast iron with the workability of wrought iron, making it far stronger and more resilient, with a keener edge than either, including bronze. The Spartans were also the first military leaders to equip all their warriors with steel. Its use survived the end of their world and into ours, where it became the mainstay of the Industrial Age and fundamentally molded modern society.

By the ninth century CE, Germany and Scandinavia were beginning to recover from the lingering Dark Ages that still befuddled the rest of Europe, as evidenced by a Rhinelander genius who singlehandedly changed the course of history. For two hundred years, Ulfberht's edged weapons empowered the Viking Age, arming the Northmen to overcome numerically superior opponents from the British Isles to Byzantium with the greatest swords ever designed. As many as 170 of them have since been found—mostly in Norway and Finland, many buried with their Norse owners—and their unique combination of strength, lightness, and flexibility is still impressive. "The swords were far better than any other swords made, before or since, in Europe," states Alan Williams, an archaeo-metallurgist and consultant to London's Wallace Collection, where he studied a typical specimen.[8]

For generations following Ulfberht's time, his name was still inscribed on subsequent examples of the blade type he invented, becoming a kind of trademark used by subsequent metalworkers who carried on his secret manufacturing process centuries after his death. Known blast furnaces operating between the ninth and twelfth centuries were Catalan forges, capable of a maximum high temperature no greater than thirteen hundred degrees Fahrenheit, less than half as much needed to liquefy iron. It would appear that Ulfberht discovered a greater heat source or some compensating component of which historians are unaware. He would have needed something powerful enough to imbue the blades carrying his name with three times greater carbon content than all other swords forged during the Viking Age. "We have no archaeological evidence of any crucible steel production in Europe until eight hundred years later," confessed Williams.[9] In other words, technology sufficient to make such a sword would not have become available until after the start of the Industrial Revolution, around the turn of the nineteenth century.

In a twenty-first-century attempt to discover the Rhinelander's medieval secret, a leading blacksmith attempted to re-create an authentic Ulfberht sword based exclusively on the materials and know-how available during the Middle Ages. Wisconsin's Richard Furrer devoted all his expertise to forging an accurate replica, which must reveal the hidden process of the original after which it was so faithfully patterned. Following more than a month of painstaking effort, he admitted that undertaking such a project was the most complicated endeavor of his life, and he could only complete it by resorting to modern methods, thereby violating his own self-imposed standards of historical authenticity.[10] Swordsmith Ulfberht's eleven-hundred-year-old secret is a mystery still.

## THE SVEBØLLE SWORD

Hollywood visualizations of antiquity would have audiences believe that our ancestors fought each other with little more than edged weapons. To be sure, ancient technology excelled among even these armaments, as proved by the discovery in Poland of a Keltic ax from the Hallstatt period, circa 800 to 400 BCE. "Metallurgical examination has shown that the socketed head of the axe," explained *New Scientist* magazine, "was forged from a block, which had been formed by welding together two dissimilar metals. This proves that the iron workers of twenty-five hundred years ago must have been able to distinguish between two different iron alloys, and it presupposes a high degree of metallurgical knowledge."[11]

The most recent example, and among the most extraordinary, came to light in northwest Denmark during December 2018. A pair of amateur archaeologists searching for lost coins with a magnetometer found the thirty-two-inch-long weapon only a foot beneath the ground near the small village of Svebølle before donating it to Zealand's Vestsjælland Museum. Curator Arne Hedegaard Andersen states that their rare find dates to Phase IV of the Nordic Bronze Age, between 1100 and 900 BCE. The Svebølle sword is remarkable not only for its virtually pristine condition but more so because, incredibly, the cutting edge has lost nothing of its original sharpness after three thousand years. This is a world record for tools or hand weapons of any kind and proof that

Figure 10.5.
The Svebølle sword.
Photo courtesy of the
Vestsjaelland Museum,
where the sword
currently resides.

ancient metallurgists applied a lost technology far more advanced than anything comparable since. What secrets they knew to perfectly preserve an unprotected blade buried under twelve inches of earth for three millennia vanished with the sudden collapse of Bronze Age civilization.

How the Danish sword has retained its original sharpness after the past twenty-nine hundred to thirty-one hundred years baffles metallurgists. The enduring process of its manufacture is superior to anything of the kind known today.

## THE GREATEST MILITARY INVENTOR?

*This would seem fantastic! One would think that modern engineers had exploited these forces to the nth degree, but the truth is, that outside the turbine, the ancients can teach us a thing or two.*

JULES VERNE, UPON LEARNING OF LATE
NINETEENTH-CENTURY TESTS CONFIRMING
THE REALITY OF ARCHIMEDES'S THIRD-CENTURY-BCE
SOLAR-, GRAVITY- AND WATER-POWERED INVENTIONS.
QUOTED BY DAVID HATCHER CHILDRESS,
*TECHNOLOGY OF THE GODS*

Iconic weapons such as those previously discussed are more famous than the far greater variety of sophisticated, often advanced arms available to fighting men during Classical and pre-Classical times. An illustrative example was the Siege of Syracuse, a true clash of high technologies that took place twenty-two centuries ago. Although most of Sicily was Roman at the time, a powerful and independent Greek kingdom dominated its eastern coastal area, offering Carthaginian aggressors threatening the Italian mainland a potentially open back door. To close it permanently in 213 BCE, an army led by Marcus Claudius Marcellus besieged by land and sea the port city of powerfully built fortifications, massive walls, and determined warriors commanded by skilled officers.

What particularly concerned Marcellus, however, was the presence of a seventy-eight-year-old man in charge of Syracusan defenses—Archimedes, the Leonardo da Vinci of Classical times, whose genius, if applied to military matters, might overcome conventional attempts at encirclement. Accordingly, Marcellus came equipped with state-of-the-art equipment such as the *sambuca*—a floating siege tower with grappling hooks—and ship-mounted scaling ladders lowered by pulleys onto city walls. He hoped these innovations would surprise the defenders and quickly overcome them. But before his battle cruisers and troop carriers could land, they came under concerted attack from detachments of history's first operational steam cannon. Using only heat and water as a ready supply for high-pressure steam from enormous boilers, salvos of stones as large as volleyballs were rained on the invading vessels. The steam cannons operated in concert with heavier artillery that hurled five-hundred-pound boulders over great distances with precision accuracy afforded by range finders that enabled gunners to adjust for leverage. Badly suffering from the unremitting barrage of shore batteries and in the face of mounting losses at sea, the Romans pushed on, their surviving ships arriving under the very battlements of Syracuse.

"At the same time," writes the Roman historian Plutarch, "huge beams were run out from the walls, so as to project over the Roman ships. Some of them were then sunk by great weights dropped from above, while others were seized at the bows by iron claws or by beaks like those of cranes, hauled into the air by means of counterweights until they stood upright upon their sterns, and then allowed to plunge to the bottom, or else they were spun round by means of windlasses situated inside the city and dashed against the steep cliffs and rocks which jutted out under the walls with great loss of life to the crews. Often there would be seen the terrifying spectacle of a ship being lifted clean out of the water into the air and whirled about as it hung there, until every man had been shaken out of the hull and thrown in different directions, after which it would be dashed down empty upon the walls."[12]

According to science reporter Asim Qureshi, "the Claw was an

Figure 10.6. The Claw

application of the two laws of Archimedes; the Law of the Lever and Law of Buoyancy; recent tests show that building this live crane device was possible at the time."[13]

Meanwhile, some of the Roman sambucas got through, but as their troops stormed the outer fortress, they were cut down in a dense cross fire of iron darts simultaneously launched from literally hundreds of small catapults, known as scorpions, shooting from protected loopholes in the city walls. Thanks to Archimedes—the wily inventor of these effective anti-invasion measures—the city of his birth withstood and continued to defy the best efforts of its powerful opponent. The siege bogged down to a stalemate, with the Romans prevented from forcing their way into the city and the Syracusans, minus outside help, unable to compel the enemy to withdraw. Time was nonetheless working against Marcellus, because the blockade he imposed—already over budget and rapidly becoming financially unsustainable—was never tight enough to entirely stop supplies from reaching the defenders. If the Syracusans continued to hold out indefinitely, he would have to lift the encirclement for lack of funding, evidence of weakness the observant Carthaginians would take advantage of for seizing Sicily, a last stepping-stone to the Italian mainland. Desperate for a decisive victory, the proconsul launched an all-out naval operation aimed at overwhelming Syracusan defenses through sheer force of numbers in ships and men. So large was his flotilla that even the combined firepower of the city's steam cannons and long-range catapults could only slow but not halt its progress.

"When Marcellus had placed the ships a bowshot off," the Byzantine scholar Tzetzae wrote in his *Chiliades* (*Book of Histories*) about Archimedes, "the old man constructed an array of mirrors, which were moved by means of their hinges and certain plates of metal. He placed it amid the rays of the sun at noon, both in summer and winter. The rays being reflected by this, a frightful, fiery kindling was excited on the ships, and it reduced them to ashes, from the distance of a bowshot." Tzetzae's succinct account is not half of what befell the attacking Romans. When the bulk of their warships towing siege towers, followed closely by troop carriers and landing craft, came within 550 yards of Archimedes's coordinated mirrors, sails burst into sheets of flame while men were blinded or burned alive to a crisp, like ants shriveling up in the sun's rays focused through a magnifying glass. Panicked sailors and marines jumped overboard, abandoning their fire-ravaged vessels adrift at sea. "Thus," concluded Tzetzae, "the old man baffled Marcellus by means of his inventions."[14] (See plate 8.)

In 200 BCE, just a dozen years after the Siege of Syracuse, the Greek mathematician and geometer Diocles wrote *On Burning Mirrors,* suggesting that the militarized *speculum* (Latin for "mirror") was still recognized as an operational weapon and subsequently put to peaceful purposes on the Aegean island of Crete. Temple points out that "the reason why the soil there was so dark was that the ancient Greeks had repeatedly burnt it by walking round the fields holding burning glasses and directing the focused rays at the ground." This local folklore suggests to him "the use of burning glasses to start the fires of stubble on top of which the Cretans pile cuttings from the tops of pine trees for better effect; after stubble is burnt, the ground beneath really does look black."[15] Thus, perennial oral tradition underscores the plausibility of ancient solar power, despite persistent disbelief of conventional modern scholars.

The earliest surviving account of Archimedes's heat ray in action was recorded by the second-century Roman rhetorician Lucian in his *Hippias* and later by the Greek physician Galen. Tzetzae's Byzantine predecessor, Anthemius of Tralles, wrote in *On Mechanical Paradoxes* "a full description of the construction of a burning-mirror according to the principles of Archimedes, but greatly improved. . . . [Anthemius] constructed his own multiple mirror in emulation of him."[16] Anthemius was the architect of Istanbul's Hagia Sophia, among the greatest cathedrals on Earth.

But modern skeptics disagree. They argue that such a long-range thermal weapon did not exist, simply because, in their opinion, it *could* not exist. Reflecting sunlight on a large scale over distance would have been, and still is, incapable of raising temperatures sufficiently high to ignite fires, as apparently demonstrated by recent re-creations designed to test any possibility for solar power the ancient Syracusans may have deployed in the third century BCE.[17] However, results were invalid because these controlled experiments ignored the basic details clearly enumerated by Tzetzae eight and a half centuries ago. A more faithful simulation was undertaken by Ioannis G. Sakas, a Ph.D. in mechanical and electrical engineering, which he taught at the Air Force College of Greece in Athens before becoming an engineer at the Electric Power Corporation there.

On November 6, 1973, at the Skaramagas-Athens Naval Base, Sakas conducted his own experiment in ancient solar weaponry. As Temple describes it, "seventy mirrors were held by the same number of sailors at an average distance of fifty-five meters [180 feet] from the target, which was a small, wooden, moored boat 2.3 meters [7.5 feet] in length and covered in tar. Within only a few seconds, the target gave off smoke. Three minutes later, the entire side of the boat facing the mirrors was in flames. The experiment was a complete and dramatic success," even though conditions were not ideal, with only partial sunshine.[18] "So," Sakas concluded, "I proved experimentally as well that it was possible for Archimedes to set the Roman fleet on fire."[19]

Archimedes had been preceded by 226 years, when "one of the greatest figures in the history of French science" arranged forty-eight little flat mirrors "in such a way," writes Temple, "that they could be twiddled and teased with the greatest of ease to be pointing at a particular spot." In 1740, Georges-Louis Leclerc, Comte du Buffon, directed his reflectors and melted within minutes a large tin container weighing six pounds. Encouraged by his success, he used his thermal array to liquefy or incinerate a number of different materials, such as planks and metal objects, in a variety of tests. "No one who was familiar with them at the time," Temple continues, "was in any doubt that the principle of Archimedes's burning-mirror was viable. In 1747, when Buffon suddenly ignited a piece of wood one hundred fifty feet away with his mirrors, he had very nearly replicated the achievements of Archimedes in terms of distance and efficacy."[20] Edward Gibbon, famous for *The Decline and Fall of the Roman Empire,* believed that the repetitive results of Leclerc's experiments proved not only that the ancient death ray was possible but also likely.

## INCENDIARY MIRRORS

Though many of his ideas were original, Archimedes was not alone in understanding the principle of solar power and its application. At Delphi, home of the ancient world's most important oracle, the sun-god's sacred altar fire was traditionally ignited, beginning about 1500 BCE, "by metallic mirrors," in the words of the Greek historian Plutarch. This method was used because, activated as it was by solar rays, it was considered the most pure means of honoring Phoebus-Apollo at his chief shrine. Plutarch explains that if the holy flame went out,

> it must not be kindled again from other fire, but made fresh and new by lighting a pure and unpolluted flame from the rays of the sun. And this they [the Delphic priests] usually effect by means of metallic mirrors, the concavity of which is made to follow the sides of an isosceles rectangular triangle, and which converge from their circumference to a single point in the center. When, therefore, these are placed opposite the sun, so that its rays, as they fall upon them from all sides, are collected and concentrated at the center, the air itself is rarefied there, and very light and dry substances placed there quickly blaze up from its resistance, the sun's rays now acquiring the force of life.[21]

Such incendiary mirrors appear to have been in use throughout the Late Bronze Age, as suggested by the contemporaneous Thesmophoria, held annually to celebrate human and agricultural fertility but restricted to female participants. At this popular religious festival, "the women did not use fire, but the sun's heat, for cooking their meat," according to Oxford Classical scholar Lewis Richard Farnell; "the sun's fire was purer than that of the domestic hearth."[22] The earliest explicit written evidence of a magnifying device may be found in Aristophanes's 424 BCE comedy, *The Clouds,* when one of his characters asks, "Have you ever seen a beautiful, transparent stone at the druggists', with which you may kindle fire?" This line implies that solar-powered incendiary contrivances were in common use at the time.[23]

Theophrastus, the early third-century-BCE successor to Aristotle, wrote that "fire can be ignited from rock crystal and from copper and silver reflectors, when prepared in a certain way."[24] Temple quotes Charles Vallancey, a nineteenth-century British authority on Irish antiquities, "that the Druids [Keltic followers of a shamanic cult with roots in the Neolithic Period] used crystals as burning-lenses 'to draw down the Logh, the essence of spiritual fire,' in religious ceremonies."[25] It would appear that solar power was used mostly for religious purposes until it was first weaponized during the Syracuse campaign.

In 1669, the German polymath Athanasius Kircher related "an experiment of his own, whereby he produced a heat intense enough to burn, by means of five mirrors directing the rays of the sun into one focus. He supposes that Proclus by such means might have set fire to Vitalian's fleet."[26]

The Proclus mentioned by Moses Cotsworth, author of *The Rational Almanac,* was a scientist and teacher of Anthemius cited previously and who, in 496 CE, aided in defeating the rebellious general at sea by "launching upon the enemy vessels from the surface of reflecting mirrors, such a quantity of flame, as reduced them to ashes," in the words of the Byzantine historian Johannes Zonaras.[27] Operational deployment of an effective thermal weapon not only preceded Proclus but may have predated Archimedes himself. A Late Bronze Age version was mentioned by the important Roman philosopher Macrobius Ambrosius Theodosius in his early fifth-century *Saturnaliorum Libri Septem* (*Seven Books of the Saturnalia*). Book I, chapter 20 tells of how "the men of Gades sailed out to meet [an enemy king commanding his invasion fleet] with their ships of war. Battle was joined, and the issue of the fight was undecided, when the king's ships suddenly took to flight and at the same time burst into flames without warning and were consumed. The very few enemy survivors, who were taken prisoner, said . . . that of a sudden their own ships had been set on fire by a discharge of rays like those which are represented surrounding the head of the sun."[28]

# 11

# Children of the Sun

*Any sufficiently advanced technology is indistinguishable from magic.*

ARTHUR C. CLARKE, *PROFILES OF THE FUTURE*

Two hundred eighty years after the clash of military technologies at Syracuse, a former navy and army commander of Imperial Rome, turned naturalist, transformed the principles of Archimedes's invention from the arts of war to the healing arts. In *Natural History,* Pliny the Elder tells of how patients being treated for severe cuts were firmly bound to a couch or chair, rendering them immobile, beside a glass globe mounted on a platform standing on caster wheels, allowing it to move in any direction. Sunlight entering the specially designed, water-filled sphere concentrated into a single heat ray the physician adjusted and focused on the wound, efficiently cauterizing it. Thus was applied the solar-powered equivalent of modern-day laser surgery almost two thousand years before the latter procedure was invented.

The modern city of Cadiz was known as Gades in early Classical times by Phoenician conquerors occupying the Spanish city after the earlier destruction of Atlantis. In the *Kritias* dialogue, Plato lists Gadeiros as the Atlantean ruler of southwest coastal Spain before 1200 BCE. Two centuries earlier still, sacred fires at the site of the Delphic oracle were rekindled by "drawing the pure and unpolluted flame from sun-beams," according to Plutarch.[1] "These new flames," writes John Perlin for *Whole Earth*, "were generally kindled with concave brass mirrors."[2]

If not merely coincidental, but due to transatlantic influences from the ancient world long before the Spanish Conquest, "Incas of Peru similarly ignited their holy fires with solar energy. Believing themselves the Children of the Sun," Perlin continues, "they celebrated the summer solstice with great solemnity. Temple virgins concluded the ceremony by flourishing their concave, silver mirrors, mounted on gold, gem-encrusted frames. They focused the sun's rays onto cotton wool, which burst into flame. As the solstitial flame had to be lit on that day and no other, if the sun didn't shine, the virgins made fire the secular way, rubbing two sticks against each other. But they shook in fear on such occasions, taking it as an evil omen, for, in the words of James Frazer [famed author of *The Golden Bough*], 'they said the Sun must be angry with them, since he refused to kindle the flame with his own hand.'"[3]

Ancient American thermal mirrors appear to have come about during the early pre-Classical or Formative Period, but production of significantly improved versions surged circa 1200 BCE. These incendiary reflectors belonged to numerous parallels connecting the Mexican Olmec culture with China's Shang Dynasty, which collapsed around the same time. Notable mariners, the Shang controlled coastal regions of the Bo Hai Gulf, which gave them access to the Yellow Sea for transpacific voyaging to the western shores of Central America. While mainstream archaeologists balk at the mere suggestion of Chinese seafarers to Mexico before the Spanish Conquest, far less technologically endowed Polynesians were renowned for traversing thousands of miles of open water in outrigger canoes long before the Spanish nation even came into being. Denying Shang Dynasty sailors at least the equivalent ability to navigate similar distances is a form of academic bias, especially when it is so effectively contradicted by an abundance of cogent, contemporaneous comparisons linking ancient Asian and Mesoamerican civilizations.

"In the ancient Chinese kitchen, for example," observes Perlin, "a burning mirror was as common as a pot or pan. On sunny days, the son in charge of lighting the family stove took the concave mirror outside and concentrated the sun's rays onto kindling. As soon as the family stove fired up, the women could cook."[4]

Military applications for reflectors are recalled by archaeology reporter Ellen Lloyd: "Ancient Chinese legends describe a *Ying-Yang* mirror that was carried by warriors to burn the enemy."[5] Imperial armies were outfitted with six-inch-diameter, circular, concave, highly polished bronzes hung around the neck. Just before battle, if the angle of the sun worked to their advantage on cloudless days, whole corps simultaneously directed glaring sunbeams from hundreds of coordinating reflective plates into the eyes of their foes, at least temporarily blinding them. The same arrangement, more tightly focused, inflicted incapacitating burns on concentrations of opposing troops already hemmed into positions of low mobility. Whether the early Mesoamericans weaponized solar energy is unknown.

More certainly, the Olmec used sand, hematite, ilmenite, and magnetite powder—the most effective abrasive materials—for polishing iron ore to produce a durable, non-tarnishing, metallic, highly reflective surface. The Olmecs knew not to use iron pyrite because it degrades with time. Most of these mirror stones were sawed from a larger section of rock before being configured into an oval shape. "Their concave fronts are as precisely ground as modern optical lenses," according to Richard Diehl, a leading authority on Olmec culture. "The curve of each mirror is unique and tailored to the stone from which it is worked. Although the elliptical mirrors are parabolic, the circular mirrors have a spherical concavity, and are particularly effective at lighting fires."[6]

The front mirror face was concave with a highly polished lens, while the beveled edge of the mirror was convex. "Of four large mirrors found at Arroyo Pesquero in Veracruz," writes John B. Carlson, a specialist in Olmec mirrors, "two were circular and were excellent sources of ignition. The concave lenses of these mirrors were found to

Figure 11.1. Aztec obsidian mirror that passed into the possession of Elizabethan court alchemist John Dee. Now in the collection of the British Museum. Photo by roseandsigil.

form parabolic reflectors. The borders of each of the La Venta mirrors formed a circle or an ellipse, and they usually had different focal lengths for each axis."[7] Olmec reflectors commonly ranged up to twelve inches across, but some were more than three feet in diameter. The degree of craftsmanship exhibited by these ancient mirrors is extraordinarily high, even compared to present-day examples made with the assistance of computerized machining. The Olmecs certainly employed some form of mechanical technology for grinding and polishing. Archaeologists have recovered literally hundreds of Mexico's pre-Columbian reflectors, including specimens from subsequent Mayan and Aztec civilizations.

A deity of the latter culture suggests possible connections with Atlantis through the solar mirror. Xiuhtecuhtli, the Aztec god of fire, is portrayed on the Codex Vaticanus B igniting flames from a mirror with one hand while holding his staff of command topped with a deer's head in the other. In Aztec myth the deer signified some catastrophic deluge that destroyed a former kingdom, dragging it to the bottom of the sea where Xiuhtecuhtli still dwells in its ruined palace. In temple art he is depicted holding in his left hand a shield covered by a thin gold plate adorned with five green stones—the four cardinal directions with a center stone—arranged in the form of a cross signifying Aztlan, his drowned homeland, once known as the Center of the World.

The green stones were *chalchihuites,* associated with his wife Chalchiuhtlicue, the goddess who changed victims of the Great Flood into fish. The same transformation appears in the deluge myths of the Babylonians and American Lakota Sioux. Chalchiuhtlicue was honored during an annual ceremony in which priests collected reeds, dried them out, and placed them inside her shrine. As writing utensils, the reeds symbolized wisdom and the Place of Reeds, Aztlan, her overseas' homeland. Temple art represented Chalchiuhtlicue seated on a throne, around which men and women were shown drowning in huge whirlpools. Her name, Our Lady of the Turquoise Skirt, may refer to the feminine Atlantis, Plato's Daughter of Atlas, in the midst of the sea.

Chalchiuhtlicue's myth is a self-evident evocation of the cataclysm that destroyed Aztlan. And Xiuhtecuhtli's fire-starting mirror appears to have been an example of technology brought to Mexico from the Atlantean old country by its culture-bearing survivors. That such an object should be independently associated with Atlantis on opposite ends of the world—the Roman Macrobius and the Aztec Xiuhtecuhtli—underscores its possible technological origins there and subsequent migration in the hands of survivors eastward to Spain and westward to Mexico.

While no unequivocal evidence has so far been found for weaponizing solar mirrors in pre-Columbian times, their military deployment is nonetheless implied by a prominent Mesoamerican figure. The Aztec god of war was Tezcatlipoca, meaning "Smoking Mirror" in the Nahuatl language (see plate 9). His very name describes the polished object as something more than a tool for shamanic rituals or prophecy, perhaps as an instrument for setting fires. In temple art, he is often shown carrying a shield and holding arrows or a spear in his right hand, with a fan of feathers surrounding a mirror.

Tezcatlipoca was an incarnation of the preceding Maya K'awil, himself derived from an even earlier Olmec deity whose name has been lost—all of them nothing more than cultural inflections of the same war god. This succession of a bellicose immortal wielding his heat ray paralleled the unbroken production of obsidian mirrors from pre-Classical to post-Classical times, spanning 3,500 years or more. Given such a prolonged, continuous history, the transitional usage of burning reflectors from ceremonial to military applications undoubtedly took place.

With the fall on either side of the Atlantic Ocean of pre-Columbian and, earlier, Western European Classical civilizations, solar technology was lost in subsequent dark ages until it was independently reinvented centuries later by English experimenter Samuel Parker. He designed and constructed a glass lens "three feet in diameter," according to Rev. J. Joyce, who personally examined the instrument and described it for *London's Scientific Dialogues* in 1844. Joyce goes on to explain that

> when fixed in its frame, it exposed a clear surface of more than two feet eight inches in diameter, and its focus, by means of another lens, was reduced to a diameter of a half an inch. The heat produced by this [when exposed to sunlight] was so great that iron plates were melted in a few seconds. Tiles and slates become red hot in a moment and were vitrified, or changed into glass. Sulfur, pitch, and other resinous bodies were melted under water. Wood-ashes and those of other vegetable substances were turned in a moment to transparent glass. Even gold was rendered fluid in a few seconds. . . . A piece of wood may be burned to coal, when it is contained in a decanter of water.[8]

Temple describes the ancient applications of solar energy that long preceded Parker's reinvention as "'light amplification by stimulated emission of radiation,' the initial letters of which phrase form the acronym laser. No sun is needed anymore, but the mirror is still there, for the coherent beams of laser light are emitted only after going back and forth in a tiny chamber between mirrors. Archimedes lives on!"[9]

Archimedes did not, however, survive the Siege of Syracuse his innovative designs successfully defended. The Syracusans were subverted by a single act of treason that allowed General Marcus Claudius Marcellus to take the city with relative ease. Finally victorious, he ordered his men to capture Archimedes alive and unharmed. A legionnaire discovered the aged scholar at his workshop, deeply engrossed in a scientific problem of some kind and unwilling to leave before he solved it. The impatient Roman forthwith slew the old man in cold blood for resisting arrest. That, at any rate, was the official report. More likely, having found the Greek genius responsible for hideously blinding and burning to death so many of his comrades, the soldier avenged them by stabbing Archimedes to death. His fate foreshadowed future wars, down to modern times. Overreliance on technology, no matter how far advanced over one's enemies, cannot ultimately prevail against human betrayal.

About 140 years before, Archimedes's fellow Greek scientist, Aristotle, observed that energy from the sun evaporates and purifies water. His insight prompted the invention of the solar still, a water purifier powered by sunlight. It used the sun's heat to evaporate water, leaving salt, bacteria, and dirt behind. The water vapor then cooled and returned to a liquid state and was collected in a clean container. This simple but effective technology provided drinking water for the dry plains of interior Greece, the Egyptian desert, central Asia Minor, and other parts of the ancient Old World, where rainfall was infrequent and water resources were scarce. As an example of either independent invention or cross-cultural influence, Aristotle's fourth-century-BCE contemporaries of pre-Inca Peru—in the Jarabarriu, or final stage of the Chavín culture—likewise employed condensation traps for the distillation of fresh water in arid regions of the Andes Mountains. The important function of these solar stills explains why ancient South Americans referred to drops of water as "tears of the sun."

"Now researchers are bringing this technology into the modern age, using it to sanitize water at what they report to be record-breaking rates. By draping black, carbon-dipped paper in a triangular shape and using it to both absorb and vaporize water, they have developed a method for using sunlight to generate clean water with near-perfect efficiency."[10]

A single modernized solar still the size of a small refrigerator can generate three to five gallons every twenty-four hours—good news for the inhabitants of drought-ravaged lands or the thirsting human and animal survivors of natural disasters, which often leave no drinkable water in their wake. Aristotle's twenty-three-hundred-year-old discovery is revived, applied, and modified to aid living creatures in the twenty-first century. Yet it is not the only such ancient world legacy that has come down to our time.

Archimedes's solar weapon that was powerful enough to incinerate a Roman invasion fleet 2,200 years ago has taken the form of today's lenses in solar furnaces, which employ large parabolic arrays of mirrors; some facilities are several stories high. They focus sunlight to a high intensity for industrial purposes, instantly producing extremely high temperatures without the need for fuel or large supplies of electricity. Their productive application contrasts with sunlight's military capabilities to exemplify the amorality of great power, which is, in itself, neither good nor evil, save only in how it is used.

# 12
# Stone into Glass

*If we have learned one thing from the history of invention and discovery, it is that, in the long run—and often in the short one—the most daring prophecies seem laughably conservative.*

ARTHUR C. CLARKE, *THE EXPLORATION OF SPACE*

Scotland's Craig Phadrig is an early Dark Ages' site crowning a forested hill rising 564 feet above the western edge of Inverness, Britain's northernmost city. It overlooks the Beauly Firth inlet to the north and the mouth of the River Ness to the northeast. The view—as panoramic as it is commanding—suggests the old structure's original military intentions. The ruin itself seems unexceptional in every respect. Its inner walls of crudely piled rocks enclosed an oval area 246 by 75 feet, rising an unimpressive three feet, eleven inches high. Beyond it lies another outer rampart with sections of a third to the east.

King Bridei mac Maelchon was supposed to have ruled over the Keltic Picts from this place for thirty-four years during the late sixth century, and Pictish metalworking tools, plus French pottery of two hundred years later, have been found here, but nothing more. These common details are incidental to the prosaic hill fort's true significance, which only appears on closer examination of its clumsy, unmortared stonework: huge blocks had been fused with smaller rubble to form a hard, glassy mass. The rockface had been literally melted into vitrification.

This is "a molecular change in the surface of a rock caused by high temperatures, which transform the naturally rough surface to form a bright and shiny finish," explains archaeological researcher Brien Foerster. "This molecular modification caused by [high] temperatures produces a skin or surface layer on the rock. . . . The combined use of molding and heat have given the rough stone a mirror-like finish [and] its metallic sheen."[1]

Craig Phadrig, of all the other seventy or so such locations in Scotland, is among the best preserved, a relatively pristine representative of the Highlands' so-called vitrified forts. How their prehistoric builders achieved, applied, and sufficiently sustained temperatures well above the 1,000 degrees Fahrenheit required for vitrification was at odds with known Keltic furnaces, which reached no higher than one quarter of that intensity. However, science writer Brian Dunning, executive director of Skeptoid Media, reports that as recently as May 2018, archaeologists from Forest Enterprise Scotland, working with Stirling University, believed they had solved the mystery.

> The team of experts studied the vitrified fort known as Dun Deardail, in the Highlands near Ben Nevis [at 4,413 feet, Scotland's highest mountain], and have concluded that they can explain how its stones became molten and melted. . . . They believe that a large-scale wooden structure over the stone walls was set alight and the blaze reached such a temperature that it burned the stones. . . .
>
> The study has shown that a timber superstructure, which included ramparts and towers, was set alight and the resulting blaze heated the stones. The fire was so intense that is was able to melt stones because of the anaerobic environment that developed as the flames burned down into the stones. The absence of oxygen in the anaerobic conditions made the fire much more intense and allowed

it to reach the temperatures that would have burned the slabs until they melted and fused.

We've learned that the technology required to create the vitrified forts was not extraordinary.[2]

Sadly, the University of Stirling experiment failed to vitrify anything more than a small handful of rubble, far short of the vitrification covering one or even the smallest of Scotland's six dozen forts; the hardworking archaeologists were simply unable to keep their inadequate fires burning long enough for sustaining the necessary temperatures. Their attempt was, moreover, unnecessarily redundant and served only to underscore a similar experiment already undertaken eighty-four years earlier by Vere Gordon Childe, an archaeologist at the University of Edinburgh and London's Institute of Archaeology, and Wallace Thorneycroft, Fellow of Scotland's Society of Antiquaries.

In March 1934 they "set about trying to replicate the process that led to the vitrified stones of Scotland coming into being," writes author Nick Redfern. "They carefully constructed a series of walls that were comprised of fire-clay bricks, timber, and basalt rubble. They then proceeded to place no less than four tons of brushwood, and extra timber, against the walls and set them on fire."[3]

"The experimental wall was six feet wide and high," according to the 1966–1967 edition of *The Proceedings of the Society of Antiquaries of Scotland,* "with horizontal timbers interlaced with stone slabs. After ignition through brushwood fires around the wall face, the wall began to burn and after three hours it collapsed. The core of basalt rubble became red-hot, probably reaching 800 to 1,200°C, and after excavation the bottom part of the rubble was found to be vitrified, with rock droplets and casts of timber preserved."[4]

A few melted droplets were the sole results of more than four tons of burning brushwood and extra timber. Clearly, a concentrated, far more powerful, longer-lasting heat source had vitrified Craig Phadrig and its associated fortresses. Building on the Childe and Thorneycroft effort, Ian Ralston (at Edinburgh University's Department of Archaeology since 1985, currently head of the School of History, Classics and Archaeology) undertook an even more ambitious project in northeast Scotland during 1980, when he built his own twenty-five-foot-long partial re-creation of a stone fort. An episode of *The Mysterious World of Arthur C. Clarke* covered the experiment.

> Professional dry-stone wallers toiled for days to build the wall of rock laced with timber [which was set alight]. After several hours and many tons of wood, a load of old furniture has to be commandeered from the local dustman, as the only way to keep the temperature up. Later, another consignment of wood, the sixth of the day, arrives to keep the fires burning. As night falls over Aberdeen, weary helpers begin to realize the true extent of the mystery of the vitrified forts, to wonder not only how the fort builders could achieve the searing temperatures needed to melt the rock, but how they managed to drag vast quantities of wood up to the tops of the hills with only primitive transport. The morning after . . . twenty-two hours after the first fire was lit . . . at first sight, the result looks disappointing. There are no ramparts of fused stone. The search is now on for any rocks that have melted.[5]

The handful of specimens Ralston retrieved from the blaze fit into the lid of a small cardboard carton with room to spare. He did indeed prove, however, that stone could be melted by piling on flaming timbers. He likewise demonstrated that burning at least half of Scotland's original thirty-thousand square miles of pine forests would have been necessary to vitrify its seventy or more hill forts, as established by the ratio of his Aberdeen fire to the very few vitrified pebbles and drops recovered. His experiment also showed the obvious: namely, the coolest part of such fires occurs at their base, where heat efficiency is lowest and chances of resulting vitrification are minimal.

Official radiocarbon dates obtained by his academic colleagues at various vitrified sites range from the sixth century BCE to fourth century CE. This unmanageably broad and vague time span enfolds numerous cultures that rose and fell across northern Britain; this fact makes creating whatever connections with anyone to the vitrified forts impossible to ascertain and therefore useless. Ralston himself confessess that "the process has no chronological significance, and is found during both Iron Age and Early Medieval Forts in Scotland."[6] Moreover, C-14 testing cannot date any of the vitrified locations, save only by presumed reference from organic materials found on site. As such, half-devoured chicken bones radiocarbon-dated at Craig Phadrig to 300 BCE mean only that someone enjoyed an Iron Age meal there; concluding from them that the structure was actually built at that time is precipitously jumping to conclusions, minus any basis in applicable data.

Due to the sealant nature of their vitrification, the forts themselves are "virtually impenetrable to erosion, meaning that the true age of these miraculous structures may be far, far older than we are led to believe,"[7] concluded Ralston. They are, after all, cultural anomalies, possessing nothing in common with constructions of the Keltic, Pictish, or Early Medieval Scotts, who were credited them without credible cause by archaeologists. Obviously these uncharacteristic places belonged to an older period. The forts were more likely built by a Bronze Age society that left jars of vitrified food inside the remains of a dwelling destroyed by fire, circa 1200 BCE in Cambridgeshire County, England. This period witnessed widespread burning across Europe and the Near East.[8]

Among the findings at the Cambridgeshire site were intricately decorated tiles made from lime tree bark, indicative of a high culture. As recently as 2016, Scottish archaeologists discovered one of the largest Bronze Age wheels to have ever been unearthed anywhere in the world near the same excavation. The wheel measures 1 meter (3.28 feet) in diameter and 3.5 centimeters (1.38 inches) thick. Although mainstream scholars presume the vitrified forts are exclusively Keltic, especially Pictish, the same structures are found outside Scotland in County

Londonderry and County Cavan, Ireland. They also occur in other parts of the world, sometimes far removed from the British Isles. There are more than two hundred alone on the European Continent in France, at Sainte-Suzanne (Mayenne), Châteauvieux (near Pionnat), Péran, La Courbe, Puy de Gaudy, and Thauron.

Germany is rich in vitrified forts, such as those found in Saxony's Oberlausitz, near the Polish frontier; in Silesia and Thuringia; in provinces on the Rhine, especially near the Nahe; at Ucker Lake; and in Brandenburg, where walls are formed of burned and smelted bricks. Broborg is a vitrified hill fort in Uppland, Sweden. Others are found in Hungary and the Czech Republic. While Keltic peoples may have taken up residence in some or even all of these locations over time, nothing identifies the actual builders or their real origins.

Contradicting conventional identification of vitrified forts entirely with Europe's Iron Age and Early Medieval Period, unmistakable evidence of a military installation's rock face having been deliberately melted during prehistory was excavated in Ohio in 1890 by our country's foremost archaeologists of the time, E. G. Squier and Edwin Davis. The stone fort they investigated—dismantled in the following century—was near Bourneville. "It occupies the summit of a lofty, detached hill twelve miles west of Chillicothe," according to a contemporaneous article in *American Antiquarian*. The following description of the Bourneville site is a mirror image of Craig Phadrig and most European hill forts.

The hill is not far from forty feet in height. It is remarkable for the abruptness of its sides. It projects midway into the broad valley of Paint Creek and is a conspicuous object from every point of view. The defenses consist of a wall of stone, which is carried around the hill a little below the brow, cutting off the spurs, but extending across the neck that connects the hill with the range beyond. The wall is a rude one, giving little evidence that the stones were placed upon one another, so as to present vertical faces.[9]

*American Antiquarian* goes on to report Squier and Davis's observation that the Ohio structure exhibited

the marks of intense heat, which has vitrified the surfaces of the stones and fused them together. Strong traces of fire are visible at other places on the wall, the point commanding the broadest extent of country. There are two or three small stone mounds that seem burned throughout. Nothing is more certain that that powerful fires have been maintained for considerable periods at numerous points on the hill.[10]

## PRE-AZTEC HEAT RAY

Remarkably, the sole representation of ancient technology responsible for vitrification in both the Old and New Worlds may occur, not in Scotland or Germany, but at one of Mexico's most important archaeological locations. Northwest of Mexico City, at the ruins of the pre-Aztec city of Tula, towers a pyramid topped by four thirteen-foot-tall basalt columns, identically sculpted in the image of ceremonially dressed men standing at attention. Each one grasps in his right hand a peculiar triangular object, the index and middle fingers passing through a small hoop or guard of the handle, their thumb on a singular element, suggesting a depressor switch. The pistollike article unique to these colossi is nowhere else portrayed in Mesoamerican art and remains unidentified (see plate 11).

Author Colin Wilson writes that "one of the *pilasters* [rectangular, supporting roof columns] has a peculiar carving [in bas-relief] of a man wearing a segmented suit with what looks like a kind of backpack. In his hands he is holding the same tool—the one that resembles a pistol in its holster—and is pointing it at the rock face in front of him; a surging flame is bursting out of the barrel of the pistol."[11] Is this the illustration of an ancient vitrifying device in action? If so, does its sidearmlike reappearance on Tula's anthropomorphic columns identify them not as

Figure 12.1. A faithful rendition of Tula's unusual bas relief. Image courtesy of artist Laura Beaudoin.

warriors, but construction workers? Or did the fire-spewing instrument they hold double as a handheld flamethrower?

Before attempting any definitive answers, let us regard the image in the context of its surroundings. Between 900 and 1150 CE, a people remembered as the Toltecs built Tula, the largest city and the most powerful kingdom in Mesoamerica. Their capital covered some 5.5 square miles, populated by approximately sixty thousand residents, with another twenty-five thousand subjects in the surrounding 386 square miles. The city's centerpiece was a five-tiered step pyramid for its quartet of *atlantes*—monumental statues of identical warriors—which originally served as columns supporting the roof of a temple (fig. 12.2). In front of their pyramid is a large vestibule forming a space (today occupied by broken pillars) with Building C, which is a large structure, perhaps a palace.

Tula was totally abandoned by 1150 CE for reasons unknown, because Itzcoatl (meaning "Obsidian Serpent" in Classical Nahuatl) destroyed all history books (codexes) after founding the Aztec empire 277 years later. The monumental structure on which the colossi stand is known as the Pyramid of the Feathered Serpent. They signify the four cardinal directions, rendering Tula the Center of the World. The atlantes are also representations of the god Tlahuizcalpantecuhtli, who is the Morning Star, Venus, an incarnation of Quetzalcoatl, the Feathered Serpent founding father of Mesoamerican civilization and the bringer of high technology from his distant homeland, Tollan, which was engulfed by a natural catastrophe. Was the vitrification process part of the cultural gifts he shared with native Mesoamericans?

Building C is directly across from this pyramid and is known as the Burnt Palace, because "walls and floor were burned bright red, and some of the stones had vitrified surfaces," according to archaeologists Victoria Bricker and Jeremy Sabloff.[12] Mainstream scholars assume that the structure was probably incinerated by enemy invaders, an unlikely speculation given that no other buildings in Tula were fire-damaged. Moreover, its ruins resulted not from military action but instead were caused by severe earthquake activity over the centuries. The Aztecs, who rose to power after Tula shut down, did not oppose its inhabitants but, on the contrary, lauded them as masters of the arts and sciences.

Figure 12.2. One of Tula's towering columns. Photo by AlejandroPZ.

In "The Prophet," the Aztecs said of the Feathered Serpent:

And his people, they, the Toltecs, wondrous skilled in all the trades were, all the arts and artifices. And as master craftsmen worked they. And in Quetzalcoatl all these arts and crafts had their beginning. He, the master workman, taught them. Nothing pleasing to the palate, nothing helpful to the body, ever lacked they there in Tula. Masters they of wealth uncounted. Every need was satisfied them. In the days of ancient Tula, there in grandeur rose his temple, reared aloft its mighty ramparts, reaching upward to the heavens.[13]

Throughout the Valley of Mexico, the very name *Toltec* was synonymous with an extraordinary artisan or highly skilled worker. The Toltecs had a monopoly on the production of pottery made with gray-green plumbate, a salt compound formed of lead oxide, which they imported from southern Guatemala. "Plumbate pottery was one of the most distinctive style pottery of its time," writes archaeologist David Oldham, "and is considered the only true vitrified (glazed) pottery in pre-Columbian America. An orange-colored pottery of this kind decorated in a great diversity of styles is associated with the Toltecs, as is a dark-colored pottery with a glossy appearance and incised ornament (plumbate ware, see plate 10). Widely traded, this ware is characterized by its shiny glaze-like surface that results from the special types of clay used."[14]

Vitrified pottery exclusive to Tula, where the only vitrified building in Mesoamerica is located, is the same site illustrated with the representation of a device spewing fire. These converging elements suggest that the Toltecs possessed a kind of blowtorch for the vitrification of plumbate pottery, the basis of their commercial prosperity (and therefore deserving of memorialization in the hands of monumental statues at the Pyramid of the Feathered Serpent), and for vitrifying their second most important building, the Burnt Palace.

Vitrification took place on a far greater scale in ancient South

America, at the Incas' most important sacred centers. Visitors to their Peruvian capital at Cuzco may still see the great pre-Conquest walls of Loreto Street, their vitrified blocks fitted together with a jewelers' precision.

On-site investigation of Cuzco's granite walls convinced researchers Jan Peter de Jong, Christopher Jordan, and Jesus Gamarra that "some sort of high tech device was used to melt stone blocks, which were then placed and allowed to cool next to hard, jigsaw-polygonal blocks that were already in place."[15] Near the city is Amaru Machay, the Cave of Serpents, a subterranean temple of worked andesite, an extremely hard stone that is difficult to carve but nonetheless melted under controlled high-heat conditions.

Andesite was also the construction material of choice for creating Sacsayhuamán (the Hawk), an Inca citadel built with more than six thousand cubic meters of stone on the northern outskirts of Cuzco. Their surfaces are externally smooth and shiny with vitrification, which was used to lend the stonework cohesion strength and precision. While the Incas occupied these impressive locations, they did not build them.

Even orthodox scholars admit that Sacsayhuamán was erected by construction engineers of the little-known Killke culture that flourished in the Cuzco area centuries before the Inca conquered it. When tour guide Brien Foerster visited Amaru Machay, he observed how "the sculpted surfaces . . . with the heavy weathering patterns, show clearly that this place is much older than the presence of the Inca, [who] arrived here in 1200 A.D. But any real thinker will note that the weathering patterns of the stone itself predate them by a very long period of time."[16]

Ancient vitrification anteceded the Incas in the Andes, just as it had the Kelts in Europe, suggesting that both peoples were preceded by the same advanced civilizers capable of melting stone on both sides of the Atlantic Ocean. Just who these technologically superior culture-bearers might have been cannot be determined by any physical evidence but may only be ascertained by comparing the folk traditions of the societies closest to them.

# 13
# Electric Power

*In science, it is a service of the highest merit to seek out those fragmentary truths attained by the ancients, and to develop them further.*

JOHANN WOLFGANG VON GOETHE,
*MAXIMS AND REFLECTIONS*

In the late spring of 1936, workmen for the Iraqi State Railroad Department were restoring an ancient gravesite exposed after a hillside had been washed away by severe flooding near the village of Khujut Rabu, outside Baghdad. On June 14, they unearthed a curious, light-yellow, baked-clay vase, its former neck apparently broken off at the top. Iraq Museum curator Wilhelm König observed that

> in it, held by a kind of stopper of asphalt, was a completely oxidized iron rod, the top of which projected about one centimeter [0.4 inch] above the stopper and was covered by a yellowish-grey, fully oxidized, tin coating of a metal which looked like lead.
>
> The bottom end of the iron rod did not extend to the bottom of the cylinder, on which was a layer of asphalt about three millimeters [0.1 inch] deep. The question as to what this might be received the most surprising answer. After all the parts had been brought

148

together and then examined in their separate parts, it became evident that it could only have been an electric element. It was only necessary to add an acid or an alkaline liquid to complete the element.[1]

In fact, the object's sheet-copper tube had been originally soldered on its end with a sixty-to-forty lead-tin alloy, "which is comparable to the best solder we have today," remarks Brad Steiger.[2] Someone knew precisely what he or she was doing centuries ago. König dated the simple battery to circa 150 CE, given the Parthian context in which it was excavated. The Parthians were an imperialist people who dominated Mesopotamia during the second century CE. The style of the Khujut Rabu vase, however, belonged to their successors, the Sassanids—the last pre-Islamic kings—who ruled Persia from 224 to 651 CE.

## IT STILL WORKS!

Even so, that was twelve hundred to fifteen hundred years before Italian physicist Alessandro Volta officially invented the first electrical battery in 1799. König's theory was put to the test in 1954 when Willard F. M. Gray, an electrical engineer for General Electric Company's Pittsfield plant in Massachusetts, created an exact replica of the Khujut Rabu artifact. "The dimensions had been given by König," reported science writer Willy Ley, "and the composition of the metals, established analytically, was reasonably close to that of commercial sheet copper and iron rods of today, so there were no special difficulties as far as materials were concerned."[3]

Gray used a solution of copper sulfate as a likely electrolyte, a liquid that contains ions and can be decomposed by electrolysis for powering a battery. Electrolysis is chemical decomposition produced by passing an electric current through a liquid containing ions, which are themselves electrically charged atoms. The precise re-creation produced a sufficient charge to electroplate a small metal object. Subsequent testing found that fruit juice worked just as well. They employed wine, lemon juice,

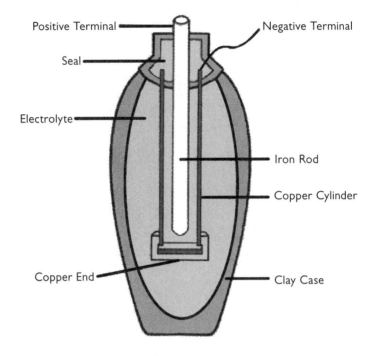

Positive Terminal
Negative Terminal
Seal
Electrolyte
Iron Rod
Copper Cylinder
Copper End
Clay Case

Figure 13.1. Illustration of the Baghdad Battery

grape juice, and vinegar as an acidic electrolyte solution to generate current from the differences between the artifact's electrode potentials of its copper and iron electrodes. Gray's working model was put on public display at the Berkshire Museum in Massachusetts.

In 1960, John B. Pierczynski at the University of North Carolina used a 5 percent vinegar solution as the electrolyte in his own replica Parthian device. It generated half a volt of electricity for eighteen days. Four more terra-cotta jars resembling the Khujut Rabu vase had been uncovered in the vicinity of Tel Asmar, also near Baghdad. Six to eight inches high and sealed with bitumen stoppers, three contained a bronze cylinder 1.25 inches in diameter and 3 inches long. Each vessel contained one iron rod and four bronze rods for connecting all the jars together in, as König observed, "an attempt to increase the voltage of the battery" through a linked series of electrical cells.[4]

The same year, physicist Walter Winton traveled from London's

Science Museum to see for himself the allegedly ancient battery in Baghdad: "Put some acid in the copper vessel—any acid, vinegar will do—and, hey, presto!—you have a simple cell, which will generate a voltage and give a current of electricity. Several such cells connected together in series would make a battery of cells, which would give enough current to ring a bell, light up a bulb, or drive a small motor."[5] Clearly the potential for multiplied connections of Baghdad-type batteries went far beyond mere electroplating.

This same arrangement was demonstrated on March 23, 2005, for the twenty-ninth episode of a Discovery Channel program, *MythBusters*, as ten handmade baked-clay jars replicated the so-called Baghdad Battery. Lemon juice was chosen as their electrolyte to activate an electrochemical reaction between the copper and iron. Connected in series, the batteries produced four volts of electricity, power enough to electroplate a small metal item and deliver a minor electric shock to the program's cohost.

Twenty-seven years earlier, Arne Eggebrecht, an Egyptologist and director of the Roemer and Pelizaeus Museum in Hildesheim, Germany, noticed that a solid silver statuette of the god Osiris had been covered with a layer of gold that was so thin and smooth "it could not have been applied by beating and gluing techniques." Having learned of Khujut Rabu's controversial find, as an experiment, according to an article in *Science News,* "he claimed to have deposited a thin layer of silver on to another surface, just one ten thousandth of a millimeter thick" using a re-created series of the original battery.[6]

Several replicas of the original Iraqi battery produced up to 0.87 volt. "Electroplating techniques, however, generally need a current of only a half volt," according to Jochmans.[7] "While electroplating is a simple process," author Larry Brian Radka explains, "good results require careful control. If too much current is allowed in the circuit over a short time, the deposited metal will not form a smooth and adherent surface. Manufacturers of electroplated articles usually obtain the best results by using a small current [like that produced by the Baghdad Battery] over a long period."[8] Eggebrecht's experiments were conducted with the assistance of experts in electrochemistry, goldsmithing, and galvanization.

On the third episode of 1980's British television series *Arthur C. Clarke's Mysterious World,* Eggebrecht's short series of Baghdad Battery replicas effectively duplicated the suspected electroplating of the museum's Osiris. Despite similar results obtained from various tests over fifty-four years, these experiments are ignored by mainstream scholars, who do not fact-check them but instead rely on their own authority and even deception.

For example, "Paul T. Keyser of the University of Alberta noted that Eggebrecht used a more efficient, modern electrolyte, and that using only vinegar, or other electrolytes available at the time assumed, the battery would be very feeble, and for that and other reasons concludes that even if this was in fact a battery, it could not have been used for electro-plating."[9] In reality, Eggebrecht "created a voltaic cell using a jar filled with grape juice, to produce half a volt of electricity, demonstrating for the program that jars used this way could electroplate a silver statuette in two hours, using a gold cyanide solution."[10]

Ignoring this and related research, conventional academics still denigrate the Khujut Rabu discovery "as a storage vessel for sacred scrolls." Elizabeth Stone, with New York's Stony Brook University Department of Archaeology, told Public Broadcasting listeners in 2012, "I don't know anybody who thinks it's a real battery in the field. I think the people who argue it's a battery are not scientists, basically."[11] What about fellow archaeologist Wilhelm König, General Electric engineer Willard Gray, Egyptologist Eggebrecht, and others? The only persons who "are not scientists, basically" are those unwilling to consider evidence contrary to their preconceived opinions.

"The batteries have always attracted interest as curios," Paul Craddock, a metallurgy expert at the British Museum, denigrated them. "They are a one-off. As far as we know, nobody else [meaning König] has found anything like these."[12] Craddock was apparently ignorant of similar batteries found six years before the Khujut Rabu specimen came to light. In 1930, E. Kühnel of the Berlin Museum unearthed several storage jars for electric battery parts from the archaeological zone of Ctesiphon, the royal capital of the Persian empire in the Parthian and Sasanian eras, on the eastern bank of the Tigris, about twenty-two miles southeast of Baghdad.

More ancient batteries were discovered in the area before the advent of World War II. "Nobody who knows all the facts," writes Willy Ley, "doubts that they [the Mesopotamians] did have 'galvanic' batteries in Baghdad at about the time of Christ and for a few centuries thereafter."[13] Examining one of the jars excavated by Kühnel, König noticed that one contained ten copper cylinders, another held ten iron rods, and a third enclosed ten asphalt stoppers—"ten stored electric cells in a disassembled state."[14]

Actually, they functioned throughout the Fertile Crescent and elsewhere in the ancient world long before König's Sassanid specimen was built between 224 and 651 CE. Eggebrecht's Osiris statuette had been electroplated at the Nile delta 625 to more than 1,000 years earlier, circa 400 BCE. "However, electroplated objects, which presuppose the use of some form of battery," pointed out alternative science investigator Rene Noorbergen, "have been discovered in Iraq in Babylonian ruins dating back to 2000 B.C."[15] Willard Gray adds that "it seems that copper vases, some of whose ages go back four thousand years, were unearthed several years ago, which had designs plated on them in gold or silver, even some were plated with antimony [a brittle, silvery-white metalloid, with chemical properties intermediate between those of metals and semiconductors]."[16]

In truth, they were older still. Jochmans tells of how "König found copper vases plated with silver in the Baghdad Museum excavated from Sumerian remains in southern Iraq dating back to at least 2500 B.C. When the vases were lightly tapped, a blue patina or film separated from the surfaces, characteristic of silver electro-plated to copper. Martin Leavy of Pennsylvania State University confirmed from cuneiform texts dating to the third millennium B.C. that the Sumerians possessed all the necessary metals and acids that went into the construction of the old batteries."[17] These specimens were being discovered unbeknown to a New York researcher, who was then pushing back the applied knowledge of electroplating to the very dawn of civilization.

## THE SECRET OF THE STATUES

According to 1933's *Annual Log of the Scientific American Publishing Company*, Colin G. Fink brought a five-thousand-year-old secret to life through the study of ancient Egyptian vases belonging to the Metropolitan Museum of Art.

> To explain the existence of antimony-coated vessels, we must conclude that the Egyptians knew the secret of electrochemical exchange, a secret later lost and not rediscovered until the last century by Faraday [Michael Faraday, 1791 to 1867, the British scientist who discovered the principles underlying electromagnetic induction]. . . . To accomplish their electro-plating, the Egyptians must have dipped the copper vessels in a solution of antimony sulfide, vinegar and salt (sodium chloride). When this is done, an electro-chemical exchange takes place—the copper goes into the solution and the antimony becomes deposited on the vessel's surface.[18]

Fink discovered that this process electroplated a number of early dynastic statuettes, indicating long-term development of applied electrical power in the ancient world, from early chemical interaction to rechargeable storage cells. Evidence for even earlier predynastic development of electroplating was unearthed by none other than Auguste Mariette, among the most successful and important figures in the history of archaeology. After 1863, while clearing sand around the Great Sphinx down to the bare rock, he found "pieces of gold jewelry whose thinness and lightness makes one believe they had been produced by electroplating, an industrial technique that we have been using for only two or three years."[19]

His outstanding discoveries were made more extraordinary by

finding them at sixty feet beneath the surface of the Giza Plateau. There was no indication they had been deliberately placed in a deep grave or shaft. Instead, the geologic deposition required to accumulate over the jewelry indicated their burial took place approximately twelve thousand years ago. The culture—a dozen millennia ahead of its time— responsible for these electroplated artifacts is unthinkable, save only in terms of myth. The process vanished after Classical civilization fell and was only re-discovered with invention of the voltaic pile, which facilitated the next electrodeposition after fifteen centuries.

Since then, the very ancient Egyptian technique has redounded to advance the cutting edge of twenty-first-century electrical invention. Correspondent Phil Schneiderman reports in *Science and Technology* that

> to make modern-day fuel cells less expensive and more powerful . . . a team led by Johns Hopkins chemical engineers has drawn inspiration from the ancient Egyptian tradition of gilding. . . . In a modern-day twist, the Johns Hopkins–led researchers have applied a tiny coating of costly platinum just one nanometer thick—one hundred thousand times thinner than a human hair—to a core of much cheaper cobalt. This microscopic marriage could become a crucial catalyst in new fuel cells that generate electric current to power cars and other machines.
>
> The new fuel cell design would save money because it would require far less platinum, a very rare and expensive metal that is commonly used as a catalyst in present-day fuel-cell electric cars, an alternative to battery-powered vehicles. . . . By making electric cars more affordable, this innovation could curb the emission of carbon dioxide and other pollutants from gasoline- or diesel-powered vehicles. [Chao Wang, a Johns Hopkins assistant professor in the department of chemical and biomolecular engineering and his research team members,] tipped their hats to the ancient Egyptian artisans, who used a similar plating technique to give copper masks and other metallic works of art a lustrous final coat of silver or gold.[20]

# RUST-DEFYING IRON

Applied interaction of electricity with metals developed beyond jewelry-making and statue-plating to material achievements superior even to those of modern industrial science. One example is India's remarkably advanced Delhi Pillar, "a solid shaft of wrought iron," as Joseph Robert Jochmans describes it, "made up of iron discs expertly welded together in a fashion that the welding marks are hardly discernible. . . . The mystery is, one would expect that any equivalent mass of iron—subjected to the Indian monsoon rains, winds and temperatures for sixteen hundred years or more—should have been reduced to a pile of rust long ago."[21]

Figure 13.2. Delhi's Iron Pillar. Photo by Sujit Kumar.

During all those centuries of exposure to the forces of nature, it has remained virtually rust-free, unlike present iron structures, which totally disintegrate within a fraction of that time. Videographer Praveen Mohan published photographs of an iron bridge that, typically, rusted beyond repair and was condemned less than eighty years after completion in China during the 1930s. Weighing more than six tons, the dark-gray pillar stands in Delhi's Qutub complex at Mehrauli. From a lower diameter of 17 inches, the monolith tapers to 1 foot, making it appear taller than 23 feet, 8 inches high—3 feet, 8 inches of which are below ground level.

But nothing about the Ashoka Pillar hinted at the source of its unique self-preservation until the early twentieth century, when the pillar was analyzed by one of history's greatest metallurgists, Sir Robert Abbott Hadfield. Hadfield is notable for discovering manganese steel, one of the first steel alloys. He also invented silicon steel, initially for mechanical properties, which have made the alloy a material of choice for springs and some fine blades though it has also become important in electrical applications for its magnetic behavior. No one since his 1911 investigation has learned more about the subcontinent's most enigmatic object. Its "purity level is particularly surprising," Jochmans remarks, "for it was not attained in Europe until the nineteenth century, and was certainly a technological anomaly for the fifth century," when it was allegedly made.[22]

Hadfield determined that the Ashoka Pillar is composed of 99.72 percent iron, 0.08 percent carbon, 0.046 percent silicon, 0.032 percent nitrogen, 0.114 percent copper, and 0.114 percent phosphorus; almost one hundred years later, this would be the key to unlocking some of the iron pillar's secrets. When iron is exposed to oxygen and water, it decays through a chemical process known as corrosion. This oxydating process creates rust, which erodes the metal and makes it slightly but progressively smaller and weaker until any structure made of iron completely deteriorates.

Jochmans explains that when Hadfield's laboratory tests of the

Ashoka column were conducted under conditions of seventy to seventy-five percent humidity,

> he discovered that the internal, newly exposed iron rusted in four days, as any normal iron sample would. But the iron taken from the outer edge of the pillar would not rust at all. The column is unusually conductive to heat absorption and retention. This causes rapid evaporation of water droplets accumulating on the pillar, even at night. The result is the pillar has a built-in mechanism for keeping itself as dry and moisture-free as possible.
>
> In the early 1970s, G. Wranglen of the Royal Institute of Technology in Stockholm found that the entire Delhi column is covered with an oxide film of metallic sheen, blue-black in color, between fifty and six hundred millicrons (a millionth part of a millimeter) in thickness. In an experiment conducted by Wranglen at Delhi, a small portion of this film was scraped off. In one day, rust appeared on the bared iron patch below; but within a week, the rust had undergone a chemical change, turning it into a new layer of film and preventing further oxidation. Wranglen believes that the high phosphorus, low sulfur content of the iron encourages the formation of this self-protecting coating. Aiding in the process further, the outer surfaces—especially where the outer surface can be detected—have been found to contain a high percentage of silicon, a rust retarding agent. This appears to have been intentionally impregnated into the column at the time of its creation.[23]

That the riddle of Delhi's Iron Pillar was solved only after modern science rose to a sufficiently high degree parallel with the interaction of its component parts, shows that the monolith was made with a technology equivalent, though still superior, to our own. In other words, we now understand but are not yet able to duplicate the monument's anti-rusting capabilities. Having discovered their age-old secret, industrial metallurgists are painstakingly back-engineering this imperishable example of ancient know-how for twenty-first-century application.

The breakthrough came in 2002, when mineralogists equipped with chemical computer analysis revealed that an evenly coated, self-renewing layer of crystalline iron hydrogen phosphate hydrate on the exterior of the high-phosphorus-content iron pillar prevents rust. When corrosion begins to form, slag and unreduced iron oxides intervene with a chemical reaction, altering polarization and enriching the metal with phosphorus. These particles combine to act as a cathode, with the metal itself serving as an anode, for a mini-galvanic reaction during environmental exposure. The next main agent for protecting the pillar from oxidation is phosphorus, because it is an essential catalyst in the formation of a passive protective film known as *misawite*—a compound of iron, oxygen, and hydrogen in a corrosion-resistant agent that forms a barrier on the pillar's exterior between metal and rust.

Misawite increases the pillar's electromagnetic properties. Ancient Indian smiths refrained from adding lime to their furnaces because it would have carried away the misawite. The use of limestone in modern blast furnaces yields pig iron, which is later converted into steel. In doing so, most phosphorus is lost with the slag. On the other hand, the absence of lime in the slag of an ancient Indian furnace and the use of specific quantities of wood with high-phosphorus content during smelting induced a higher phosphorus content than in modern iron produced by blast furnaces. This high-phosphorus content produced rust-preventing misawite.

The most critical corrosion-resistant agent is iron hydrogen phosphate hydrate under its crystalline form, as it builds up a thin layer next to the interface between metal and rust. Alternate environmental wetting and drying cycles provide the moisture for phosphoric-acid formation. In time the amorphous phosphate is precipitated into its crystalline form, continuously coating the metal and thereby preserving it from corrosion. The more amorphous phosphate it incrementally produces, the more resistant it becomes. Over at least the past sixteen hundred years, this covering film has grown just one-twentieth of a millimeter thick. The only rust on the monolith accumulated as it was being erected and exposed to moisture in the air for the first time, when coating was thinnest and too weak to hermetically seal its exterior as did successive layering. The Ashoka Pillar has been described in some detail here to demonstrate the highly advanced capabilities of its ancient creators.

Although the secret of its preservation has finally been revealed, why this monumental object was not only infused with electromagnetic potential but also bolstered with more phosphorus than needed is another mystery sparking more questions: What was the pillar's real function? Why was it made of solid iron? Why did its builders go to such extreme lengths of truly advanced scientific application to ensure its perpetual preservation in an outdoor setting, deliberately exposed to extremes of weather? Was it designed to attract or somehow interact with lightning? If so, for what, conceivable purpose? Was it originally part of an electromagnetic device of some kind? Perhaps the most fundamental question here is why the iron pillar was made so it would not rust. Today, all electrical components are specifically manufactured to be noncorrosive, but why was such a structure needed in ancient times?

Delhi's Iron Pillar has been officially dated to 403 CE, when the Gupta empire dominated most of India. The column's indefinite Sanskrit citation of a "King Chandra" has led most professional investigators to speculate that the structure is a memorial to Chandragupta I, who died fifty-three years earlier. But Mohan and other independent experts point out that the pillar's brief text describes the extent of the dubious Chandra's empire, which encompassed all of India and Sri Lanka, while the historical limits of Chandragupta I's conquests did not comprise any southern territories of the subcontinent, nor islands in the Indian Ocean.

Because Ramachandra is described in the seventh-century-BCE epic the *Ramayana* as the ruler of a united India and Sri Lanka, he may have been the "Chandra" mentioned on the Delhi Pillar. If it was indeed associated with him, the object could conceivably date back to the turn

Figure 13.3. The Ashoka Iron Pillar with Qutub Minar.
Photo by आशीष भटनागर.

of the fourth millennium BCE, because Ramachandra's reign took place during the Indus valley civilization, which flourished at that time. One of the world's first high cultures, along with Sumer and Egypt, the Indus valley cities were legendary for their technological innovations—far greater than those associated with the Gupta kingdom—which may have included anti-rust preservation. According to Jochmans:

> What this suggests is a far older origin, older than the inscriptions that simply must have been added on to it at a later date—older perhaps by several thousands of years. This is borne out by the fact that no other Indian iron works dating to the fifth century can compare with the Delhi Pillar. At Manud, near Dhar, are the remains of a second iron pillar called the Dhar Column. It once stood over fifty feet tall, but now lies broken in three pieces, with a total length of forty-three feet, four inches. It too was made with welded discs, and it too has a high purity level of iron, though not anywhere near as high as the Delhi Pillar.
>
> The one difference is the Dhar Column is heavily corroded, its surface pitted, and there is evidence it collapsed about the fourteenth century from welding weaknesses compounded by advanced rusting. It is clear the Dhar Column was a fifth century attempt at copying the far older Delhi Pillar—an attempt that failed in time, because it did not incorporate secrets of metal preservation unsuspected by the fifth century metallurgists, nor detected by them as the studied the Delhi model.[24]

Was the Ashoka Pillar part of a Tesla-like electromagnetic complex, as suggested by its proximity to Qutub Minar? This is a former Hindu temple appropriated by late twelfth-century Muslim invaders, and it has since been officially, if erroneously, referred to as a minaret. But why was the 239-foot 6-inch tower built precisely ten times as tall as the Ashoka Iron Pillar? Is their height relationship part of some larger connection forming an original shared purpose, since lost?

# 14
# Organized Lightning

*Electricity is really just organized lightning.*

GEORGE CARLIN, *LAST WORDS*

Almost certainly lost was the original Baghdad Battery that Wilhelm König discovered in 1936. It disappeared, along with thousands of other priceless artifacts, from the National Museum amid a frenzy of looting unleashed by America's Iraq invasion sixty-seven years later. Thus, the last, scientifically advanced remnants of one of humanity's first civilizations scattered into oblivion, forty-five centuries after they were invented. The Persian empire's one-to-four-volt galvanic batteries were adequate for electroplating small, metallic art objects, although not much more.

But if even these low levels of applied electrical power were attained, might their ancient creators have taken developments significantly further? Jochmans writes that "the finds at Tel Omar and Ktesphon imply that methods were being employed to increase output beyond the three-volt maximum of a single pot battery, and that the batteries were being mass-produced. What had they been used for, besides electro-plating?"[1]

A convincing answer has been provided by a world-class authority on the subject, a retired broadcast engineer with a lifetime career in electronics. Painstakingly combing through his personal library of more than five thousand source materials, Larry Brian Radka eventually discovered the electrical secret of the greatest of the Seven Wonders of the Classical world. The Lighthouse of Alexandria (see plate 12) was commissioned in 290 BCE by Ptolemy I Soter (Savior), successor of the city's eponymous founder, Alexander the Great, but completed about twelve years later by Ptolemy II Philadelphus. A promontory known as the Heptastadion (meaning "Seven Stadia"; a *stadium* was a Greek unit of length), spanning more than three-quarters of a mile, connected Alexandria with Pharos, located on the western edge of the Nile delta. Its name derived from the monumental structure that rose upon the small island: *pharez,* Egyptian for "look-out place," similar to the Greek verb *pharos,* meaning "to shine."

The Heptastadion's east side became the Great Harbor, now an open bay; on the west side was located the port of Eunostos, with its inner basin, Kibotos. Standing on a 98-square-foot base, three tapering tiers rose in succession from a lower square section with a central core, a middle octagonal section, and, at the top, a circular section. Its apex was positioned with the largest mirror ever built in antiquity, at 94.5 inches in diameter, unsurpassed for more than twenty-two centuries, until installation of the 200-inch Hale Telescope mirror at Southern California's Mount Palomar Observatory in 1949. Messenger gods resembling mermen and one Triton statue adorned each of the building's four corners, guarding the cardinal directions, with a colossus of their father, Poseidon, standing proudly, emblematic trident in hand, over the very top of the lighthouse. It was built mostly with solid blocks of limestone, interlocked and sealed together by molten lead against the site's severe weathering. This ingenious process was so successful, it endured 1,234 years of relentless wave action, in contrast to twenty-first-century skyscrapers, which commonly begin deteriorating within a decade or less after their completion. Ptolemaic Egypt's skyscraper was 387 feet high, but, owing to the elevation of the island on which it stood, towered 600 feet above sea level, making it the tallest man-made structure on Earth for millennia to come.

Figure 14.1. The Pharos of Abusir, an ancient funerary monument thought to be modeled after the Pharos at Alexandria, with which it is approximately contemporaneous. Photo by Gene Poole.

This height advantage allowed its beacon to be seen an average of 32.5 miles away, even farther during exceptionally clear nights. For example, in the mid-first-century CE epic *Pharsalia,* the Roman writer Lucan tells how Julius Caesar saw the Pharos light on his seventh night at sea from Troy, which would have put him about 60 miles from Alexandria at the time, according to early Classical epoch sailing speeds.[2] By comparison, Minnesota's Split Rock Lighthouse, located on the North Shore of Lake Superior, operated the world's most powerful beacon in 1910, when its official range covered a maximum distance of twenty-two miles. To be sure, its Alexandrian precursor was a terrific achievement by any standard, but therein lies the Pharos mystery.

Archaeologists commonly posit that a large flame fueled by prodigious stockpiles of cut timber was the Alexandria Lighthouse beacon. But, Radka points out, Egypt "hardly had any trees, except for mainly scrubs, like acacia and tamarisk [which make poor kindling]. Egypt's lack of wood, in fact, prevented it from building even a semblance of a formidable navy in antiquity. Mr. Maurice pointed out: 'There was one, insuperable objection to their maintaining any considerable navy; I mean, the total want of timber for its construction and repair, of which the whole country was so entirely destitute, that even the boats on the Nile were obliged to be fabricated either of baked earth glazed and varnished, or of rafts sewn together with papyrus.' Furthermore, no practical sources of trees existed nearby, which could sustain a continuous, yearly blaze on the Pharos Lighthouse. Coal would not have solved the problem. It was hardly known in the Mediterranean area."[3]

*Naptha,* a Classical epoch term for natural gas, was occasionally ignited as a weapon in wartime conditions but proved unstable or capricious, even under military control, and unsuitable for any other purpose. Radka explains: "We have no records of any attempts to harness it for ancient lighthouse fires. Pitch, widely used in ancient torches, was also not an appropriate fuel for lighthouse beacons," because they were often extinguished by sudden gusts of wind or rain if exposed or smoked so heavily their rapidly accumulating soot sullied and ultimately obscured any glass cover. Notwithstanding all these unsolved problems with an open fire blazing away on the Pharos and an appropriate fuel to maintain it, we have one more curious but rejected suggestion. "Dried animal dung could have been a possible solution to the problem and is still widely used in native houses today," wrote Peter Clayton, "but, once again, the sheer quantity required presents problems." Furthermore, Emil Ludwig claims, "An open wood or pitch fire would have shone only seven miles."[4]

The very magnitude of an enormous flame powerful enough to be seen at a distance of more than 32 miles, all night, every night, year after year, predisposes its total, unrestricted exposure to the elements; otherwise, the immensely high temperatures generated by such a huge, steady fire must destroy any enclosure, no matter how well ventilated.

Lucan, in fact, describes the Pharos beacon as a "lamp." Not only would the vast required quantity of fuel, whatever its nature, necessitate unsustainably gargantuan resources, especially in treeless, coalless Egypt, but its continuous conveyance from the ground, straight up 380 feet to the insatiable beacon, would have been no less unmanageable. In all the original source materials describing the Lighthouse of Alexandria, not one so much as hints at any colossal logistical campaign ever undertaken to maintain its operation. Given these limitations, Radka determined that the Pharos could have been lit only by an alternate power source.

> Pliny expresses a fear, lest its light, which, seen at a distance, had the appearance of flames, should, from its steadiness, be mistaken for a star; but assuredly he would have not spoken in such terms of the wavering, irregular and fitful light of an ordinary fire. We conclude, therefore, that its lighting apparatus was more complex than has generally been supposed.
>
> In view of the well-attested "Baghdad Battery" and others like it, there is no reason to believe that the ancient Alexandrians could not have built and installed a similar battery in antiquity to power the searchlights on the spacious Pharos Lighthouse. They would have needed, however, a means of charging the battery, and we can find no evidence that they developed a dynamo or any other type of motorized generator to do the job. Nevertheless, they could have easily employed either primary batteries or thermo-electric generators (thermopiles) . . . to accomplish the task. Building simple devices like these were hardly beyond their capabilities. . . . The thermo-electric generator operated on the principle that the heating of a certain combination of two, dissimilar metals generates a voltage, enough to easily charge batteries.[5]

Radka cites the Clamond thermopile, which, as long ago as 1879, produced 109 volts, with an internal resistance of more than 15 ohms.

Figure 14.2. The Clamond thermopile

He says, "This was a serious source of power. . . . It was an expensive unit to build, but cost would have been no obstacle for a wealthy ruler of any ancient city like Alexandria, which relied on a bright navigation light for its urban prosperity and commercial survival."[6]

It then follows, from the credible availability of a simple thermo-electric generator, that the Alexandrians from the early third century BCE attached to it an arc light as their lighthouse beacon. The step from battery to arc lamp would have been—in fact, *was* during the Industrial Age—a small one, and natural. In 1802, Humphrey Davy, a British chemist, invented the first modern electric battery. When he almost immediately thereafter connected wires to it and a piece of carbon, the carbon glowed, producing light. His invention was known as the electric arc lamp. The electrodes of its ancient Alexandrian predecessor were also carbon rods that, when touched together, allowed a relatively low voltage that would ignite a continuous spark between their end points. The rods were then slowly drawn apart, allowing electrical current to heat and sustain an arc of electrified air across the growing gap. The carbon vapor in the arc was highly luminous, resulting in a bright light.

Figure 14.3. Arc light results when opposing carbon rods reach their proper separation distance. Photo by Zaereth.

Because the rods were slowly burned away during use, the distance between them required regular adjustment to maintain the arc—too far apart, the arc light lacked sufficient ions and collapsed; too close together, the ions compressed into too much heat and quickly burned up the carbon rods. This gradual, almost constant, somewhat delicate alteration was fine-tuned by either human operators or through the predetermined adjustment of a magnetized spacing device, a kind of continual vise that maintained enough pressure on the rods for moving them together at a proper pace. The device served to keep up with the burning deterioration of the rods while preserving an optimum space between the tips of both carbon rods for a steady arc light.

Such a self-compressing vise was well within the technological capabilities of third-century-BCE Alexandrians, because magnetism was long recognized and applied throughout the ancient world, occasionally in ways that have only been approached, but not yet equaled, in our time. Modern mastery of computerized electromagnetic fields is capable of suspending a small, lightweight, iron object in space. "It seems amazing but nevertheless true," according to the website Above Top Secret, "that, in antiquity, there were temples erected and constructed in such a way that by the use of magnetism the deity of those places was made to levitate in free air. It would seem that loadstone, a naturally magnetic mineral, was carved and placed within these temples in an arrangement which allowed an iron statue of the temples deity to float."[7]

About 580 CE, the Latin scholar and statesman Cassiodorus told of how "in the temple of Diana [before it was transformed into a Christian church] hung an iron cupid without being held by any band."[8] In his eleventh-century work *A Concise History of the World,* Byzantine historian Kedrenus wrote that a sacred art object in the Serapeum at Alexandria was "suspended by magnetic force."[9] This was almost certainly the same statue of the god Serapis that was erected by an Egyptian priest for Ptolemy II Philadelphus, the same king who completed construction of the Pharos Lighthouse. The third-century-BCE historian Manetho explained his grasp of magnetism by writing that "iron drawn by a stone [magnetite] often follows it, but often also is turned and driven away in the opposite direction."[10] Pliny, too, stated that "the temple of Arsinoe was to have been vaulted with magnetic stone, in order to receive a hovering statue of Arsinoe made of iron, according to the arrangement of Ptolemy Philadelphus."[11] Queen Arsinoe I was Ptolemy's sister.

It is clear that magnetic power was being used in Alexandria just when the Pharos was being built and need arose for a magnetic adjustor of its arc light. This light alone would have produced an intensely bright beam sufficiently powerful to reach the Pharos's thirty-two-and-a-half-mile range, without either the impossible demands or destructive heat of a huge blaze, yet smaller and cooler enough to have fit into Lucan's *lampada* while matching Pliny's description of the Alexandrian beacon seen at a great distance not as a flickering flame but more like a steady beam of starlight. But arc-light technology was not restricted to the Pharos Lighthouse. About 380 CE, Libanius, a Greek teacher of rhetoric, described Antioch, a Roman city on the eastern side of the Orontes River, in the south of Turkey: "The light of the sun is succeeded by other lights, which are far superior to the lamps lighted by the Egyptians on the festival of Minerva at Sais. The night with us differs from the day only in the appearance of the light."[12] Radka comments that "his words, 'far superior,' and his comparison of his city's lights to the 'light of the sun,' suggest they shown much more brightly than the dismal candles and oil lamps of his time—but electric arc-lamps certainly would have explained his terms."[13]

Just one hundred years later, the lights went out in Antioch with the demise of Classical civilization, while the arc light know-how that lit up the Pharos for the previous 780 years was lost. When Muhammad al-Idrisi, an Arab Muslim geographer and cartographer, saw the now dilapidated lighthouse around 1155 CE, he reported in his *Book of Pleasant Journeys into Faraway Lands* that "its fire burns night and day for the guidance of navigators, and is visible at the distance of a day's sail . . . By day, you may distinguish its smoke."[14] W. H. Davenport Adams, a lighthouse and lightship historian, writes, "This latter passage shows that if any better mode of illumination had once been in use, as we are inclined to believe, it had been discontinued, or its secret forgotten by the degenerate successors of the Alexandrian Greeks."[15]

By the time Idrisi laid eyes on the Pharos, a severe earthquake had already damaged the technologically attenuated, under-maintained lighthouse two hundred years before, when its immense reflective mirror shattered and the colossal statue of Poseidon was shaken from his topmost position, tumbling 378 feet to the ground. The year 1303 witnessed a renewal of seismic violence that further weakened the ruin, triggering its abandonment. Reduced to a stubby remnant by another tectonic event twenty-three years later, this, too, vanished during the 1480 construction on the monument's surviving larger platform, which used some of the original limestone blocks for building a medieval fort. In 1968 a few more pieces of lighthouse masonry were identified by scuba divers off the island of Pharos (see plate 13).

As the need for safe navigation and the commercial prosperity it brought had called the Lighthouse of Alexandria into existence, so the internal conditions of deep darkness that prevented the tomb and temple inscription of religious texts for survival in the afterlife inspired the ancient invention of artificial illumination. As long ago as 1894, this possibility occurred to the renowned astronomer and antiquarian Sir J. Norman Lockyer when he visited Egypt: "In all freshly opened tombs there are no traces whatever of any kind of combustion having taken place, even in the innermost recesses. So strikingly evident is this that my friend, M. Bouriant, while we were discussing this matter at Thebes, lightheartedly suggested the possibility that the electric light was known to the ancient Egyptians."[16] Breached or violated structures are commonly smudged with torch soot residue but never, as stated, "in all freshly opened tombs."

Kenyon reports that "technology used by craftsmen two thousand years ago to apply thin films of metal onto their statues surpassed modern standards for producing DVDs, solar cells, and electronic devices."[17] The statement refers to a July 2013 article in the professional journal *Accounts of Chemical Research*, which concludes that "the high level of competence reached by the artists and craftsmen of these ancient periods . . . produced objects of an artistic quality that could not be bettered in ancient times, and has not yet been reached in modern ones."[18]

Conclusions are based on electron-microscope examination of gilded statuettes displayed at the Cairo Museum and associated with the Twentieth Dynasty pharaoh Ramses III. His own tomb in the Upper Nile valley suggests that the Egyptians possessed an artificial light source of some kind, because all four walls of the subterranean vault were profusely decorated with sacred art and highly detailed hieroglyphic passages from the Book of the Dead. Archaeologists found no evidence that torches ever entered the sepulcher, nor was its ceiling smudged by either taper smoke or ancient efforts to scrub it clean. Alternative illumination of some kind must have been available by the early twelfth century BCE. If not, how then were artists able to paint such elaborate and fine art across so many hundreds of square feet?

Although Egyptologists closed to any consideration of contrary evidence continue to scoff at the very notion of high technology in antiquity, they are still unable to solve the riddle that puzzled Lockyer more than 125 years ago. Their official explanations of artwork by torchlight were long ago debunked, not only for total absence of the merest spot of soot on ceilings but also for lack of any indication that such residue

had been ever cleaned away during the ancient past. Moreover, the prodigious temperatures generated from what must have otherwise been at
least several pitch-fueled firebrands simultaneously flaming in a stone
crypt or temple would have filled these confined, unventilated spaces
with clouds of dense, toxic smoke and depleted their oxygen in a matter
of moments, rendering working conditions impossible.

"Furthermore," Radka adds, "the artisans could not have removed
the soot from the ceilings and walls after finishing their tasks, because
they would have had to clean up the smudge with the same, smoke-
belching lights that produced it."[19] Arguments that interiors were decorated and inscribed before the structures' roofs were added, allowing
the inscriptions to be made in broad daylight, were also shown as baseless suppositions when reexamination of various examples of monumental architecture from different dynastic periods revealed that their total
construction had been uniformly completed before any chambers were
adorned.

Contorted theories endeavoring to prove that pharaonic Egyptian
interior designers organized gangs of slaves positioned to hold mirrors
reflecting sunlight from outside a tomb down into its subterranean
depths, enabling artists there to proceed with their work, only show
to what preposterous lengths mainstream scholars will go to avoid
discussion of electrical possibilities. These are based on more than
assumptions but physical evidence at one of the best-preserved temple
complexes in Egypt.

15

# Inner and Outer Enlightenment

*Knowledge has been suppressed throughout the last two thousand years. It is sometimes said that history is written by the winners of wars, rather than the losers. Given the amount of known, war-oriented political propaganda still popular as "history" in this century, we should consider much of ancient history in this light.*

DAVID HATCHER CHILDRESS,
*TECHNOLOGY OF THE GODS*

Covering 430,557 square feet, Dendera is a collection of chapels and shrines constructed from the beginning of dynastic history—perhaps even before—and all the millennia through to the Ptolemaic kingdom (305 to 30 BCE), which is represented in most of Dendera's surviving monuments (see plate 14). A necropolis running along the eastern edge of the western hill and over the northern plain dates from the Early Dynastic Period of the Old Kingdom (circa 3000 BCE), but nothing else from that remote epoch is in evidence.

This city of the dead nonetheless complements Dendera's original schematic, which was already eight or more centuries old. It was found by accident in the Sixth Dynasty royal palace archives of King Pepi I Meryre sometime between 2332 and 2287 BCE, when he reigned over Egypt. Many years after the original temple had fallen into ruins, he reconstructed it according to the rediscovered "plan written upon a goatskin scroll from the time of the Companions of Horus."[1] This is a remarkable scrap of information, because the Semsu-Hor, as they were known in the ancient Egyptian language, were the founding fathers of Nile valley civilization during the late fourth millennium BCE. In Manetho's *Aegyptiaca* (History of Egypt), written circa 250 BCE—a major chronological source for the reigns of the pharaohs—the Followers of Horus are described as immigrants from Sekheret-aaru (Field of Reeds), a name characterizing the island kingdom's profuse learning, because reeds were used as ink pens. A "field" of them signified general mastery of the written word.[2]

Manetho locates Sekheret-aaru in the far western ocean, where it was lost beneath the waves during a terrible cataclysm, but only after the Semsu-Hor escaped eastward in their ships to the Nile delta. There one of their descendants, Hor-Aha, became the premiere pharaoh of the First Dynasty circa 3100 BCE. There is, after all, at least a fundamental resemblance between the Temple of Hathor at Dendera and the early First Dynasty Neith-hotep *mastaba* (meaning "house for eternity," a type of mud-brick tomb in the form of a flat-roofed, rectangular structure with inward-sloping sides) on the west bank of the Upper Nile, believed to have been built by Hor-Aha. This comparison implies at least some substance for the subterranean inscription in the temple about the Followers of Horus.

The chamber walls of the Temple of Hathor at Dendera feature large, singularly unusual stone panels carved in low relief depicting a series of strange activities most Egyptologists insist comprise nothing more than symbolic depiction of a *djed* column (a pillarlike image representing stability) with a lotus flower spawning a snake within, thereby representing standard aspects of Egyptian myth. Hathor, the divine mother of Horus, sits enthroned at the far-left end of the southern crypt panel, watching a man of some authority (judging from his wig) standing behind an elongated, tubelike structure containing a snake. The serpent's head points toward the tube's broader end, its tail at the opposite narrower end, clasped in the petals of a lotus. The stem curves around beneath the tube to connect with the center of a rectangular platform surmounted by Shu. This god of the air supports with his upraised hands the wider end of the tube. Below the center of the tube kneels a servant, his hands palms up toward the larger, standing figure.

This scene is exactly reproduced in reversal, except for Shu's replacement by a djed column and a shorter, downward curve made by the lotus flower into the platform on which the tube is mounted. A second panel portrays two men carrying a long snake, from the closed mouth of which descends a wavy, vertical line representing either water or energy. Directly in front of this dribbling serpent is a little rectangular table, the small-scale representation of a solar goddess with upraised arms sitting on its top. To the right stands a man holding another tube identical to the pair shown in the southern crypt panel as an undersized female attends to his feet.

A third panel shows two men standing in profile with the same kind of large tubes; they differ from each other only in the djed columns supporting them. The first touches the broad end of the tube with upraised hands; the second does not have arms. Under the first tube, on the flower stem, kneels a little male figure offering a jar—hieroglyphically associated with a human heart—to the much larger standing man. A couple of similarly small male figures join hands while kneeling on the lotus stem beneath the second tube, before which a miniature version of Shu sits facing the tube atop a rectangular structure. Behind him is a taller, nonhuman figure, although shorter than both standing men, holding up a large blade by each hand in front of the lead tube.

The long-tailed creature has the body of a baboon and a toadlike head wearing a wig of authority. An accompanying wall text reads, "Your name is perfect, Upu. Your face is [that of] a frog."[3] He is a composite being and an incarnation, avatar, or servant of Heqet, the second wife of Shu, goddess of spiritual rebirth and childbirth. Upu's two apparently edged weapons depicted in the Dendera reliefs are actually the surgical knives an Egyptian physician used to sever a newborn's umbilical cord, simultaneously crossing them together over the navel string and cutting it in a fast, clean procedure.

In dynastic myth, frogs were associated with birth and rebirth, as a result of the profusion of these animals along the Nile River banks, and symbolized Heqet herself. Baboons were known to sometimes gather in early dawn to observe sunrise; hence, their imagery was used by Egyptian temple artists to signify solar worship, personified in Upu. All his combined attributes are cogent to the surrounding wall texts, which, as described in more detail below, celebrate the birth of the sun god. While tourists of the Temple of Hathor are mystified by such arcane imagery, some of its resemblance to modern electrical illumination devices is inescapably self-evident for most visitors.

The Hall 5 reliefs appear to portray a pair of men standing behind "two enormous light bulbs," writes Corliss, "each containing a snake-like

Figure 15.1. The Hall 5 reliefs at Dendera.
Photo by Lasse Jensen.

filament and voltage electrical insulators. Furthering the electrical interpretation are long cables connecting each 'bulb' to a central power source. One has to admit that a flavor of high technology pervades this twenty-one-hundred-year-old scene preserved in the Dendera Temple."[4]

## ARTIFICIAL LIGHT

Official interpretations or academic denial alone cannot dispel such a practically universal impression. True, the illustrated supports are recognizable versions of the djed pillar, usually but not invariably identified with Osiris, the god of regeneration. But it was also the emblem of Ptah, the Memphite patron of craftsmen, the divine artificer associated with the high technology of ancient Egypt. Indeed, its very name derives from the dynastic word for Memphis: *Hikuptah,* meaning "Home of the Soul of Ptah." This entered Classical Greek as Aiguptos, then Latin as Aegyptus, which developed into English as Egypt. "Ptah is the creator-god par excellence," asserts Anthony S. Mercatante, author of *Who's Who in Egyptian Mythology.*[5] Ptah's association then with the Dendera Light through his djed symbol is appropriate to a technological interpretation, which receives further support in the lotuslike "bulbs" because this flower connotes the brightening of light. The snakes inside the lotuses are likewise apt, since they epitomize power.

Given their individual meanings, these well-known symbols at least suggest high-tech lighting at the Nile valley in dynastic times. While most of the figures and objects are recognizable enough, nowhere else throughout the Nile valley are they similarly portrayed in the company of these perplexing tubes. Their appearance at Dendera is absolutely unique. Yet this sacred chapel complex is itself the perfect setting for presenting visual representations of artificial light, because the Temple of Hathor encloses the darkest interior of perhaps any other public religious building in Egypt. Construction of its highly detailed yet pitch-dark spaces could only have been carried out under constant bright conditions, never in the flickering shadows of a sputtering torch.

If the oblong objects depicted on the walls of the Temple of Hathor are indeed electric lightbulbs, then the extensive written narrative accompanying these atypical reliefs should define them as such. The hieroglyphs describe the large tubes as devices, which played a role in a New Year festival circa 54 BCE and the Night-of-the-Child-in-His-Nest pageant commemorating the birth of Ra, the sun god. Both of these important occasions attracted vast throngs of celebrants with ornate ceremonies, taking place, as their names indicate, after dark.

The wall texts go on to delineate the strange tubes and their various details, identifying each one in the first-century-BCE[6] Egyptian vernacular equivalent of modern technological terminology. They are described in a hieroglyphic banner running across the top of the southern crypt chamber's south wall as component parts belonging to a combined purpose; namely, the achievement of Nehebkau, or the "bringing together" of the *ka* (divine spark) and the *ba* (soul) for the creation of *akh* (light). Although this plain statement could hardly be clearer in identifying the depicted tubes as instruments of illumination, skeptics insist that such enlightenment must have been strictly allegorical, not technological.

To settle the matter, Peter Krassa, editor of the prominent Viennese newspaper the *Kurier,* sought expert opinion from Walter Garn, a consulting electrical engineer at Siemens, Europe's largest industrial manufacturing conglomerate. Garn was later project manager and chief of the development division at ELIN, another electric megacorporation, where he oversaw power plant operations in Austria, Switzerland, Scotland, Thailand, Turkey, India, and Indonesia. Without ever having previously looked into the issue, Garn initially took on faith the mainstream archaeological dismissal of any discussion regarding ancient Egyptian electrical technology as the pseudoscientific drivel of fringe theorists.

But he began to reconsider academic consensus opinion about Dendera's controversial images after learning how John Harris, the Lord Alliance and professor of bioethics and director of the Institute for Science, Ethics and Innovation at the University of Manchester in

England, "concluded that they appear to be the ancient equivalent of technical equipment used by today's scientists."[7] Garn was then sufficiently intrigued by photographs of the Temple of Hathor's panels to accept Peter Krassa's challenge by undertaking a close examination of them for the purpose of either confirming or denying their electrical potential.

Beginning in 1982 he constructed a sixteen-inch working model of one of the "tubes" portrayed on the walls of the Dendera crypt to test such a possibility and answer the question: Did ancient Egyptians master electricity, as suggested by bas-relief illustrations at the Temple of Hathor? "To seriously consider replicating their accomplishments," states Christopher Dunn, a machinist, tool-and-die maker, and

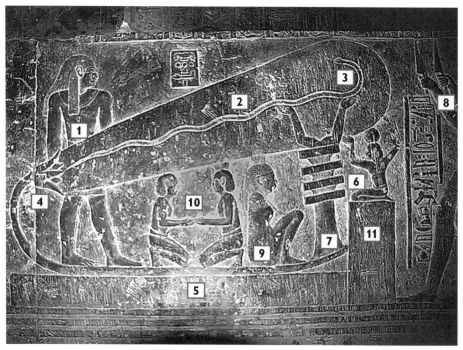

Figure 15.2. Schematic showing potential lightbulbs from the Temple of Hathor. The schematic shows: 1) priestly operator, 2) ionized gas, 3) electrical discharge (the serpent), 4) cable connector (the lotus), 5) electrical cable, 6) Shu, god of the air, as a support, 7) metal anode electrode (djed pillar), 8) electrical resistors as Heqet's upheld pair of metal blades, 9) support, 10) positive/negative polarity, and 11) electrostatic generator. Photo by Roland Unger, labels added.

manufacturing engineer since the 1970s, "is a step toward understanding their advancement."[8] Garn's feasibility study was meticulously patterned after all visible details, changing or adding nothing. Doing so, he was guided by the reliefs themselves to make a precise correspondence among every depicted element with the electrical component of an artificial light source.

For example, the arms of the djed pillar (its mandated reproduction in gold, an ideal conductor material) are analogous to the metal anode electrode, while ka, the divine spark, on its knees was power from an electric battery of the kind described in chapter 14. Skeptics cast doubt on ancient Egyptian ability to craft glass envelopes that were the uniform configuration and large size of the seven tubular objects pictured on the Temple of Hathor's panels. But glaziers in the Nile valley already had at least fifteen hundred years of experience before the Dendera reliefs were created in the mid-first century BCE. After Garn completed his downsized, though painstakingly accurate replica and switched it on, even he expressed surprise when the tube filled with light.

Because scientific experiments must be repeated to confirm their results, he went to the trouble of building a second model, again crafting all parts exclusively from those portrayed at the Temple of Hathor. When it, too, illuminated in an identical manner, questions concerning the depiction of artificial light devices on the crypt's wall were answered in the affirmative. Garn noted:

Accurate illustrations like these would be impossible without a basic knowledge of electrical engineering. Too many technical details simply fit the picture. The wall reliefs show precisely presented details that, in my opinion, can only be reproduced so precisely if very precise knowledge of electrical processes is available. Without elementary knowledge of electrical engineering, such drawings would not be possible, because too many technical details are the same.

[Explaining how his replicas worked, Garn said], if you remove air from the glass bulb that has two metal parts extending inside, discharges will occur at a lower voltage. At a pressure of 40 *torr* [a low-compression level], a line of light will wind its way from one metal part to the other. If the vacuum process is continued, the line widens further, until it eventually fills out the entire glass bulb— exactly as the images in the underground chambers of the Hathor Temple suggest.[9]

Garn's working models and the relief images they duplicated are modern and ancient versions of a forerunner of the modern cathode-ray television tube, the so-called Crookes tube named after English physicist William Crookes. In 1875 his invention was used to discover the properties of cathode rays through a glass bulb inserted with two metal electrodes—the cathode and the anode—one at either end. As a high voltage was applied between these electrodes, cathode rays were projected in straight lines from the cathode (see plate 15).

Jochmans writes:

> When the tube is in operation the beam is created where the power cord enters the cathode tube at the opposite end. In the image of the temple [at Dendera], the electron beam is represented as an extended snake. The tail of the snake begins where a cable from the power box enters the tube, and the head of the snake touches the opposite end, and in Egyptian art, the serpent was the symbol of divine energy.[10]

Given these temple illustrations of electrical devices, their dominance by Hathor is particularly appropriate because she was the goddess of miners, who perhaps depended on artificial illumination as much in antiquity as they do today. In any case, the Dendera light performs identically to a Crookes tube, which it correspondingly resembles. According to Jochmans, another electrical engineer, Michael R. Freedman at the University of Illinois-Urbana, "believes that the solar disc on Horus's head [as depicted on Dendera's final Temple of Hathor relief panel] is a Van de Graaff generator, an apparatus that collects static electricity."

This instrument enters into a power-generating relationship with Upu. The figure's mythological role, described above, as a frog-headed, baboon-bodied servant of the birth goddess Hequet doubles in applied science as an electrical component.

"Under actual conditions," Jochmans clarifies regarding Professor Freedman's observation, "the static charge built up on the knife [the first of two held up by Upu] from the generator would cause the electron beam inside the Crookes tube to be diverted from the normal path, because the negative knife and the negative beam would repel each other. In the temple picture, the serpent's head in the second tube is turned away from the end of the tube, repulsed by the knife in the baboon's hand."[11]

Going to the heart of the matter, Dunn asks us to "consider the simple fact that these hidden symbols of technology became evident and understandable only through the use of modern technology and its standards of exactness and consistency."[12] Dunn was seconded by Pavel Smutny, a Slovakian electrical research engineer: "If we see plans for the Valley Temple of the Sphinx, or of the Mortuary Temple at Chephren's pyramid, or also the Osireon at Abydos, to a person familiar with the basics of computer techniques, or, even better, to a person experienced with construction of microwave circuits in bands above 1 *Gigahertz* (GHz), he will tell you that these plans are schemes of PCBs (boards for electronic circuits)."[13]

Smutny says, in effect, that the electrical technology documented on the Temple of Hathor was not limited to Dendera but known and applied at other major sacred sites in the Nile valley. Indeed, modern electronics validates ancient myth in what was formerly regarded as the anachronistic bas-relief representation of a dynastic Egyptian holding a lightbulb. "While technologists compare the image in this wall carving with what they know of science," writes Dunn, "Egyptologists interpret these images with what they know of ancient Egyptian symbolism."[14] At Dendera, both converge to reveal the truth about its controversial stone panel reliefs.

The African Creation Energy website draws the controversy's ultimate conclusion in light of Garn's experimental models.

> Comparative analysis of the components as described in the text of the Dendera lights match electrical engineering components, which can be used to construct a cathode ray tube electrical lighting device. In considering the artifacts known as the Dendera lights for present and future practical application, it is undeniable that a cathode ray electrical light source can be constructed describing the components needed to build the technology, using the terms as described in the text accompanying the Dendera lights' reliefs.[15]

But what possible use could the ancient Egyptians have had for a Crookes tube? It could not be for studying the properties of cathode rays, anymore than stage directors of modern-day light shows are interested in the same lasers used by surgeons to cauterize wounds. When the artificial lights portrayed at the Temple of Hathor are regarded within the context of the hieroglyphic instructions sharing the same walls, it becomes apparent that Dendera's Crookes tubes were special-effects instruments to help dramatize the nighttime New Year festival and especially the Night-of-the-Child-in-His-Nest pageant celebrating the birth of Ra, the sun god. The great glass bulbs not only filled with serpentine light but also could be made to dazzle a wide variety of internally glowing fantasies by artistically manipulating the agitated electrons using handheld pieces of magnetite, which electromagnetically interfaced with and contorted the charged light.

During the late nineteenth century, William Crookes popularized different models of his invention by similarly dramatizing them, according to his entry in Wikipedia: "By the time they [the electrons] reached the anode end of the tube, they [the electrons] were going so fast that many flew past the anode and hit the glass wall. The electrons themselves were invisible, but when they hit the glass walls of the tube they excited the atoms in the glass, making them give off light or fluoresce, usually yellow-green. . . . The colorful glowing tubes were also popular in public lectures to demonstrate the mysteries of the new science of electricity. Decorative tubes were made with fluorescent minerals, or butterfly figures painted with fluorescent paint, sealed inside. When power was applied, the fluorescent materials lit up with many glowing colors."[16]

If future archaeologists sifting among the ruins of modern civilization were to find broken laser lights amid debris from a twenty-first-century rock concert, the excavators might conclude that its long-dead stage managers, while technologically adept enough for the practical application of electrical power, used it only for special effects at public gatherings. So it follows that the Dendera lights might convince some contemporary investigators that dynastic Egyptians never harnessed electricity for anything more than wowing audiences at their religious spectaculars.

We do know that the ancients understood it well enough to also electroplate some of their art objects, illuminate at least one of their cities (Antioch), power the Pharos Lighthouse, and treat various illnesses with electromagnetic therapy, as described in chapter 6. These achievements are advanced enough in themselves, but what other examples of related high technology could our ancestors have possessed? How else they may have employed electricity we may only learn with the unearthing of some future discovery.

# 16

# Mega Structures

*[They] seemed to be triumphing over us, asking: "Guess how this engineering work was done!"*

THOR HEYERDAHL, *EASTER ISLAND*

The Greek Parthenon in Athens is world famous, but less appreciated today are its original pair of colossal doors. Each one stood 30 feet tall, was 7 feet wide 2 feet thick, and was made of solid oak inlaid with gold and ivory panels. Despite their estimated combined weight of 20 tons, which required teams of roped horses to open and close them, the doors were capable of being swung back and forth on metal hinges for 2,025 years after they were mounted in 438 BCE.[1]

Conquering Ottoman Turks used the former temple as a mosque and ammunition dump, which exploded in 1687, blowing off the great doors. These had been stripped long before of their chryselephantine panels, which were cut up for timber. How two ten-ton doors could have been hoisted with precision for mounting on hinges strong enough to bear such an excessive weight burden over the course of more than twenty centuries utterly contradicts everything known or assumed about construction technology from the fifth century BCE. More remarkable by far was a much older and greater engineering triumph.

On the Atlantic coast of France lie the remains, broken into four

Figure 16.1. Full-scale reproduction of front entrance doors of
the Athenian Parthenon at Nashville, Tennessee.

pieces, of a single monolith that originally stood 67.5 feet high on a peninsula overlooking the Bay of Quiberon. The Broken Menhir of Er Grah or Le Grand Menhir Brise, as it is sometimes called, was the tallest of nineteen standing stones nearby, erected circa 4700 BCE. The exceptionally heavy stone was transported six miles from a rocky outcrop located at Locmariaquer.

According to Alexander Thom, a professor and chair of engineering science at Brasenose College University of Oxford, "a prepared track (of timber?) must have been made for the large rollers necessary, and a pull of perhaps fifty tons applied (how?) on the level. Many explanations have been advanced, but they all fail to account for the sheer size of the stone or indeed for its position."[2] He correctly identified it as a lunar marker, from which the monolith would have been able to calculate the moon's 18.6-year cycle.

This was achieved by observing the menhir from different vantage points in the surrounding countryside. Thom predicted the locations of these sites and found ancient markers at several of them, confirming his hypothesis. He also made predictions for the directions of eight additional observation points, of which six are prehistoric mounds or standing stones. One of them is ten miles distant. As such, the Er Grah Menhir is the tallest, heaviest gnomon ever made; a gnomon is the projecting piece on an astronomical device that determined specific celestial alignments.

Figure 16.2. The grand menhir Er Grah stood in a row of
19 giant standing stones, erected ca. 4700 BCE in Brittany France.
Image by Kenny Arne Lang Antonsen & Jimmy John Antonsen.

John Michell, an English author and prominent figure in the Earth mysteries movement, found a British Admiralty report of 1659 describing a local shipwreck, which noted how Le Grand Menhir Brise was standing and clearly "visible from the scene of the wreck." He further pointed out that an early eighteenth-century painting depicting the Broken Menhir of Er Grah places its fall sometime between 1659 and 1725. He concluded from this narrow time parameter that the monolith toppled on December 27, 1722, when a severe earthquake affected much of western Europe. Subsequent computer modeling supports his conclusion, based on the pattern in which the stone fragments fell to the ground.

Before his death in 2009, Michell wondered if there was still more to Le Grand Menhir Brise than lunar alignments: "The transport of such a large stone from such a distance indicates both that the location was important to the builders and that the type of stone was."[3] Sculpted bas-relief—badly eroded and now only faintly visible—cover the Menhir of Er Grah's entire surface with the Mané-Rutual, or plough ax. This image may have signified at least part of Le Grand Menhir Brise's other, heavenly function: the Plough is a large asterism in the constellation Ursa Major, better known today as the Big Dipper, while an ax was a Neolithic symbol for lightning.

Was the Er Grah Menhir set up as a colossal lightning rod 6,450 years before Benjamin Franklin reinvented a much smaller version of such a device in 1749? Standing at the highest point in its location for many miles around and specially chosen for its rose quartz granite— veined in crystal with piezoelectric qualities—Le Grand Menhir Brise may have not only oriented itself with the sky but may have summoned its electrical power; to what end, ceremonial or otherwise, is a mystery. This conjecture was given significant support in December 2019, when geographical surveys of another New Stone Age monument revealed its close association with lightning.

Referred to as Site XI, just one megalith remains from a hillside stone circle on the west coast of Lewis, an island in the Outer Hebrides, off Scotland. At the center of the location, investigators uncovered a sixty-foot-wide, star-shaped mark scorched millennia ago onto the bedrock by either a single extraordinarily energized lightning bolt, or, more probably, a number or series of average, less potent strikes occurring over the course of many years. The heavenly impact was so powerful that it transformed the ground itself into a magnetic anomaly.

Site XI is one of several Neolithic positions on Lewis, all of them built from coarsely crystalline foliated rock mixed with metamorphosed quartzite and mica schist. These component minerals, including large, crystalline grains and visible veins, combine to make Lewis gneiss exceptionally piezoelectric—chief cause perhaps for selection of this particular island as the most proper setting in which to establish a temple that would attract lightning. Something of this geophysical relationship between piezoelectric stone and lightning may have even been handed down over time in the very word *gneiss,* as it derives from the Middle High German noun *gneist,* meaning "spark."

Richard Bates, a geoscientist at Scotland's St. Andrews University, commented that the stone circle at Site XI was constructed either to commemorate an unusually large lightning strike that had been observed on the isle of Lewis or was purposefully built to attract lightning.[4] The latter supposition implies that its Neolithic builders possessed sufficient working knowledge to raise a megalithic lightning rod some five thousand years ago. Whatever its purpose, it must have consistently performed as designed because the monumental device was in use for at least fifteen centuries before being abandoned by its attendants at the close of the Late Bronze Age, a period of geological and climatological upheaval that afflicted the Northern Hemisphere circa 1200 BCE.

Perhaps Er Grah and the Hebridean location are not anomalies but instead typical of megalithic sites everywhere across Britain and Western Europe: all were constructed of piezoelectric stone designed to summon God from heaven in the tangible form of lightning. No less confounding was how New Stone Age engineers could have erected the 330-ton monolith and precisely maneuvered its position with such astronomical exactitude that it accurately aligned to the eight positions of the moon plus the lunar cycle. When standing, the Er Grah Menhir weighed as much as the 143-foot-long submarine USS *F-3 (SS-22) Pickerel* or the *Kyotoku-maru,* a 197-foot-long Japanese trawler.

## SUPERHUMAN TOOLING

Any objective observer of monumental structures such as the Greek Parthenon or Brittany's Le Grand Menhir Brise cannot help but be persuaded that they could only have resulted from the mastery of highly advanced building materials worked by power machining that is still deemed impossibly ahead of its time by mainstream scholars. A simple case in point is the lathe, a machine for shaping wood, metal, clay, or other substances by means of a rotating drive turning the piece being worked on against changeable cutting tools. Controversial evidence for its European invention dates to a Mycenaean site in central Greece circa 1400 BCE.

In any case, possible lathe technology was lost with the violent end of the Bronze Age for at least the next eight hundred years, until the Etruscans were using it in Northern Italy to fashion beautifully turned wooden bowls. Lathes disappeared again, this time for thirteen centuries, after the Classical world fell, reemerging about 1800 to make the Industrial Revolution possible. The device then gained a reputation as the "mother of machine tools" for its capacity to spawn the invention of other machine tools. It and its progeny are still very much part of modern manufacturing.

Contemporaneous with the lathe's debatable Greek origins, it surfaced in Atlantic coastal Mexico among Mesoamerica's founding fathers. Whether its reappearance among the Olmec was a case of independent invention by an unquestionably creative people or a cultural legacy they received via Bronze Age visitors from the ancient world, clearly machined specimens are publicly displayed at the Museo de Antropología de Xalapa in eastern Mexico. Outstanding examples "are perfectly circular objects made out of obsidian," in the words of Brien Foerster, an authority on megalithic structures in the Near East and Central and South America. "Though not extremely hard a stone, obsidian is very brittle, and these pieces are extremely thin." The objects in question are themselves difficult to identify in many instances, resembling spools, spindle whirls, and clublike batons fashioned with astounding precision. Several rings of some kind have been cut to two millimeters—that is, 0.0787402 of an inch—thin. "An engineer who was with us on the January 2018 tour," Foerster continues, "who is a manufacturing expert, stated quite emphatically that they could not have been made by hand." He cites a black vessel "perfectly bilaterally symmetrical and highly polished, which could only be achieved with the use of a high-speed lathe and at least tungsten carbide tools, or perhaps even diamond ones. The Olmec did not even have knowledge of bronze."[5]

Ancient machining on an opposite scale of exactitude occurred a world away from Mexico, in the Nile valley. It is here that history's supremely monumental achievements still bear the unmistakable earmarks of applied technology far beyond conventional experts to credit, much less explain. No one has done more, however, than Christopher Dunn to demonstrate just how the dynastic masterpieces were so finely rendered, with tools only a modern craftsman, not a mechanically inexperienced Egyptologist, could recognize, such as a crowned statue of Pharaoh Ramses II at Luxor. Dunn writes:

> Creating such an object today using modern computers, software and computer numerical controlled (CNC) machines would present some significant challenges, to be sure—but not as much head scratching would be involved today as there would have been forty years ago, when I first entered the manufacturing trade as a young apprentice.
>
> Applying the tools of fifty years ago to the Ramses challenge would severely tax craftsmen skilled in manufacturing, and the tools and instruments necessary to ensure such precise geometry would

not even be in a sculptor's toolbox. . . . The tool marks visible on the Ramses statues in the Temple of Luxor do not have the appearance be being made by chisels and hammers of any kind.

In other words, the technological means needed to only possibly duplicate the Ramses statue did not exist until the late twentieth century. If no hand tools were ever capable of sculpting such a work of art, then the only explanation left to explain its existence lies in advanced machining.

If we are driven to the conclusion that the symmetrical accuracy of the Ramses statues could be achieved only with the assistance of mechanical axes that guide the tool along a predetermined path, then the striations found around the eyes would not be surprising. The marks follow a path that a guided tool would follow to create these features. We should also note that these marks are not visible to the naked eye but instead were captured by a 15.2 mega-pixel camera using an ultra-violet filter.[6]

The scope of achievement here may be only fully appreciated when we realize that the microscopically detailed artworks were cut from hard granite, "which was not fashioned into statues until the development of more modern power tools with steel bits."

For the first time in more than three thousand years, something of the nature of the tool that gave birth to the colossi begins to reemerge. Dunn continued, "The measurement reveals a tool size of approximately 0.30 inch (7.62 millimeters) x 0.180 inch (4.572 millimeters). From a technical perspective, these dimensions are probably for a tool that is performing finish cuts. . . . The dimensions applied to the outline of the jaw on Amenophis III [a statue at the Temple of Mut in Thebes] indicate a precision of plus or minus 0.006 inch (1.52 millimeters), which, on a human scale would be 0.01 inch (0.254 millimeter), or half the thickness of a thumbnail."[7]

Of all the many hundreds, perhaps thousands of examples of dynastic temple art graphically representing a broad variety of physical tasks engaged in by Egyptian workers, not a single instance depicts them sculpting anything. Instead, they are invariably shown only finishing a statue. It is as though some organized crafts or guilds—like those of the Middle Ages, when becoming an apprentice was to enter a process of strictly confidential initiation—insisted upon protecting certain trade secrets by forbidding their visual portrayal. The surviving results of an ancient tool that was the precise opposite of that which worked the Amenophis statue came to Dunn's attention in a trench surrounding an unfinished obelisk lying prone in a dynastic quarry at Aswan.

He saw that "the tool that cut the trench left horizontal marks that are familiar to machinists and are consistent with either a tool that is drawn out of a hole and then reinserted to begin cutting again, or with a tool that cuts while performing a horizontal, sweeping motion, or both. . . . The horizontal striations are typical in cutting when the feed of a tool that is removing material pauses along its path, withdrawn to remove waste, and the interruption of the tool leaves a mark on the surface."[8]

The tool that left such telltale marks was, as Dunn describes it, a "mega-saw" like the one at Abu Roash, 37.5 feet across: "While the TBMs [tunnel boring machines] that bored through the English Channel were twenty-seven feet in diameter, objective evidence shows that the ancient Egyptians used mega-saws for cutting granite, limestone, and basalt that exceeded that diameter. We can calculate the size of these saws by the impression they left on the granite block."

He noted "a radial undercut at one end of the trench, which is indicative of a circular saw's action. . . . The tool marks on the stone at Abu Roash provide evidence for the movement of the tool that cut the granite. . . . The evidence shows that they were using processes that modern manufacturers may yet need to discover."[9] They have, at any rate, discovered that the same kind of high-speed lathes that left their self-identifying tool marks up and down the Nile valley were also at work more than three thousand miles away, in the south of India.

The 860-year-old Hoysaleswara Temple has been almost entirely carved by power tools, from its massive columns to 0.12-inch stone figures. Its approximately 340 large reliefs depicting Hindu legends, countless smaller complexly designed friezes narrating Hindu texts such as the *Ramayana* and *Mahabharata,* and highly detailed, intricate reliefs were all cut by a variety of machining technologies. The sacred site impressed late nineteenth-century art critic James Fergusson as a "marvelous exhibition of human labor to be found even in the patient east, and surpasses anything in Gothic art."[10]

Before 1550 CE, Hoysaleswara was twice sacked and plundered by Muslim armies, consequently falling into a state of ruin and neglect. During the course of its 1862 restoration, British archaeologists were persuaded by earlier materials surfacing amid mid-twelfth-century-CE rubble that the official completion in 1160 CE actually represented occupation by conquerors of the Hoysala empire, who claimed the temple, including its name and history, as their own. "What makes you think they are only nine hundred years old?" asks commentator Larry Croft. "Could these masterpieces even be thousands of years old?"[11] As such, Hoysaleswara may be far more venerable than generally suspected and could consequently owe its construction to different culture creators.

In any case, many thousands of minute circular lines closely resembling grooves in a phonograph's long-playing disc record encircle each of the temple's great pillars and are identical to machining tool marks recognized today as turning stripes made by a lathe (see plate 16). In order to do so, the twelve-foot-long, three-foot wide pillars would each have had to have been laid horizontally in a lathe not only strong enough to support the multiton blocks but also sufficiently powerful for rotating them at high speed, thereby enabling a bit of harder stone to incise the grooves seen on the columns.

Such a procedure is extremely challenging if not virtually impossible to complete with so perfect a regularity as displayed inside the Hoysaleswara Temple, even by modern machining methods. A hypothetical alternative might envision the pillar mounted horizontally in place, while a mobile lathe, circling round and round its circumference, incised the surface. If such a preprogrammed, automated tool existed in the deep past, it has not been reinvented since. Whatever one might imagine, the pillars' turning stripes could not have been executed by hand using any kind of handheld tool with the consistently spaced regularity found at Hoysaleswara.

As such, its creation could only have come about through the application of a construction technology at least the equal to, but more likely the superior to, state-of-the-art manufacturing in the twenty-first century. Near the pillars is the seven-foot-tall statue of a god, his crown adorned with five miniature human skulls. Each one is 25.4 millimeters in diameter and has been hollowed out, though not separately, because they are part of the same single piece of stone belonging to the sculpture; in other words, the little skulls were not worked away from the statue and then attached to it, because they have never been cut out of the lithic matrix of which the carved figure and the skulls are part.

Accordingly, hollowing out one-inch-wide spheres with their backs attached to the stone from which they have never been removed is outside the operative parameters of any conceivable tool, let alone some sculptor wielding a handheld chisel. More incredibly, the original artist carved a contoured gap less than 0.12 inch wide between the statue's forehead and the base of its crown—something beyond the limitations of known human technology until the introduction of laser saws within the past fifty years.

This impossibly small gap between the sculpted god's forehead and his crown is not only anomalous at the temple but also separates two necklaces around the neck of another statue portraying a nearby female figure. The mirrorlike quality of extraordinarily high polishing displayed by monolithic representations of Hoysaleswara's bulls could only have been achieved by the ancient equivalent of a modern rotary burr (see plate 17). Commentator Aaron Martin, a machining metalworker for twenty years, states that a deburring tool could not have polished the large taurine statues, as "no metal tool could ever hold up to any stone for any length of time. Polishing takes many, many steps of incremental grits to achieve a polished surface. Polishing the surface would be actually not very technical, just tons of elbow grease."[12]

True, but the bull monuments were carved from soapstone, which was soft enough to allow for the kind of polishing a high-speed tool was capable of making. Because India was, appropriately, the largest single source for diamonds in the ancient world, construction engineers throughout the subcontinent would have always had a ready supply of the mineral on hand for their power tools when cutting and polishing stone. No less fittingly, Hoysaleswara's divine patron was Masana Bhairava, the god of measurement, depicted by a relief statue at the site holding in his right hand nothing less than a reduction gear of the kind used in modern power drills.

This is no baseless fantasy or misinterpretation of a spiritual symbol. It is the clear reading of a recognizable object composed of a pair of concentric circles; the outer one with thirty-two teethlike features, the inner with half as many. This two-to-one ratio is the same found in current planetary gears. These are combined gears consisting of a central wheel around which another larger wheel revolves. With this fundamental reduction gear literally in hand, the significance of Masana Bhairava's sculpted appearance at Hoysaleswara could hardly be more obvious.

## ADVANCED MACHINING
## FOR COLOSSAL CONSTRUCTION

Ancient India's high technology was not confined to the mainland. Unique examples top a massive plateau formed from magma of an extinct volcano towering 660 feet above the central jungle plains of Sri Lanka (see fig. 16.3 and plate 18). It is known as Sigiriya, or Lion Rock, for a monumental pair of leonine claws flanking the public entrance to zigzagging, steel stairways installed by the State Bureau of Tourism.

The only way to reach the summit of Sigiriya is a two-hour climb. The formation's vertically sheer sides render the almost perfectly flat summit otherwise inaccessible. Weary sightseers may rest from their

Figure 16.3. The summit of Sigiriya is surmounted by a construction
project as ancient as it is enigmatic. Photo by Sean Kommer.

arduous ascent at the so-called Mirror Wall to gaze at vibrantly colorful frescoes, remnants of many more that formerly covered almost the
entire western face of Sigiriya within a space 460 feet long by 130 feet
high. Resuming their upward trek, hardy backpackers eventually reach
the top of Lion Rock, where its ruins are officially characterized as the
remains of a combined palace and fortress, although physical proof
exists for neither description.

Undeterred by a lack of evidence, local archaeologists have
dreamed up fantasies for tourist attractions of imperial personages,
like the bejeweled ladies portrayed by the lower-down frescoes flitting
through a sumptuous playground in the sky of gardens, fountains,
bridges, banquet halls, and harem quarters. The thorough absence
of such an opulent estate disappoints visitors unprepared to behold
instead stark brick foundations missing any hint of former glory. A

large stone rectangle containing water is supposed to have been a royal swimming pool but was actually a reservoir—the world's largest monolithic tank at ninety feet long, sixty feet wide, and seven feet deep. To create it, thirty-five hundred tons of solid granite were excavated in the same manner a scoop digs out a block of ice cream in long, smooth, continuous ruts. These are the only tool marks present at the reservoir. No indication of chipping, impact, or indentation made by handheld chisels is present.

Instead, the bottom and sides of the monolithic tank have been machined by some inconceivably powerful dredge, robust enough to have dug out thousands of tons of the world's hardest building stone. The reservoir is itself a complex hydraulic system of interacting canals, locks, and drains. These keep it automatically filled with water year-round, even throughout Sri Lanka's excessively dry summers, yet prevent overflowing during heavy downpours of the rainy season. This self-sustaining engineering marvel still functions properly after centuries of continuous operation. It is, however, just one component among numerous stone walls, pavements, platforms, pyramidal edifices, hollow squares, and larger windowless buildings occupying an archaeological zone approximately 1.5 miles long by 0.6 of a mile across.

If their original purposes seem obscure, more so is the means of their construction. Sigiriya has always lacked enough clay for producing its combined structures' three million or more bricks. They could have only been made 660 feet below and then brought to the summit. But how? Only the most skilled, best-equipped mountain climbers could attain it by scaling Lion Rock's almost perfectly vertical slopes, until the location's first stairs reached the top from ground level, beginning in the mid-twentieth century. Hauling up millions of bricks to the building site in man-powered hoists during antiquity does not seem feasible, suggesting instead some kind of huge automated conveyance beyond imagining. There are additionally innumerable fifty-pound steps made from milky white marble—a hard, crystalline, metamorphic form of limestone not native to central Sri Lanka.

Marble for Sigiriya had to be imported over hundreds of miles through virtually impenetrable jungle and then lifted hundreds of feet to the construction area by the tens of thousands without breaking or chipping. While unknown numbers of laborers were needed to handle these materials plus the reservoir's 3,500 tons of excavated granite, how an entire workforce was transported to the lofty summit, along with heavy tools, and how so many men were regularly supplied after arriving there (Lion Rock offers neither fruit trees nor soil for growing crops) defies explanation. No less inexplicable are the numerous grooves and circular or rectangular holes cut all over Sigiriya.

If their original purposes or meanings are mysterious, their execution forms a greater riddle, because most of them have been incised far up the sheer face of the plateau where no provision of any kind allowed their makers the merest foothold or standing place in utterly inaccessible areas. The linear cuts, being vertical, could not have been used for drainage nor served as steps, because they begin high above ground level and then unaccountably terminate hundreds of feet beneath the summit. All these enigmas—the futuristic reservoir perfectly cut from a single field of granite; mass-importation of marble across impassable terrain; the lifting of thousands of workers, along with their tools and at least three million bricks, 660 feet to the top of a volcanic formation; provisions required for perhaps many years while they undertook building the monumental structures—may only be understood within the context of some advanced technology applied in various forms by advanced culture-bearers at Lion Rock. But who was capable of such material greatness?

The site was supposedly selected by Kashyapa I for his new capital sometime before the king took his own life in 495 CE. Recorded eight hundred years after the fact (if fact indeed it was) by a Buddhist monk naturally opposed on religious grounds to pagan monarchs (especially if they committed the sin of suicide), his explanation for the construction achievement at Lion Rock additionally contrasts with the lower level of Sri Lanka's known building skills in the late fifth century. A small fortress was, after all, constructed around that time at Lion Rock, lending at least partial credence to Kashyapa's relocation there. But the unimposing citadel is stylistically different from and structurally inferior to the monumental structures that dominate the plateau top. Some twelve hundred years before King Kashyapa's time, a major Sanskrit epic referred to Lion Rock as Alakamandava, the City of the Gods, built fifty centuries ago.

The *Ramayana* appears spot on, because the earliest physical evidence for human habitation in central Sri Lanka, at the Aligala rock shelter just east of Sigiriya, is dated to the Mesolithic Period, or India's Middle Stone Age, circa 3000 BCE. This year connects the *Ramayana*'s City of the Gods with Lion Rock through the Indus valley civilization, which underwent one of humanity's first urban expansions around the turn of the fourth millennium BCE. Revealingly, Indus valley city planning at famous archaeological sites like Harappa or Mohenjo Daro, with their emphasis on rectangular mud-brick structures and large-scale water reservoirs accessed by descending steps, is identically reflected at Sigiriya.

Although the *Ramayana* was written no earlier than the seventh century BCE, about eight hundred years after the Indus valley civilization came to an end, the epic's hero, Rama, lived in 2500 BCE, at the zenith of that earlier culture. It seems likely, then, that Sigiriya was a sister city of Harappa and Mohenjo Daro and was constructed with the same advanced technology that made them the extraordinary metropolitan centers of pre-Hindu India. During 2002, UNESCO listed Lion Rock as a World Heritage Site. Until little more than 170 years before, Sigiriya had been overgrown, lost and unremembered even by local natives, for five centuries.

In 1831, Major Jonathan Forbes of the British Army's 78th Highlanders happened to pass by while returning on horseback from a ride to the town of Pollonnuruwa, about thirty miles away. Intrigued, he scaled the strange, natural formation's perpendicular north face, with no small effort, to eventually arrive at the bush-covered summit and its silent ruins. But the ancient high-tech methods responsible for building Sigiriya are still forgotten. Better remembered is Surang Tila, the largest sacred structure among the Sirpur Group of Monuments, an archaeological zone in northeastern India.

The temple's flight of thirty-seven steep, relatively well-preserved courses of limestone steps, bulges radically only in a large section flanked by a wall, the lasting effect of a massive earthquake that struck the area in the eleventh century CE. It was the only building throughout the area that was not demolished at the time, due to Surang Tila's singular precautions. The stairway's partial and unusual deformation can be explained by a unique cement paste, resilient and stronger than modern concrete, that binds the entire temple and preserved the structural integrity of its foundations during the catastrophic seismic event. The invention and application of this construction adhesive appears to have been one of two measures specifically designed to render the sacred center earthquake resistant.

The other is a series of several square shafts, each one sunk vertically almost seventy-five feet into the earth at various strategic points around the temple. The air pockets thus created by these shafts absorbed and dissipated tectonic vibrations that would have otherwise shaken Surang Tila into a heap of ruins. An inscription found during excavations there in 2004 convinced archaeologists that the site is no more than twelve hundred years old, even though the discovered epigraph states that the temple was only in operation during the eighth century CE. In fact, it is described by the *Mayamatam* texts, dated to a period circa 2500 BCE that coincided with the zenith of the Indus valley civilization, an innovative high culture mentioned in association with Sigiriya. Surang Tila was not, however, the only earthquake-proof sacred center created by the ancients.

# 17

# Ancient Engineering

*The relevance of ancient megalithic construction and precision cutting of igneous rock relies on engineering principles, not on geology or Egyptology.*

CHRISTOPHER DUNN,
*LOST TECHNOLOGIES OF ANCIENT EGYPT*

A famous example of megalithic construction appears a world away, high in the mountains of Peru at the Incan citadel of Machu Picchu. Its window and doorway spaces, forming a quadrilateral with two parallel sides, are familiar to tourists and archaeologists who dismiss the arrangement as nothing more than a cultural design feature. In reality it is substantially more: a trapezoidal configuration tends to disburse tectonic vibrations toward its broader and more stable base, dissipating them upward along sloping sides into the upper lintel, which, because smaller, is prone to less violent movement than the top of a square or rectangle, with improved structural resistance to collapse (see fig. 17.1, p. 204, as well as plate 19).

But these tetragonal apertures are only part of Machu Picchu's earthquake-proof construction. Its self-evident designation means "high peak," but the location has been known to Quechua-speaking natives from time out of mind as the Place of the Dancing Stones. This name never meant much to Renán Alvarez, a guide with forty years of

Figure 17.1. Earthquake-resistant stonework at
Machu Picchu's Temple of the Sun.

experience, who was caught with his gaggle of foreign tourists at the center of Machu Picchu on the morning of December 11, 1982, when one of the most powerful earthquakes in Peruvian history badly shook the entire Andes mountain range. As his clients panicked around him, he reasoned that there was no better place to die and observed his chaotic surroundings with calm detachment.

Especially fascinating were the blocks that made up the site's walls and buildings: they were sliding powerfully back and forth, whole courses of them, not brokenly or in confused self-destruction but as though choreographed in repeatedly controlled motion. Not one of the megalithic stones fell out of place or disjoined itself as entire lengths of unmortared masonry undulated violently like enraged boa constrictors. The moment seismic activity abruptly ceased, all the blocks, on cue, slid in one simultaneous movement precisely back into their former placement. "They looked as though they had never budged the

Figure 17.2. Earthquake-resistant Andean stonework.
Photo by Martin St-Aman.

second the earthquake stopped," remembered Alvarez. "Nobody else there at the time seemed to notice, but I understood then why the Indians called Machu Picchu the Place of the Dancing Stones."[1]

The stonework has been engineered to counter tectonic energies, not by resisting but by moving with them, in the manner of a ship at sea riding safely along with the flow of high waves rather than sideways and consequently being struck and damaged by them. Oceanic waves are very similar to seismic waves, as the builders of Peru's Incan capital understood. Their pre-Columbian ramparts at Cuzco are composed of undulating courses of megalithic stone paralleling the pattern of seismic waves, thereby disbursing and diffusing otherwise destructive energy throughout the length of the walls. These structures still stand after surviving centuries of seismic violence, while twenty-first-century buildings fall to earthquakes every year.

## BRIDGING A MONUMENTAL PAST

Isolated in its mountain fastness, Machu Picchu was originally connected to the outside world by a rope bridge traversing the Urubamba River, southeast of Cuzco. Not reinvented in the West until 1801, Incan suspension bridges were the greatest structures of their kind, spanning longer distances over wide canyons, deep gorges, and broad rivers than other bridges of their era anywhere in the world. They were made of *ichu*—a tough, native grass—woven into powerful bundles. Large rope cables were then formed from smaller ropes woven of llama and alpaca wool, together with ichu and cotton. These attached to stone pillars or towers on either side of the crossing. Thick cables were stretched to form handrails and the floor of the bridge, which was then covered with flat wood panels (see plate 20).

Tests conducted on cables from the sturdiest Incan bridges—which additionally incorporated leather, vines, and branches—by MIT professor John Ochsendorf showed that they were capable of supporting two hundred thousand pounds and "could bear the weight of columns of soldiers," G. Wayne Clough reported in *Smithsonian Magazine*.[2] To carry these one-hundred-ton loads, often over the course of centuries, the suspension bridges were extremely strong. The Inca made about two hundred of them, some more than 150 feet in extent, longer than any stone bridges on Earth at the time. The rope bridges' only disadvantage lay in their restricted, early-morning passage.

During most of the day, strong winds set them wildly swinging like hammocks. An impressive "old bridge," as it was known in Quechua, began at the main road north from Cuzco. Before the close of the nineteenth century, all 161 feet of the Mawk'a Chaka collapsed into the Apurímac River after three hundred years of continuous traffic, inspiring Thornton Wilder's 1927 novel, *The Bridge of San Luis Rey*. Despite the undoubted greatness of the Inca of Peru's enduring rope bridges, they were preceded and eclipsed by a single project located on the south bank of the Usumacinta River, in the state of Chiapas on the Mexican side of the international border with Guatemala.

At about 700 CE thousands of workers at Pa'Chan (Broken Sky), an ancient Mayan city known today as Yaxchilan (Green Stones), constructed "the longest bridge in the world until 1377, when Italians built a fortified stone bridge with a span of seventy-two meters [236 feet] over the Adda River at Trezzo, Italy," as elucidated by James A. O'Kon, a registered professional engineer. He tells how the project was "a long-span,

Figure 17.3. Yaxchilan's modernlike suspension bridge.
Image courtesy of James O'Kon.

rope-cable suspension bridge across the Usumacinta River. The rope-cable support system was supported from tall composite stone and cast-in-place concrete bridge towers and anchored by stone mechanisms and the north and south abutments. . . . The center of the north bridge pier is 63 meters [207 feet] in distance from the center of the south bridge pier."

At its highest point the bridge was "approximately 22 meters [72 feet] above the riverbank at low water level," reports O'Kon.[3] Yaxchilan's suspension bridge held the record as the longest span on Earth for 677 years, partly because Mayan engineers had by then developed structural mechanics for multistory buildings—such as their 212-foot-tall Tikal Temple IV in Guatemala, built during the same period—that were not exceeded in height until Chicago completed the world's first skyscraper in 1885.

Impressive as the Incan and Mayan suspension bridges may have been, they were a fraction of the length of history's longest floating bridge, built nearly twenty-five centuries ago by the Persians. In 480 BCE, their second invasion attempt of Greece needed to cross the Hellespont (at today's Dardanelles) from Asia into eastern Thrace, in what is now western Turkey. But to do so, a bridge of unprecedented proportions was required for allowing the transfer of King Xerxes's troops, animals, and supplies. While he and his forces were marching from the city of Sardis far to the south, he sent orders ahead for the construction of two bridges spanning Abydos, then an important Black Sea harbor, to the opposite side near Sestos, another city on the European side of the Hellespont.

The spans were supposed to be ready for crossing when Xerxes appeared with his forces so as not to lose the initiative of their incursion. The day he arrived, however, the king was appalled to see that his recently completed bridges had been utterly destroyed by a powerful storm the night before. Enraged, he had their engineers beheaded, then summoned fresh replacements to build a pair of stronger bridges in record time. They were constructed by lashing together 674 ships, bow and stern anchors lowered to securely immobilize the vessels. Their 1,348 heavy anchors were cast from 202 tons of iron, and 186.5 miles of white flax and papyrus went into making ropes for two bridges.

Stretching from shore to shore, these cables were tightened by large winches to prevent any movement by the ships, moored one to the other in a long curve by a large number of hawsers instead of single cables. Laid across the cables were wooden planks covered with soil kept in place by layers of brushwood to form a dirt roadway. The bridges' 5,610 cubic feet of wood combined for a total weight of 142.5 tons. The supply bridge was 1.25 miles long. Its soldierly counterpart ran for 1.6 miles. Both were necessary: to ensure that the head of the Persian army's elongated column of troops was properly provisioned with food and water, warriors and supply personnel marched parallel along their respective bridges.

As some indication of the Persian numbers threatening Greece, crossing the Hellespont took them seven days and nights. The army used the northeasterly bridge, and the enormous crowds of attendants and baggage animals took the southwesterly bridge. The king's floating enterprise was a success, and his engineers kept their heads. "Over this bridge," writes L. Sprague de Camp, "Xerxes' vast army—perhaps more

Figure 17.4. The Persian army's floating bridge.
Image from A. C. Weatherstone in Walter Hutchinson's
*Hutchinson's History of the Nations* (London, Hutchinson & Co., 1915).

than one hundred fifty thousand soldiers, and several times that number of non-combatants—passed in safety, most of them to leave their bones in the stony soil of Hellas."[4]

Even their historic construction achievement, however, had been dwarfed millennia before by a colossal masterpiece that connected the Indian subcontinent with the island of Sri Lanka. Although today in ruinous condition, it still spans more than thirty miles of open sea and is known throughout India, if not the outside world, as Rama Setu (Rama's Bridge) after the prince of an ancient kingdom.

His engineering wonder is described in the *Ramayana,* a Sanskrit epic dated to 700 BCE, and, like Homer's *Iliad* a century earlier, preserved in writing the oral traditions repeated over the course of untold previous generations. It tells in some detail how Rama Setu was previously surveyed and planned, then built with "mechanical contrivances" that regularly deposited great boulders atop a framework made from fourteen different kinds of timber planks laid out on a natural sandbar

Figure 17.5. Rama's Bridge, as seen between India and Sri Lanka from Space Shuttle *Endeavor* during STS-59. Photo by the Earth Science and Remote Sensing Unit, NASA Johnson Space Center.

resting in shallow water.[5] Completion included a topmost course of wide, flat stones standing three feet above the surface of the Indian Ocean.

The *Ramayana* goes on to state that the bridge was built in a one-to-ten ratio, the same ratio found at the site today. It opened on September 20, 5076 BCE, when continental troops stormed across the 1.8-mile-wide causeway to invade Sri Lanka, the project's original purpose. This date is geologically contemporaneous with the installation of boulders at Rama Setu.[6] Remarkably, the shoal they sit atop is three thousand years *younger;* it accrued from gathering sand progressively piled up by powerful sea currents carried against subsurface foundations after the structure fell out of use, about 2000 BCE, and regular maintenance ceased.[7]

While time parameters for both bridge construction and its original written account are closely complementary, their late sixth-millennium-BCE provenance is perplexing. No society associated with collaborative enterprises carefully planned and designed to achieve a particular aim on such a monumental scale is known to have flourished in India seven thousand years ago. At that time, Neolithic agriculture had only just begun in the Indus valley region, where a high culture capable of successfully undertaking Rama Setu would not appear for another fifteen centuries, at Harappa and Mohenjo Daro. Perhaps Rama's Bridge is the sole surviving physical evidence for some technologically progressive civilization yet to be discovered by archaeologists.

Partially due to the structure's lack of identification with any recognized culture, it was long dismissed by skeptics as nothing more than a natural formation, although they were never able to point out a similar nonartificial example. Their dilemma was not eased by S. Badrinarayanan, former director of the Geological Survey of India, who announced that the structure cannot be a natural formation in view of a loose sand layer *beneath* corals running the feature's full length. Coral typically forms *above* rocks.[8]

But Landsat photographic surveys in 1988 established the feature's true character (see plate 21). "These results," observed the Science Channel, "suggest that the structure in the satellite image is not natural, but built by humans."[9]

Alan Lester, a professional geologist, senior instructor, and research associate in the Department of Geological Sciences at the University of Colorado Boulder, concluded that the great, regularly spaced stones in the ancient bridge "have been brought from afar and set on top of our sandbar island chain."[10]

Rama Setu was rendered finally impassable by a destructive typhoon in 1480 CE. Even before then, gradual sea-level rise had dropped most of its topcover stones to their current positions, averaging three feet beneath the surface of the sea.[11]

## HOLDING IT ALL TOGETHER

Some fifty-seven centuries after Prince Rama's time, on the other side of the world, Yaxchilan's bridge over the River Usumacinta came about during the reign of a no less ambitious leader. Itzamnaaj B'alam II was responsible for a monumental building program that also included the erection of magnificent temples with richly incised lintels, hieroglyphic stairways, and carved stelae—stone columns engraved with commemorative inscriptions and relief designs—transforming the center of this great Mesoamerican metropolis.

Many of these structures were themselves made possible thanks to the invention of Mayan cement, "which was also used as stucco coating, mortar, paving, and other building applications," writes O'Kon. "Fabrication of cement was developed by Maya technicians before 250 B.C. using an innovative fabrication process that was still in use until the twentieth century. . . . The durable, cast-in-place concrete construction of the monumental structures and their survival is a testimony to Maya building technology. . . . Maya technicians produced the same, technical process for fabricating hydraulic cement as that used by modern technology, but the Maya technical achievement was more than twenty-one hundred years in advance of modern technology."[12]

But how they concocted their good-quality concrete is an enigma, because no known Mesoamerican furnace was powerful enough to attain the necessary high temperatures. O'Kon explains:

The basic principles required to produce hydraulic cement consist of two major efforts, the mining of limestone and the ability to elevate the temperature of the limestone to a temperature level that will melt the raw materials and induce the chemical conversion into cement clinkers. . . . However, the Maya natural environment did not offer fuels that burn at high temperatures, such as coal or natural gas. The only major fuel source available to the Maya was timber, which grew abundantly in the forest. The use of timber alone, as a fuel source, cannot achieve the fourteen hundred fifty degrees Celsius temperature required to melt limestone. Wood burns at three hundred to five hundred degrees Celsius, much lower than the threshold for melting limestone. . . . It is unknown how the Maya technicians developed the geometry of the ingenious cement kiln assembly that enabled them to convert raw limestone into hydraulic cement.[13]

The magnificent span at Yaxchilan was preceded fourteen hundred years by the Pons Subiacus, a rope-and-timber connection over the Tiber, crossing the river at Insula Tiberina. An important landmark from the earliest days of the Roman republic, the world's first suspension bridge was built about 700 BCE. Romans also constructed the earliest large and lasting stone bridges, most of them with their own concrete, which, strange to tell, they invented about the same time Mayan cement came into being in the mid-third century BCE. Another case of independent innovation, or could it be due to transatlantic cultural diffusion? Industrial researchers are still busy at work trying to find the lost secret of *opus caementicium* and replicate it for contemporary use, because Roman concrete was superior to modern Portland cement.

According to a report in Vintage News:

Because of its unusual durability, longevity and lessened environmental footprint, corporations and municipalities are starting to explore the use of Roman-style concrete in North America, substituting the coal fly ash with volcanic ash that has similar properties. Proponents claim that concrete made with volcanic ash can cost up to sixty per cent less, because it requires less cement, and that it has a smaller environmental footprint, due to its lower cooking temperature and much longer lifespan. Usable examples of Roman concrete exposed to harsh marine environments have been found to be two thousand years old with little or no wear. Finally, microscopic studies identified other minerals in the ancient concrete, which show potential application for high-performance concretes, including the encapsulation of hazardous wastes. The results of the study show how these improvements could be adopted in the modern world and, in particular, how they could result in a significant reduction of environmental damage caused by the manufacturing of concrete.[14]

Paulo Monteiro, a professor of civil and environmental engineering at the University of California, Berkeley, states that "manufacturing Portland cement accounts for seven percent of the carbon dioxide that industry puts into the air. In the middle twentieth century, concrete structures were designed to last fifty years, and a lot of them are on borrowed time."[15]

As mentioned above, cement requires heating a mix of limestone and clay to 1,450 degrees Celsius. When that happens, significant amounts of carbon are released into the atmosphere. Roman cement, on the other hand, used much less lime and needed to heat the limestone to just 900 degrees Celsius, which was not only more economical, because less fuel was required, but also made a far less negative ecological impact.

Figure 17.6. Among Imperial Rome's earliest and greatest concrete triumphs was the Coliseum, completed under Emperor Titus in 80 CE. Photo by Jerzy Strzelecki.

"Stronger, longer-lasting, modern concrete, made with less fuel and less release of carbon into the atmosphere," concludes Matt McGrath, environment correspondent for the British Broadcasting Corporation, "may be the legacy of a deeper understanding of how the Romans made their incomparable concrete."[16] Its superior durability derived in part by incorporating pulvis puteolanus, ash, and sand from the volcanic beds of Pozzuoli, near Naples. The brownish-yellow-gray dust with a high content of alumina and silica prevented cracks from spreading and made opus caementicium more resistant to saltwater than modern-day concrete.

Volcanic tufa was often used as an aggregate, while gypsum and quicklime served as binders. Results flourished in monumental works of art like the Pantheon, topped by the world's largest and oldest unreinforced concrete dome. Roman cement was so inherently strong, it needed no reinforcing iron or steel. After the disastrous fire of 64 CE, when extensive sections of Rome were destroyed, reconstruction was carried out with brick-faced concrete because it allowed buildings to shift slightly during subsidence or even moderate earthquakes, thereby accommodating stresses and enhancing the overall strength of the structure.

Although many of Rome's buildings sustained serious cracking from a variety of causes over time, they nonetheless continue to stand to this day. The Romans took their development of concrete another step further by inventing marine cement, which actually set under water. They found that seawater reacts with a mixture of volcanic ash and quicklime to create a rare crystal called *tobermorite,* which resists fracturing. Tobermorite has a greater strength and durability than any modern equivalent.

"It's the most durable building material in human history," Philip Brune, a researcher at DuPont Pioneer who studies the engineering of ancient Roman monuments, told the *Washington Post.* "And I say that as an engineer not prone to hyperbole."[17] Modern concrete, however, deteriorates within decades after exposure to water.

Jay Bennett of *Popular Mechanics* writes:

Ancient Roman concrete was more durable than any developed before or since. Now, some researchers are wondering if the secrets of this ancient building material could help us adapt to a world of rising seas. As global temperatures rise, sea ice is melting and causing the sea level to rise at a faster rate than during the 1900s . . . there is a high likelihood that rising sea levels will force us to reinforce infrastructure around coastal cities. Venice is already sinking. One of the most direct solutions for a coastal city is to construct a seawall. These structures do not need to hold back the ocean constantly, but rather are built to block the water from the city during high tide and storms that can cause flooding.

It turns out the ancient Romans had the perfect recipe for water-resistant concrete. . . . Researchers studying ancient Roman concrete suggest the material could be imitated with modern resources to build seawalls around cities at risk of flooding from the ocean. . . . If cities around the world are forced to build seawalls due to rising oceans, a version of Roman concrete could provide an alternative to steel structures. This enduring concrete only hardens and becomes more durable as it is exposed to the saltwater of the sea. . . . With the waves rising around us, we could have more need for this concrete than ever before.[18]

So far, however, research chemists are unable to determine the correct water/cement ratio of marine cement, although they have concluded that it was far more durable than modern-day concrete based on specimens submerged under the Mediterranean Sea for the past two thousand years at Baiae, a first-century Roman harbor in the northwestern region of the Bay of Naples. Current cement harbor construction has a maximum life span of one hundred years, and then only if regularly maintained. In contrast, Roman harbor installations have survived twenty centuries of chemical attack and wave action underwater, with no regular maintenance since they were built. It was marine cement that allowed Roman engineers to construct their famous bridges, many of which still stand.

The earliest known instance of underwater opus caementicium on a large scale took place at Caesarea Maritima, built on the northern coast of what is now the state of Israel, between 22 and 10 BCE. De Camp told of how ancient marine cement "formed a synthetic rock as hard as most natural rocks. In fact, samples of Roman concrete that have come down to modern times in buildings, conduits and the like are harder than many natural rocks would be after so many centuries of exposure."[19] In fact, it is cement that allowed Roman genius free reign to materialize some of the world's grandest monumental structures.

## ANCIENT ENGINEERS

No Roman construction was greater than the temple complex of Heliopolis Syriaca, built not in Rome, strangely enough, but on a remote eastern border of the empire between two mountain ranges in the Beqaa Valley, about fifty-three miles northeast of Beirut, Lebanon, at a place called Baalbek. Its enormous Temple of Jupiter, completed circa 60 CE, stood on a broad platform of stone raised another 23 feet above the preexisting foundation left by a former culture. Three gigantic passageways the size of railway tunnels run through the foundation for unknown purposes. A wide staircase provided access to the newly elevated platform, which measured 156.5 feet by 288 feet on top.

The temple was encircled by a peristyle—a row of pillars surrounding a space within a building, such as a court—of fifty-four unfluted Corinthian columns, ten in front and back and nineteen along each side. Three more temples, equally splendid though not as large, were dedicated to Venus, Mercury, and Bacchus. The architrave—a main beam resting across the tops of columns—and frieze blocks weighed up to 66 tons each, and one corner block weighed more than 110 tons; all of them raised to a height of more than 62 feet above the ground. The ancient walls

Figure 17.7. Baalbek's Temple of Jupiter. Image from Bruno Schulz, *Baalbek: Ergebnisse der Ausgrabungen und Untersuchungen in den Jahren 1898–1905*, 3 volumes (Berlin, Theodore Wiegand, 1921–1925).

surrounding Heliopolis Syriaca had a circumference of nearly four miles. It was situated on an immense raised plaza erected 16 feet over an earlier T-shaped base consisting of a podium, staircase, and foundation walls.

These walls comprise twenty-four monoliths, each weighing 330 tons. The tallest retaining wall, on the west side, has a second course of monoliths containing a trílithon of three stones in a row. Cut from limestone, each one weighs 888 tons and is more than 62 feet long, 14 feet high, and 12 feet wide. A fourth, still larger block, called the Stone of the Pregnant Woman, weighing 1,100 tons, lies uncut from the bedrock at a nearby quarry.

Author Hugh Newman told *Atlantis Rising* readers that

late in 2014, in the ancient quarry at Baalbek, the largest worked monolith in the world was discovered. The newly-found megalith weighs, it is estimated, an astonishing five hundred tons more than the former record holder, the Stone of the South, or Hajar el Hibla, from the same quarry, a massive twelve hundred forty-two tons. . . . Professor Janine Abdel Massih and the German Archaeological Institute made the new discovery, which has now been calculated to be sixteen hundred fifty tons. . . . Measuring 19.6 by five by six meters [64.3 by 16.4 by 19.7 feet], its profile reveals not only enormous size, but precision stone working, like that found in ancient Peru and Egypt. . . . The largest stone at Stonehenge weighs around forty-five tons. The new discovery is over thirty-six times as heavy.[20]

Not one of Baalbek's stones was too ambitious for their ancient engineers, who did not transport them to the temple complex probably because both developed serious cracks. "The biggest stone that we know of, ever moved by the Romans," says Newman, "was the Laterno obelisk, but in 27 B.C., Augustus Caesar ordered that a much larger obelisk

Figure 17.8. The largest monolith found at Baalbek.
Photo by Ralph Ellis.

(some estimates claim as much as four hundred fifty-five tons) be transported, but his engineers failed miserably, and that two hundred-thirty-ton ones were moved instead."[21]

The Romans invented and long used the most powerful crane in the ancient world. But even multiple combinations of such a machine would have been far too weak for hoisting any one of the 888-ton stones in Heliopolis Syriaca's trílithon, much less budging the 1,300-ton specimen left behind in the local quarry. Even today, only the Liebherr mobile crane, the world's most powerful version, can lift the Stone of the Pregnant Woman, but not the 200-ton-heavier block. Picking up the trílithon's 888-ton megaliths was not possible again until the late twentieth century, while the only machine capable of hoisting the 66-ton architrave reappeared around 1890. How, then, was it possible for a preindustrial people living two thousand years ago to move such impossibly heavy stone?

Referring only to the third largest of Baalbek's cut blocks, the Stone of the Pregnant Woman, Newman found mainstream archaeology's explanations unacceptable. "Forty thousand workers would be needed in order to move this huge mass. The question is, how could such a multitude have had access to the slab in order to move it? Moreover, even in this brilliant era of technology, there is not a crane in the world today that could raise this monolith from the quarry."[22]

The gigantic Temple of Jupiter and all of Classical Heliopolis Syriaca were built upon much earlier, far more monumental foundations belonging to a style entirely different from Imperial Roman construction. "These older works were not built by the Romans," states Brien Foerster, "but discovered by the Romans."[23] Who these original engineers may have been, the obvious power of the machinery they possessed, and how, why, and when they came to apply it in Lebanon's Beqaa Valley defy understanding. All that may be inferred from the surviving evidence at Baalbek is that a pre-Classical culture operated a construction technology more advanced than our own.

# 18
# Subterranean Cities

*The ancients can still speak to us with authority, even on the themes of geology and chemistry, though these studies are thought to have had their birth in modern times.*

HENRY DAVID THOREAU,
*THE JOURNAL OF HENRY DAVID THOREAU, 1837–1861,*
EDITED BY DAMION SEARLS

Carved from igneous rock, the ancient, well-preserved remains of more than two hundred subterranean cities, each one at least two stories deep, have been discovered in a historic area of Turkey known as Cappadocia. Some forty of these sanctuaries are sunk at three or more levels. Others descend in eight to twenty connected stories, with large chambers cut out of the rock for livestock, food stores, and human occupants. Underground aquifers and ventilation shafts, respectively, provided water and air. But what kind of ventilation could have effectively and continuously circulated sufficient fresh air for thousands of persons in residence as deep beneath the surface of the Earth as eighty to two hundred feet?

This question is severely complicated by the presence of livestock herds, whose methane emissions would have made life impossible for humans living with the animals in close proximity. Perishable supplies sufficient to feed an urban population daily over a protracted period of time demanded inconceivable solutions for food preservation and storage. And what of sewage disposal? Or lighting? To have carved out of the ground sunken urban projects on the vast scale of Cappadocia's subterranean cities with only the bronze hand tools supposedly available to its builders is staggering enough to consider. But seeing to the basic needs of entire populations twenty stories beneath the Earth's surface would have been at least as challenging. These fundamental questions could only have been properly answered by the application of a high technology far beyond the context of the times in which they were posed. Some solutions, at least, are self-evident, such as a huge, rolling stone capable of securing an entrance against enemies (see plate 22).

Many of these subsurface sanctuaries were used by early Anatolian Christians as hiding places from marauders or persecutors. Christian motifs, on the other hand, rarely appear at the lowest levels of the sites. The vast scale of these underground cities and the architectural prowess needed to construct them thus lead some scholars to speculate that these sites were not built by the early Christians but rather by some much more ancient culture.

Turkey's subterranean mystery began thirty million years ago, when a trio of monstrous volcanoes—much later to be named Erciyes, Hasan, and Melendiz Dadlari—erupted simultaneously. They blanketed much of Cappadocia, in central Turkey, with a 328-foot-thick layer of tufa. Tufa is a soft, easily worked, reddish lava rock some preindustrial construction engineers considered ideal for their purposes. During 1963 a resident of Derinkuyu, a town of more than ten thousand inhabitants in what today is called Nevsehir province of Turkey, was tearing down a wall of his house in the process of expanding the place. To his amazement, a broad section of tufa unexpectedly collapsed, exposing a dark, gaping cavity. He entered it with a flashlight, its beam playing over the interior of a spacious, self-evidently artificial chamber skillfully cut out of the living rock. The homeowner immediately notified local authorities.

Days later archaeologists arrived from Ankara, 390 miles away, but they were no less baffled by the accidental discovery. Their surprise ballooned into astonishment when cleaning the chamber revealed a corridor leading to an adjacent room. And then another, and another. Continuous excavation over the next six years laid bare series upon series of private domiciles, regular apartments with separate living quarters, including bathrooms. Niches had been cut into the walls, presumably for storage, perhaps for the display of ancestral or religious objects or possibly statuettes, though none were found. A network of high, broad passageways connected shops, wineries, chapels, communal or confer-ence chambers, hospitals, libraries, workspaces, oil presses, animal sta-bles, cellars, schools, bakeries, immense food bins, granaries, dinning halls, administrative centers, rubbish containment areas, arsenals, bar-racks, and tombs (see plate 23).

Wells provided fresh, flowing water throughout the complex, which was efficiently air-conditioned by regularly sunk ventilation shafts, fifty-two of which have been located so far. The longest known example sinks perfectly straight to 180 feet deep. The site's largest feature is a spacious room with a superbly carved barrel-vaulted ceiling on the sec-ond floor that archaeologists speculate was used as a religious school; smaller adjacent chambers to the west may have been studies. A verti-cal staircase from the third to fourth levels connects with a corridor descending to the lowest level, where it opens onto a cruciform alcove. There are eighteen stories in all, going down 280 feet beneath the sur-face and connected by steps and stairways regularly cut into the rock.

Each floor could be efficiently sealed off from the rest in the man-ner of a ship's compartments by massive hatches (circular doors) capa-ble of being rolled across the access to every passageway. These circular doors range from 3 to 5 feet across and 1 foot to 20 inches thick. They weigh between 440 and 1,102 pounds. A small hole drilled at the pre-cise center of all "millstones" allowed for the insertion of a handle used to open or close them. Although many floors remain unexca-vated, archaeologists have nonetheless learned enough from investigat-ing the multilevel urban center to realize that it once accommodated between thirty-five thousand and fifty thousand residents. Nothing like it had ever been seen before. But more surprises were to come.

A third-floor tunnel closed by debris, when excavated and explored, ran north in a straight line for more than three miles to yet another underground city. Kaymakli appears to be smaller, with the uppermost five of its six levels excavated to date, although its resemblance to Derinkuyu leaves no doubt that both sites belonged to the same people. Also known as Ozluce, Kaymakli differs chiefly by its engineers' choice of variously colored tufas for obvious aesthetic effect, a preference extended to the main entrance formed by a pair of serpentine arches made of intertwining basalt. Passing through them, a fifty-foot-long passageway terminates at a millstone door of solid granite—at nearly six feet across, larger than any counterpart at Derinkuyu. Expanding their research, investigators were shocked to discover that Kaymakli-Ozluce was just one of five interconnected cities with a total estimated capacity of one hundred thousand inhabitants.

Even these, however, were not the only such locations nor even the largest. Others in and around Nevsehir include Özkonak, in the northern slopes of Mount Idis, capable of supporting sixty thousand persons for up to three months without resort to outside supplies. A unique feature of Özkonak is its built-in communication system of speaking tubes connecting all ten levels, down to more than 130 feet. The subterranean location was found in 1972 by Latif Acar, a local farmer who, curious to learn why his excess crop water continued to mysteriously disappear into the ground, dug a shallow hole that opened into the roof of the complex's largest room.

Three years later another buried metropolis inadvertently came to light just outside the village of Tatlarin, at a hill known for time out of mind, for no previously apparent cause, as the Castle. So, too, the people of Derinkuyu traditionally and appropriately knew their town as the Deep Well, countless generations before the mid-twentieth-century discovery of its lost ruins. Despite the passage of unknown centuries and their accompanying cultural amnesia, something of vanished antiquity still resonates in local place-names. Turkey's most recent subterranean site was discovered during June 2017 outside Kayseri, a large, industrialized city in central Anatolia. Composed of fifty-two chambers and wider than a football field, the complex is larger in area than either Derinkuyu or Kaymakli. How many more mysterious urban centers remain to be found is anyone's guess. Altogether, archaeologists count more than two hundred of them in the area between Kayseri and Nevsehir.

About forty underground cities contain three floors; fewer have just two levels each. Estimates place Cappadocia's subterranean population at about three million residents. Even if this figure is substantially reduced, because not all the subsurface living centers were simultaneously inhabited nor even built at the same time, it still represents a staggering number of persons who chose a molelike existence. What could have compelled them to make such a drastic decision? Who were they, and how long ago did they excavate their incredible underground urban warrens? How could these subterranean cities have survived major or even total destruction by earthquakes in seismically active Turkey? Strangely enough, none of them shows any such damage.

While adequately provided with water and ventilation, their lighting source is another mystery. Candles and torches—even dim lamps—for so many thousands of residents dwelling hundreds of feet from the surface would have consumed considerable oxygen in a very short time. Strangely, no wax or oil residue or lanterns have so far been found at any of the sites below the second or third strata. Some ceilings at the topmost floors evidence scorching by torches, but these marks do not occur at lower levels, where lighting was most needed but the torches' flames would have consumed most of the breathable air in a fairly short period. So what, then, did the lower-level inhabitants use for illumination?

For some years after Derinkuyu's emergence, it and other companion settlements were assumed to have been built by Christians as places of refuge from Persian Sassanid raiders from the late fifth to early seventh centuries CE. Retrieved monastic artifacts from the Middle Byzantine period appeared to confirm this interpretation. The area of Cappadocia in question had been converted four hundred years earlier by Saint Paul himself, according to legend, and walls belonging to the upper stories of some subterranean locations are decorated with Christian religious imagery. But archaeologists soon noticed that the Christian influences were intrusive and only infrequently penetrated deeper than the uppermost levels. Derinkuyu's bottom-floor cruciform alcove was not necessarily Christian, because cruciform designs, even similarly configured chambers, were of course commonly associated with solar symbolism, predating Christianity by millennia.

Examples are found at the numerous cruciform passage graves of west Wales and Orkney, built during the later Neolithic period beginning around the mid-fourth millennium BCE, and often, like Ireland's Newgrange, deliberately oriented to sunrise on the winter solstice. Scholars interested in the Turkish sites additionally pointed out that the earliest known written reference to Derinkuyu was composed by Xenophon, the famous historian and philosopher. In *Anabasis,* he described an entire Greek expedition against the Persians in Asia Minor, where he and his comrades stumbled upon the underground city, already old and abandoned around the turn of the fourth century BCE.[1] He assumed it had been built by Phrygians some three hundred years earlier, an official position later taken by the Turkish Department of Culture.

The Phrygians were close relatives of the Greeks and had a homeland in the southern Balkans where they were originally known as the Bryges. In possession of an advanced Bronze Age culture, they contributed importantly to pre-Classical and Classical music, including the so-called Phrygian mode found in Greek marches, and the invention of the famous aulos, a reed instrument frequently taking the form of twin pipes. For causes unknown, they migrated en masse across the Hellespont into Asia Minor, probably not before the mid- to late fourteenth century BCE, when they changed their tribal name to Phrygians and declared themselves allies of Troy. Ilion's Queen Hecuba, who reigned during the Trojan War, was of Phrygian descent. In the political vacuum following that conflict, the Phrygians established a state for the first time, building Gordium, in Cappadocia, as its rich capital.

Throughout the following centuries, their kingdom rose to military, political, economic, and cultural splendor, until it and much of Asia Minor were overrun by hordes of Cimmerians. These were equestrian nomads, barbarians from Ukraine, who sacked and burned Gordium in 696 BCE. Modern scholars presume that the violent circumstances surrounding the city's demise forced its residents to devise underground shelters. While some defeated Phrygians, like Christians many centuries later, may have sought refuge from their enemies by taking advantage of the buried mazes, they were not the earliest to inhabit such places. Nor were the Phrygians, for all their civilized greatness, known for subterranean skills of any kind.

Another earlier people renowned for the excavation of long tunnels and deep storage facilities left physical evidence behind at the lowest, oldest levels throughout Nevsehir province. These were the Hittites, whose cylinder seals, inscribed monuments, and painted murals are still being found in Derinkuyu, Kaymakli, and other related underground cities. Outstanding is the stone statue of a lion, emblazoned with Hittite script, found beside one of the entrances to Özkonak. According to American traveler Jamie Mead, "the Hittites had a high standard of underground building techniques and constructed many military tunnels. The secret tunnels found in Hittite cities are called *poterns* . . . part of the defense systems . . . used to ambush attackers."[2] At the Hittites' capital city, Hattusa, they dug nine poterns, the longest being 235 feet deep.

But who were the Hittites? Their name has long been familiar for its repeated mention throughout the Old Testament. Although biblical descriptions are mostly lacking, a passage in Genesis 23:1–20 tells how Abraham purchased a cave or underground resting place for his deceased wife from Ephron the Hittite. The Hittites were otherwise absolutely unknown until the discovery of their inscription on a stone monument outside the Cappadocian town of Bogazköy (Gorge Village) by an Irish missionary, William Wright, in 1884. For the next twelve years, Turkish officialdom's hostility toward foreigners prevented further digs, until German archaeologist Hugo Winckler was eventually given permission to excavate in 1906.

He almost immediately unearthed a treasure trove of ancient documents: the Hittites' royal archive of ten thousand cuneiform tablets written in Akkadian cuneiform script but in an unknown language. But neither Winckler nor his colleagues were able to read them for more than forty years.

In late 1947 a bookkeeper at the German hospital in Istanbul awoke from a dream in which he was shown the key to translating the lost written language. With no formal training, but personally obsessed with everything Hittite, Franz Steinherr conveyed his information to professional epigraphers, who confirmed the correctness of his remarkable revelation. Since then, the previously inscrutable records have yielded a vivid picture of the rise and fall of a Bronze Age superpower—history's first true empire. Bogazköy itself proved to be near the site of the imperial capital, one of the greatest cities of the pre-Classical world. Hattusa, according to history writer Jim Hicks, "covered more than four hundred acres [464 acres, to be exact], making it much larger than the contemporary Assyrian capital of Assur in northern Mesopotamia. Dominated by palaces and temples, it was unlike any other known city of the ancient world."[3]

The city featured at least thirty-one religious buildings, the largest being more than 213,300 square feet. As Thomas Harrison, author of *Great Empires of the Ancient World,* describes it, "the palace of the king was built on the city's acropolis and now known as *Bueyukkale* (Turkish for 'big castle'). All those who had business with 'his majesty,' including vassal rulers and representatives of foreign kings, were escorted by royal attendants through a series of colonnaded courts to a large pillared hall, the focal point of the palace complex, where the king gave audience."[4]

Main access was on the south side through elaborate, high, oval, stone gateways decorated with reliefs depicting oversize warriors, lions, and sphinxes. Cemeteries, mostly containing cremation burials in funeral urns, were located outside the walls. Private homes built with timber and mud bricks accommodated a population of fifty thousand. Emperors in Hattusa, according to Hicks, ruled "from the Aegean to beyond the Euphrates in Mesopotamia, north to the Black Sea and south to the plains of Syria, where their armies encountered, contested and rolled back the borders of the rival Egyptian empire."[5]

The Hittites first entered Anatolia, Turkey's central plateau region, as an Indo-European tribe from their ancestral homelands in the steppes of central Russia about four thousand years ago. Over the centuries their population grew in numbers and sophistication through a gradual transition from nomadic to village life, adopting Babylonian cuneiform and developing the civilized arts, including their own hieroglyphic system and the first wide-scale use of iron tools and weapons. At about 1700 BCE they established their first dynasty and initiated an imperial agenda that would lead inexorably to their domination of Asia Minor and northern Mesopotamia.

Five hundred years later, in the midst of their expansion and at the zenith of their influence, the Hittite empire collapsed overnight in one of the unexplained mysteries of the ancient world. Archaeologists speculated that northern tribes of Kassite barbarians or waves of the no-less-shadowy Sea Peoples must have been responsible. But more than physical evidence is lacking for these assumed invaders. No outside enemies in the contemporary world would have been powerful enough to break up such a powerful state. Hattusa itself was virtually impregnable. Hicks writes:

> Standing three thousand feet above sea level on a rugged tableland, snow-covered in winter, scorched by the blazing sun in summer and ringed by mountains infested with wolves and bears, the Hittites' capital bore an anachronistic similarity to a medieval fortress. And a fortress it was. The site it occupied was itself a natural stronghold, a steeply sloping tongue of land set off from the surrounding country on one side by a deep protective gorge . . . and on the other side by a narrow valley. Also guarding the city were its double, crenellated

walls [four miles long, interspaced every sixty-five feet with immense guard towers manned by troops of archers]—built of massive stone, topped by brick battlements, pierced by arch-like gateways and punctuated at intervals by tall towers.[6]

Even an armed force more powerful than the Hittite army (there was none) could not have stormed so formidable a capital. It would have required a long siege, which never took place. Instead, Hattusa was instantly transformed into a vast cauldron of flame, incinerated from end to end in a flash, its stones literally carbonized by temperatures higher than anything Late Bronze Age technology was capable of generating. The city was not alone. All across the Aegean, Asia Minor, and the Near East, virtually every human settlement, large and small, was incinerated. The vast scope of such universal arson was clearly far beyond the combined military might of all contemporary kingdoms. The far-flung conflagrations were accompanied by environmental cataclysms. Earth's largest soda lake, Turkey's Lake Van, rose 250 feet in about two years. Climatologists calculated that such an increase would have required approximately 150 inches of rainfall.

Tree-ring sequences showed that climate deterioration reached its peak in Turkey from about 1185 to 1141 BCE. Major earthquake damage and fire spread through Athens, Mycenae, Tiryns, Knossos, Troy, Urgarit, and Cyprus.[7] Meanwhile, the Arabian Peninsula suffered the most extensive volcanism in its history. At its peak, Assyrian power declined precipitously from about 1208 to 1179 BCE. This is known to historians as the Bronze Age collapse. These contemporaneous natural events puzzled scholars until the close of the past century, when archaeoastronomers and geophysicists found that Earth experienced the near miss of a comet in 1198 BCE.

Swedish geologists Lars Franzen and Thomas B. Larsson felt compelled by the evidence to "propose that cosmic activity could offer an explanation for the observed changes. We even suggest that relatively large asteroids or comets (about 0.5 km diameter)" collided with our planet circa 1200 BCE. They were seconded by the American geologist Robert Hewitt, who described the end of the Bronze Age as "a catastrophe that was one of the worst in world history."[8]

He cited Greenland's Camp Century ice cores, which reveal that a global disaster threw several thousand cubic kilometers of ash into the atmosphere around that time. Michael Baillie, professor emeritus of palaeoecology at Queen's University of Belfast in Northern Ireland and a leading expert in dendrochronology, the science of dating by means of tree rings, concluded that "there were two major temperature troughs around 1600 B.C. and 1100 B.C." The latter, "the most marked one, can be traced in many other parts of the world, including Europe, the Americas, the Near East and the Antarctic."[9]

The Harris Papyrus—a well-preserved court document from the end of Egypt's Twentieth Dynasty—reports prodigious clouds of ash overwhelming the Nile valley from the west at the time of Pharaoh Ramses III's coronation in 1198 BCE. At the close of the previous dynasty (1197 BCE), Pharaoh Seti II described Sekhmet as "a circling star" that spat flames throughout the known world.[10] Another ancient Egyptian record—the Ipuwer Papyrus—describes fiery destruction rampaging across Egypt. Its veracity is underscored by a baked-clay text from the port city of Ugarit telling of Anat, a star that fell on "the Syrian land, setting it afire, and confusing the two twilights."[11]

These ancient source materials complement conclusions by modern geophysicists and astronomers, who determined that a comet event around the turn of the twelfth century BCE extinguished Bronze Age civilizations throughout the Greek Peloponnesus, Nile valley, Mesopotamia, and Asia Minor. Among the victims were the Hittites. They were the creators of Cappadocia's underground cities. But why did they construct them? To escape the ravages of their enemies, who overran the ruins of an imperial enterprise abruptly reduced to ashes by a natural catastrophe? Or to seek shelter from that cataclysm itself? Like so many other lingering questions about this lost, mysterious people, they took their answers with them into the past.

# 19
# Tunneling into Antiquity

*One only passes from the darkness of ignorance to the enlightenment of science if one re-reads with ever-increasing love the works of the ancients. Let the dogs bark, let the pigs grunt! I will nonetheless be a disciple of the ancients. All my care will be for them and the dawn will see me studying them.*

PETER OF BLOIS (CIRCA 1130 TO CIRCA 1211),
*THE LETTER COLLECTIONS OF PETER OF BLOIS,*
EDITED BY LENA WAHLGREN

Although just when Derinkuyu or Kaymakli were constructed is unknown, they were not the first subterranean settlements. A vast grid of deep tunnels was created by Stone Age workmen at least as long ago as the close of the last glacial epoch. "Across Europe," stated Heinrich Kusch, professor of prehistory at Austria's Karl-Franzen University in Graz, "there were thousands of these tunnels, from the north, in Scotland, down to the Mediterranean. They are interspersed with nooks; at some places, where areas are larger, there is seating, or storage chambers, and rooms. They do not all link up, but taken together, it is a massive, underground network."[1]

Kusch discovered the subterranean system in the mid-1980s, when he and his wife, Ingrid, were examining a shallow, well-known chamber, one among many found throughout Austria and dug during the Middle Ages in the region of Styria. A dry-stone wall at the far end of the sunken room blocked further passage, because it prevented access to Satan on the other side, according to medieval lore. With permission from local church authorities, Heinrich and Ingrid carefully dismantled the five-hundred-year-old partition, which opened up to a long tunnel entirely unlike the small chamber. Pursuing their exploration, they noticed that regular, lineal striations on the walls were consistent with tool marks made at other similar locations during the early Neolithic era, around twelve thousand years ago.

Suspicions were confirmed when the couple found a small stone cup from the same period. For the rest of the twentieth century and into the next, they expanded their subterranean investigations across Austria and Germany into Brittany and Scotland. To their surprise, literally hundreds of megalithic sites found in these widely separated countries had been positioned above or near tunnels of various lengths

Figure 19.1. Inside one of Austria's Neolithic tunnels discovered by Heinrich Kusch and his wife, Ingrid. Photo by Josef Weichenberger.

averaging about twenty-eight inches wide. "In Bavaria alone," Kusch said, "we have found two thousand two hundred thirty feet of these underground networks. In Styria, we have found a tunnel one thousand one hundred fifty feet long."[2]

He still cannot determine their function, speculating only that they may have been spiritually linked somehow with the megaliths above them, or perhaps they allowed travel on foot to avoid encounters with enemies or dangerous beasts. His findings were only published after thirty years of research. Skeptics claim that the underground features all date to the Middle Ages, although no one is unable to connect those much longer, stylistically dissimilar sections to the medieval churchmen who ordered them walled up. Ground-penetrating acoustical studies conducted by certified geologists at several randomly selected Austrian tunnels have confirmed that those diggings identified by Kusch as Neolithic were, in fact, originally excavated between five thousand and twelve thousand years ago. He and Ingrid are currently unable to determine their full extent because they continue to make new discoveries, which suggest a work extending over at least several hundred miles beneath the surface of Western Europe. More certainly, the magnitude of such an undertaking bespeaks an organized labor force and excavation technology far beyond the presumed limitations of Stone Age capabilities.

## UNDERGROUND SECRET OF THE PHARAOHS

Better known are the subterranean skills displayed by ancient Egyptian engineers, particularly at the Serapeum, the place of Serapis, the god of abundance and resurrection. His funerary complex lies northwest of the Pyramid of Djoser at Sakkara, near Memphis in the Lower Nile valley. It is a rock-cut complex of burial chambers allegedly for embalmed bulls sacred to Ptah, the god of craftsmen and architects (see plate 24).

The Serapeum consists of an underground corridor 328 feet long, flanked on both sides by crypts in which the coffins of the bulls were said to have been enclosed. They still contain what Egyptologists refer to as sarcophagi of polished black or red granite, each hewn from a single block. They average some 13 feet in length, 7.5 feet wide, and 11 feet tall. The boxes weigh seventy tons minus their lids, which are thirty tons each, equal in weight to three fully loaded Sherman tanks. The subterranean site features twenty-four boxes, implying that they may have collectively symbolized the hours in a day, though their possible association with Serapis or Ptah is unclear. Whatever initial intentions were responsible for the vast underground necropolis, its construction details are truly staggering.

While exploring the Serapeum in 1995, Christopher Dunn pressed his measuring instrument against the highly polished interior of one of the coffers.

The edge of the parallel was accurate to within 0.00002 inch (0.005 millimeter), or 1/10 the thickness of a human hair. . . . I placed the edge of my precision-ground parallel against the surface— and I saw that it was dead flat. There was no light showing through the interface of the steel and the stone, as there would be if the surface was concave, and the steel did not rock back and forth, as it would if the surface was convex. To put it mildly, I was astounded. I did not expect to find such exactitude, because this order of precision is not necessary for the sarcophagus of a bull—or any other animal or human. I slid the parallel along the surface both horizontally and vertically, and there was no deviation from a true flat surface. The flatness was similar to precision-ground surface plates that are used in manufacturing for the verification of exactly machined parts for tools, gauges, and myriad other products that require extremely accurate surfaces and dimensions.[3]

He next brought to bear a solid precision square with a fourteen-inch blade calibrated to within a 0.00005 inch, or 0.00127 millimeter. "When I shined a flashlight behind the blade, I did not detect any gap or imprecision on either the lid or the inside surface of the box."[4] Its level of perfection was inhuman. When examining the inside corners

Figure 19.2. Incredibly machined interior of a Serapeum box.
Photo by Ovedc.

of the granite receptacles, Dunn discovered that they had been evenly, smoothly, and uniformly rounded out to a radius of 4 millimeters (0.15748 inches)—physically impossible for any hand tool but clear evidence of high-powered machining at its most sophisticated.

He wondered if such a container could be exactly replicated by state-of-the-art industrial capabilities and so forwarded his collected findings and photographs of the underground necropolis to Tri-Star Corporation, a Minnesota-based manufacturer of granite surface plates, angle plates, V-blocks, and machine bases. The corporation's chief engineer responded by saying "that Tri-Star did not have the equipment to create this box, and that they would have to create it in five pieces, then ship it to its destination and bolt it together on site."[5] The external and internal dimensions of a Serapeum container deviate by 1/1000th of an inch, beyond the reach of modern manufacturing techniques. The tool responsible for such extraordinarily high precision in tight corners was the equivalent of a dentist drill capable of cutting through granite.

The site is unquestionably an underground repository for the results of some lost engineering science unmatched by all subsequent manufacturing technology, including our own. Its capacious chambers enclose stone containers of immense but finely crafted proportions said to have once entombed the mummified remains of sacred bulls consecrated to Serapis. If so, their ritual burial here was the ceremonial work of Ptolemaic cultists, who did not create but instead used the gigantic chests for religious and political purposes other than those of the original builders millennia earlier. In point of fact, no mummified remains of any animal were ever discovered in the Serapeum, although a single human burial, as described below, was found. The rest of the stone boxes were empty save three or four, which contained only ox bones.

From these singular finds, Egyptologists jump to the conclusion that every chest was a sarcophagus for its own mummy of a bull. Coffins for man or beast elsewhere throughout the Nile valley were invariably tight fitting, with just enough room for the corpse. Yet the internal spaces of those at the Serapeum greatly and untypically exceed even the largest bull. An annex built by Ptolemaic rulers millennia after the Serapeum was constructed does feature mummified bull burials, but their sarcophagi bear no resemblance to the site's far older huge granite boxes and are indistinguishable from any other cramped dynastic coffins. Clearly the massive containers served some other purpose. It might be revealed in the context of the Serapeum's surroundings at Sakkara, a vast burial ground for residents of Memphis, the capital of ancient Egypt.

Located about nineteen miles south of modern-day Cairo, Sakkara encloses the pyramids of seventeen kings—most famously, Djoser's step pyramid—in a one-by-four-mile area additionally populated by the numerous funeral monuments of high officials. As some indication of the massive expanse of the necropolis and its sustained use across the millennia, an international team of researchers in 2011 uncovered almost eight million animal mummies there. Accordingly, Sakkara was the focus of major construction efforts requiring extensive labor energies from the earliest dynasties over many centuries. How did the Serapeum fit into such a busy city of the dead?

In light of high-technological skills exhibited by the ancient Egyptians, a plausible answer was provided in 2018 by Konstantin

Borisov, a Ph.D. in electrical engineering from Mississippi State University.[6] Because they had already mastered fermentation processes for brewing alcoholic beverages and making eatable starches by their First Dynasty, he suggested that they closed bread, beer, barley, and ox meat inside the Serapeum's stone coffers. As fermentation set in, yeast began to convert the starch present in the barley to carbon dioxide gas and ethanol. Essential for yeast to grow and maintain its developing rate over time is oleic acid, present in the ox meat. Oleic acid also negates the toxic effects of ethanol, a by-product of the fermentation process.

Continuous accumulation of confined carbon dioxide gas steadily raised pressures inside the box, which was made to withstand more than sixty thousand PSI—that's two-and-a-half times as heavy as the anchor of a cruise ship, an average fully loaded cement truck, or locomotive—before its thirty-ton lid could be dislodged. Since tolerance between the cover and the rim of the box on which it rested was within one micron, the receptacle was effectively hermetically sealed, preventing any gas from seeping out and ensuring the accrual of pressure. Resistance could be increased for building higher pressures by piling additional weight atop the lid, itself designed with a raised, reinforced platform for accommodating heavy loads. Six courses of stones were, in fact, originally layered on top of at least one lidded chest, as observed by Auguste Mariette, a French archaeologist who discovered the Serapeum in 1851.

He was also the first researcher to investigate its boxes, all of them empty save one containing the mummy of Khaemweset, a king who restored the underground complex circa 1220 BCE, and another not filled with ceremoniously mummified bulls but its floor indiscriminately scattered with ox bones; these alone of all other ingredients and their by-products would not have been consumed by the yeast. Pharaonic sarcophagi were made to fit the form of the deceased and carved from local limestone, far more ready at hand and much less difficult to work than the Serapeum's untypically oversized coffers of granite and even harder diorite, transported—at what must have been extraordinary difficulty—from quarries five hundred and seven hundred miles away.

Rose granite and diorite were deliberately chosen, not only because they were supremely strong and dense enough to contain thirty tons of pressure and prevent gas from seeping through their pores but also for their high-density crystalline structure (see plate 25).

Piezoelectricity is an electrical charge that accumulates in crystals responding to applied mechanical stress. Fermentation inside the Serapeum's chests exerted pressure on their crystalline enclosure to generate piezoelectric discharges. Notches cut into the close-fitting

Figure 19.3. 1885 illustration of an extra-weighted Serapeum box.
Image from Karl Baedeker, *Egypt: Handbook for Traveling.*
*Part I Lower Egypt, with the Fayum and the Peninsula of Sinai*
(Leipsic, 1885), 382.

chambers containing the boxes are precisely parallel to the edges of each lid, allowing the covers to be rotated on the rims of the coffers, thereby exposing their interior for periodic maintenance; that is, scrubbing out residue from used-up ingredients and replacing them with fresh bread, beer, barley, and ox meat. Although French physicists Jacques and Pierre Curie are credited with the discovery of piezoelectricity in 1880, their find was preceded, according to Borisov, by ancient electrical engineers who buried two dozen massive static-charge batteries connected in series at Sakkara thousands of years ago.

No place throughout the Nile valley was more in need of such a power supply for the numerous machining tools, as described by Christopher Dunn, that built and fashioned so large a concentration of pyramids and funeral monuments at Egypt's foremost city of the dead. Walls and ceilings of royal or aristocratic burial sites there were invariably covered with lengthy hieroglyphic quotations from the Book of the Dead or other sacred texts and illustrated by paintings or sculpted bas-relief that surrounded collected grave goods, statuary, and richly decorated sarcophagi. By sharp contrast, the Serapeum's barren, rough-hewn corridors show neither polishing nor finishing.

There are no images of men or gods, no decoration of any kind, and its scanty hieroglyphs are of uncommonly poor quality, obviously added by someone centuries after the site was constructed. In short, the Serapeum less resembles a ceremonial mortuary than a purely functional utility; and that was its original identity. Its eighteen hundred years of oblivion beneath the desert sands suggest comparable power stations await their discovery at other dynastic urban centers, where evidence of monumental machining is being recognized. Skeptics argue that Borisov's characterization of the Serapeum's granite boxes as piezoelectric batteries are unlike any electric generators with which we are familiar.

"When we try to envision past energy systems," Dunn points out, "we have many layers of cultural blinders to see through. As we search through the remnants of ancient Egypt looking for the power plants that provided energy to the machine tools that accurately shaped the granite blocks on the Giza Plateau, or the granite boxes in the rock tunnels at Sakkara, we cannot assume that their power plants looked like ours, or that the infrastructure supporting the distribution of energy was the same. Considering the extremely tenuous circumstances by which inventions are developed, promoted and utilized, it would be very surprising to find an ancient artifact, or evidence of an artifact, that is identical to one we use or have used in the recent past."[7]

## EMPERORS OF WATER MANAGEMENT

A much later, if nonetheless extraordinary, excavation was undertaken by Roman Emperor Vespasian during the late first century CE. His imperial predecessors had been stymied in their efforts to save the city of Seleucia Pieria, a vital entrepôt for the commercial wealth of Asia Minor, from yearly inundation. Its unfortunate location at the mouth of the Asi River lay directly in the path of an estuary of the mighty Orontes, between smaller rivers on the western slopes of the Coryphaeus Mountains in southern Turkey on the Mediterranean coast near the border with Syria. Each spring, these rivers combined to disastrously overflow themselves and close down Seleucia Pieria with an irrepressible deluge of silt that could only be cleared at great expense. Several large canals installed to redirect flooding were annually overwhelmed despite continuous improvements.

To succeed where they consistently failed, Vespasian ordered a diversionary channel cut into the Nur Mountains more than twenty miles southwest of the port city to outflank the swollen rivers. Doing so, however, entailed digging at least three-quarters of a mile through sold rock, something even Roman military engineers had never attempted before, until technical progress in tempered steel produced mining tools unmatched for hardness until the advent of the Industrial Revolution seventeen hundred years later. Vespasian's project would not be a standard relief canal but a more complex system designed to keep pace with rising water levels by lowering them through a step-by-step integration

Figure 19.4. Ruins of the city of Seleucia Pieria. Photo by Htkava.

of cooperative components. These consisted of a water diversion system that included a regulatory dam, the first tunnel section connected by a short intermediary channel to a second section emptying into a long discharge channel.

Nothing like these advanced hydraulics had been designed before, nor would their like be applied again until many centuries after Rome fell. Work began toward the end of Vespasian's reign, but he did not live to see its completion. Nor did his son, Titus, who dispatched additional laborers, legionnaires, sailors, and prisoners of war to the Nur Mountains enterprise. Finally, after Antoninus Pius ascended the throne in 138 CE, he had his name carved in rock, appropriately enough, near the end of the discharge channel, the last piece of construction. No less properly, at the entrance of the first tunnel section, he ordained an inscription reading, "Divine Vespasian and Divine Titus made it."[8]

The lengthy, arduous project kept Seleucia Pieria free from silt and functioning year-round for the next seventeen centuries, until a new dam diverted the River Orontes away from the site of the ancient harbor in 1882, leaving the ingenious water-management complex high and dry in the Nur Mountains. The 4,593-foot-long Vespasianus Titus Tunnel was still the longest on Earth until that same year, when the Gotthard Rail Tunnel connected northern and southern Switzerland, and then only as the result of the first large-scale use of dynamite. During its ten years of construction, some two hundred men were killed and hundreds more injured, with another four shot to death and thirteen wounded by Swiss Army troops crushing a strike halfway into completion of the project.

Although all three emperors suffered much lower labor attrition during the same length of time needed to finish the Roman effort, and they never resorted to such extreme measures against their own workers, Turkey's 1,880-year-old hydraulic engineering marvel is still in fundamentally good condition. Its excavation and operation were made possible by technological advances in a remarkably similar challenge confronting the ancient inhabitants of Sichuan, China.

## THE IMMORTAL FISH MOUTH LEVEE

Sichuan China was annually deluged by the largest and longest (at 457 miles) of the Yangtze tributaries, the Minjiang, which swelled with springtime meltwater high up in the mountains and overflowed all the smaller rivers below, devastating vast croplands and inundating dozens of cities and hundreds of villages. After a particularly disastrous flood, Li Bing, the governor of Shu for the state of Qin, determined to build a massive dam against future catastrophes but was prevented by the military authorities from doing so, because keeping the waterways open was vital for supply ships carrying goods to troops on guard at the frontier. As an alternative, rather than simply damming the rampaging Minjiang, he planned instead to harness it by inventing an artificial levee for channeling and dividing the water. "Dredge the riverbed when the water is deep," was his guiding principle, "and build low dykes when the water is low."[9]

Li Bing's Dujiangyan system—named after the capital city—was originally known as the Yuzui, which translates to "Fish Mouth Levee" for its conical head resembling the mouth of a fish. It divided the water into inner and outer streams; the former was deep and narrow, while the outer stream was relatively shallow but wide. Their arrangement carried 60 percent of the river's overflow into an irrigation system during the dry season. When too much water threatened, spillage was reduced to 40 percent. An outer stream drained away the rest, flushing out much of the silt and sediment that caused the water to otherwise back up, overflow, and inundate farm fields and living areas. The Yuzui was built from hundreds of thousands of *zhulongs*—long sausage-shaped baskets of woven bamboo filled with stones—and held in place by wooden tripods known as *macha*.

The Yuzui's inner and outer streams connected with a *feishayan* (flying sand weir). Its 656-foot-wide opening ensured against flooding by allowing the natural swirling flow of the river to drain out excess water from the inner to the outer stream. The feishayan also flushed out silt and sediment the outer stream failed to catch. Construction of the Yuzui alone required thirty-eight thousand workers—mostly exiles from lands conquered by the Qin, as well as the local population—and took four years to build. But it was inoperable unless a channel could be cut through Mount Yulei for discharging excess water to the dry Chengdu Plain beyond.

The mountain proved impenetrable against third-century-BCE mining tools, and further progress on the Dujiangyan project was frustrated until Li Bing ordered several large furnaces installed above the site. They heated great bronze cauldrons of boiling water and spilled them over the rock face and immediately thereafter doused it with vats of frigid water. Alternately heating and cooling broke apart the boulders, reducing them to removable fragments, but the procedure was painstaking. The Baopingkou (Bottle-Neck Channel) took eight years of nonstop labor to penetrate sixty-six feet of Mount Yulei. With the channel completed in 256 BCE, the system was finished. It replaced

Figure 19.5. Dujiangyan's massive water-management project.
Photo by Gjl.

yearly flooding with regulated irrigation, making Sichuan province the most productive agricultural region in all China.

Some indication of the project's millennial strength came to light on May 12, 2008, when a severe earthquake cracked but did not seriously damage the Yuzui. In fact, the levee was so well made that it is still in use today, irrigating more than two thousand square miles of farmland, draining floods, and providing water resources for more than fifty cities after the last 2,276 years of continuous operation. As such, Dujiangyan is the sole surviving water-management system from antiquity. No other wonder of the ancient world continues to function as originally designed. More than two hundred years after he died, Li Bing was honored by his likeness being placed in the Min River. When the river rose above the statue's shoulders, a coming flood was indicated; falling beneath its calves, the river foretold impending drought. After the fall of the Han Dynasty, during which the memorial artwork had been commissioned, it vanished until recovered from the river in 1974,

Figure 19.6. The long-lost Li Bing statue.
Photo by Mutt.

thereafter placed on public display as the oldest known stone statue of a Chinese man.

## INGENIOUS IRRIGATIONISTS

The engineering genius of Iran's Kura-Araxes culture endures, as described by Childress: "Some three thousand years ago, the ancient Persians discovered a method of digging underground aqueducts that would bring mountain groundwater to their arid plains. Still extant and still functional, the system of irrigation provides seventy-five percent of the water used in Iran today."[10]

A no-longer-operable but yet more massive waterworks was the Pathariecolorn, described by *Scientific American* magazine as "seven miles long, three hundred feet broad, and sixty feet high," making it history's longest, widest reservoir. Although Arizona's Hoover Dam, taller at 726 feet, is the largest of its kind in the world today. With a total length of 1,244 feet and 45 feet across, it is still shorter and narrower than its ancient predecessor in Malaya Rata, a mountainous jungle area of central Sri Lanka.

"The huge tank is but one of a great many scattered over the country and had been erected for irrigation. The tank was faced throughout its entire length with layers of squared stones. It is partly in ruins, as the waters flow freely out of a huge breach two hundred feet wide, which appears to have been made centuries ago. The race that constructed these tanks has passed away, and the country where, at one time, there existed a highly civilized and skillful engineering people, is now the abode of wild Veddahs, a race whose homes are in tents, and who wander about from place to place." Robert Knox, a seventeenth century English sea captain captured by the Veddahs, knew them as "wild men" from personal experience. "An engineer has calculated that it would cost more than $4 million [$125,702,564 current value] to construct the front embankment of this huge water reservoir."[11] Today only scattered fragments of the Pathariecolorn hidden beneath undergrowth attest to the former greatness of a lost civilization.

Water management was a particularly urgent concern in western South America, where increasing drought imperiled the continuous existence of the Nazca people residing in coastal Peru more than two thousand years ago. Encroaching desert conditions challenged them to devise methods of water collection unprecedented for originality and efficacy. Most ingenious among these attempts were the *puquios* ("fountains" in Spanish, their original Nazca name is unknown)—large spiraling holes with carefully constructed rock walls (see plate 26). "Recent research based on satellite imagery," Kenyon reports, "has now established that the puquios cleverly harnessed Peru's abundant wind to lift water out of vast underground aquifers. According to Rosa Lasaponara of the Institute of Methodologies for Environmental Analysis in Italy, the system was once much more developed, and water was effectively channeled into pools and canals for many uses."[12]

The puquios are buried funnels corkscrewing into the earth,

allowing strong winds blowing over their wide openings to create a difference in atmospheric pressure for drawing natural subterranean aquifer water upward to ground level, where spillage is caught in channels leading to reservoirs for collection. Lasaponara, Nicola Masini, and their team, in cooperation with archaeologist Giuseppe Orefici, found clear evidence that the puquio system must previously have been much more developed than it appears today. Satellite imagery also revealed additional, previously unknown puquios in the Nazca drainage basin. Like ancient China's Dujiangyan levee, most of the thirty-six known puquios are still functioning and even relied upon by local people to bring freshwater into the arid desert. No puquios have been excavated so far, nor their original numbers ascertained, although Lasaponara and her colleagues are certain that the ancient Peruvians constructed a network of water-retrieval structures that was subsequently buried under the desert that inevitably consumed Nazca civilization.

# 20

# The Great
# High-Tech Mystery

*There is no question that the Great Pyramid is the most sophisticated and precise of all the structures on the Giza Plateau, and, frankly, of all buildings in the world.*

CHRISTOPHER DUNN,
LOST TECHNOLOGIES OF ANCIENT EGYPT

"Could you build Egypt's Great Pyramid today?" The question was put to Jon Adams Jerde, chief architect of Minnesota's Mall of America, the largest of its kind in the United States.

"With modern building facilities and methods," he replied, "perhaps. But if I was restricted to using the tools of the time, the answer is no."[1]

Observers such as Jerde have an appreciation of the Great Pyramid others less familiar with the scope of its construction lack. At an original height of 480.95 feet, the Great Pyramid was the tallest manmade structure in the world until New York's Flatiron Building was completed in 1902, but its volume of eighty-eight million cubic feet remained unsurpassed until larger interior spaces were created beginning in the late twentieth century.

Figure 20.1.
Author's photograph of
the Great Pyramid.

With a perimeter of 3,023.13 feet, the Great Pyramid covers 13.11 acres, a space equivalent to seven midtown blocks in New York City. Thirty Empire State Buildings could be built from all the stone in the Egyptian structure. It contains enough masonry to make not one but two walls, each three feet high and one foot wide, spanning the continental United States from the Atlantic to the Pacific Ocean. Sawed into one-foot blocks laid end to end, its stones, combined with those of its two companions, could build a wall extending two-thirds of the distance around the Earth at the equator. The Great Pyramid has more stone than all of the combined cathedrals, churches, and chapels in England.

It sits on a stone platform that is still dead level to within 0.08 inch over a distance of 758 feet, despite thousands of years of seismic activity. Its casing stones were placed with an accuracy of 0.005 inches, while gaps for mortar average 0.02 inches. The Great Pyramid contains nearly two and a half million mostly limestone blocks, each one cut and fitted to a 0.01 inch of tolerance, the same precision used by modern gem cutters.

The prominent British Egyptologist Sir Flinders Petrie marveled "at an amount of accuracy equal to most modern opticians' straight edges of such a length" in the Great Pyramid and was seconded a century later when Peter Lemesurier observed that its twenty-one acres of polished limestone outer casing "was leveled and honed to the standard of accuracy normal in modern optical work."[2] Petrie found that the so-called Descending Passage, which begins at the pyramid's north face to penetrate the solid bedrock beneath, runs 0.25 inch from absolute perfection over its entire 350-foot length.

Polished to a high degree of gloss, the eighty acres of casing stones that originally covered its exterior surfaces makes the Great Pyramid the only artificial object on our planet visible from outer space when light reflects off a side facing the sun. The stones of the Great Pyramid weigh from two to more than eighty-eight tons; an average diesel locomotive weighs twenty tons less. All were fitted to 0.01 inch between joints; a seventy-ton block cannot be tapped into place. Moreover, these heavier stones were not even used to create the lowest course of the base but were raised one hundred feet and more up the sloping face of the structure—a modern building engineer's nightmare.

It goes without saying that these construction statistics reduce to absurdity official versions of the Great Pyramid's creation with diorite hammers too ponderous for fine workmanship, copper chisels and saws weaker than the granite they are said to have cut, dirt ramps raised centuries after pharaonic civilization expired, and eighty-eight-ton blocks bound with ropes made from water reeds, grass, leather, and animal hair pulled by ill-treated slaves who fitted each of the monument's six million stones with jeweler's precision.

"Fitted together," Dunn observes, "the blocks maintained a gap of 0 to 1/50 inch, which might be compared with the thickness of a fingernail. Inside the gap was cement that bonded the limestone so firmly

Figure 20.2. Mainstream Egyptologists insist that the Great Pyramid
was made with these pathetically inadequate tools.
Photo by Jon Bodsworth.

that the strength of the joint was greater than the limestone itself. The
composition of this cement has been a mystery for years."[3]

Joseph Davidovits, a materials scientist in France known for his
invention of geopolymer chemistry, was no less impressed: "Cement
found in various parts of the courses of the Great Pyramid is about four
thousand five hundred years old, yet it is still in good condition. This
ancient mortar is far superior to cements used in construction today.
The modern Portland cement used to repair ancient Egyptian monuments has cracked and degraded in only about fifty years."[4]

The limestone used to build the Great Pyramid was available locally,
but thousands of tons of granite that went into the project were brought
to the Giza Plateau from quarries five hundred miles away—about the
same distance from Chicago, Illinois, to Memphis, Tennessee. Just the
human labor required to ferry such ponderous tonnage over vast and
difficult stretches of the River Nile, with its strong currents and sharp
bends, seems remarkably harrowing even by today's transportation
standards.

Delicately lifting and placing seventy-ton stones on what must have been enormous barges, then lifting them again to shore—all without breaking or chipping a single block—necessitates a machine technology that, at least in some respects, must have surpassed our own. Petrie stated that the Great Pyramid showed "marks of such tools as we have only now reinvented."[5]

All three major pyramids on the Giza Plateau are linked by the golden section, or ratio, as it is sometimes known—a special number found by dividing a line into two parts so that the longer part divided by the smaller part is also equal to the whole length divided by the longer part. Often symbolized using *phi,* after the twenty-first letter of the Greek alphabet, it was used by ancient architects in designing sacred architecture.

The golden section was regarded as the most desirable proportion because it is expressed in nature. It is found in cosmic nebulae, the ratios between planetary orbits, the horns of various animals, sea mollusks, the formation of the human fetus, the laws of Mendelian heredity, strands

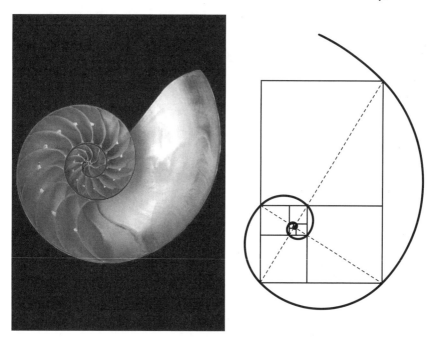

Figure 20.3. A nautilus shell and an illustration of its proportions exemplify the golden ratio. Nautilus shell photo by Sérgio Valle Duarte.

of DNA, heliotropism—the movement of flowers following the path of the sun—and whirlpools, among many thousands of examples. The pattern appears in nautilus shells; when the exterior wall is removed a cross section displays the golden section inside.

This was the Wind Jewel, a personal emblem carried by the Mayas' Kukulcan, subsequently known as the Aztecs' Quetzalcoatl—the Feathered Serpent—who long before both Mesoamerican cultures brought the principles of civilization to Mexico from his sunken kingdom across the Atlantic Ocean. Temple was the first investigator to notice "a shadow cast by the second pyramid, known as the Pyramid of Khafre, upon the Great Pyramid at sunset on 21 December. The shadow, if truncated by a vertical line running up the middle of the south face of the Great Pyramid, does actually form a Golden Triangle. There is actually a slight indentation of a few inches of the construction in the side of the pyramid, discovered in measurements made by Petrie. This apothegm, as geometers call such vertical lines, forms a right angle to transform the solstice shadow into a perfect Golden Triangle."[6] That this shadow was

Figure 20.4. The Great Pyramid seen from the Pyramid of Khafre. Author's photograph.

thrown on the Great Pyramid by the Pyramid of Khafre each winter solstice for "a perfect Golden Triangle" can have hardly been accidental and further illustrates that all three pyramids were built simultaneously at the Giza Plateau as part of a preconceived, unified plan.

Canadian historian William Fix concludes that "the technology does not exist today either to build the Pyramid or even repair it to its original specifications."[7] Of the numerous theories attempting to explain that lost technology, a proposal offered by independent investigator Edward J. Kunkel in 1950 is perhaps the most realistic. Construction engineer Arlan Andrews explains:

> Kunkel's thesis held that the inner galleries and rooms of Egypt's Great Pyramid on the Giza Plateau are the remnants of a water-pumping system originally used for supplying water to a series of locks that raised the colossal monument's ponderous, stone blocks during its construction.
>
> To test his theory, Kunkel had built a one-twelfth scale, plumbing-pipe model of how he thought the King's Chamber, Queen's Chamber, Grand Gallery, and various channels and valves and flaps would have performed more than forty-five centuries ago. To his delight, the whole thing worked very efficiently, pumping more water than it wastes, the only version of its kind that does. Based on this early dynastic design, he was awarded a United States patent for a Hydraulic Ramp Pump.[8]

In any case, Kunkel's cofferdam theory is far more credible than standard explanations of work teams laboriously hauling stone blocks hundreds of feet above the desert floor across earthen ramps. Most Egyptologists still cling to this preposterous conviction despite decades of repeated demonstration to the contrary. They rejoiced when satellite imagery in the early 1990s revealed unquestionable traces of old ramps leading to all four sides of the Great Pyramid. But their premature elation soured after excavation of the newly discovered ramps established that they were actually built and used by mid-seventh-century Arabs for stripping the pyramid of its limestone casing, which went into Cairo's early mosques.

Today even mainstream archaeologists admit that the Great Pyramid could only have been constructed with mostly skilled and semi-skilled workers, not by slave labor overseen by whiplashing aristocrats. Far more important than the technology that built the Great Pyramid, however advanced it must have been, is the pyramid's own high-tech purpose. A clue lies in a phenomenon known as piezoelectricity—the conversion of mechanical energy into electrical energy when physical stress is applied to crystalline minerals. The term derives from the Greek *piezein,* meaning to "squeeze" or "press," and refers to an electrical charge resulting from certain crystals when they are subjected to pressure.

Not all crystals are potentially piezoelectric. Of the thirty-two classifications of crystal, twenty are conductive, although most vary in their capacity for generating piezoelectricity. While not exactly rare, more or less perfectly symmetrical crystals that are particularly rutilated specimens containing some iron for heightened conductivity are less common and noted for their exceptional clarity, the result of at least partially uniformly linear striations: a half-ton pressure exerted on a 0.4-inch crystal can produce twenty-five thousand volts. In 1981, Brian Brady at the U.S. Bureau of Mines in Denver, Colorado, performed a controlled laboratory experiment that proved the electrical properties of the mineral. In subjecting a slab to extraordinarily high pressures, the granite specimen emitted an electrical spark display that was photographed and measured.

The phenomenon is not only luminous but also a real power, as Sir William Siemens demonstrated on April 14, 1859. Siemens, whose pioneering life achievements in electrical engineering won him a British knighthood and a commemorative window in Westminster Abbey, was one of the great inventive geniuses of the modern era. On a visit to Egypt, he climbed with local guides and a party of friends, fellow electrical engineers, to the top of the Great Pyramid, now a mostly flat platform of thirty feet square.

After reaching the summit, Siemens celebrated their ascent by drinking a toast from a wine bottle. As he did so, he tasted a faint electrical charge. Curious and wishing to pursue the effect further, he wrapped some dampened newspaper around the bottle, which had metal foil about the neck. When he held it above his head, the bottle quickly became so charged with static electricity that blue sparks began shooting from either end. A native guide, terrified that Siemens and his colleagues were sorcerers, seized one of the scientists and threatened to throw him off the top of the pyramid. Siemens thrust the flickering wine bottle at the Arab, who was abruptly knocked off his feet and rendered unconscious by an electric shock that leaped from the glass to the stunned guide's nose.[9]

With Siemens's experience in mind, let us examine the interior of the Great Pyramid, setting aside all previous theories to explain it. Unlike what one might expect for a "Hall of Initiation," as the structure is sometimes called, the pyramid's internal details are not meandering or complex. The vast majority of its cut blocks are calcium carbonate limestone, a perfect electrical insulator. Meanwhile, at the very bottom of the pyramid is a thirty-foot-square square hole cut into the bedrock and positioned in a straight vertical line directly beneath the apex—the same relationship between the ground (negative) and discharge point (positive) of an electrical battery. The apex, as mentioned, is today a flat thirty-by-thirty-foot square platform.

Egyptologists believe it was originally surmounted by a pyramidian, or pyramid-shaped, granite capstone, allegedly removed by Arabs in the thirteenth century. But such a capstone would have weighed more than one thousand tons—so heavy that it would have deformed the entire upper portion of the Great Pyramid. According to Arab tradition, the apex was not a capstone but a gold-sheeted chamber. Hieroglyphic symbols for the Great Pyramid as far back as those found on Old Kingdom *mastabas* (flat-roofed tombs from the late fourth millennium BCE) usually depict the apex in yellow pigment, signifying gold. The precious metal is well known for its high conductivity and integral role in the electronics industry, especially as a finish to electrical connectors.

Moving back into the structure's interior, we direct our attention to the so-called King's Chamber. It is a descriptive name only, because no human remains were ever found in this compartment. The chamber is extraordinary in that it is made entirely of granite, unlike the mountain of limestone blocks that conceal it. And even though it is buried deep within the bowels of the pyramid, the chamber has a roof. Although it cannot be seen, the roof must have been put in place for something other than keeping off the rain. The King's Chamber is seventeen feet wide, nineteen feet high, and thirty-four feet long.

Its mystery deepens with these dimensions because they perfectly express the ratio of two Pythagorean triangles, as though this very room were defining the gigantic structure enclosing it. The chamber is absolutely barren save for a solid granite basin (referred to by tour guides as the "sarcophagus") that was installed before its level of the pyramid was completed.

It is far too large to have been carried through the narrow passageway that leads to the King's Chamber.

"Without doubt," writes encylopedist William R. Corliss, "the most interesting enigma associated with the sarcophagus is seen in the drill scratches. They imply that the tubular drills used in hollowing out the

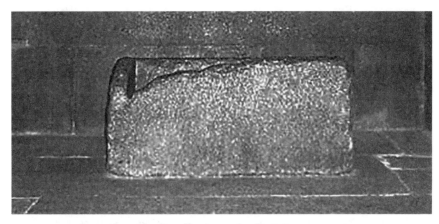

Figure 20.5. The Great Pyramid's so-called sarcophagus.
Photo by Jon Bodsworth.

Figure 20.6. The Great Pyramid's Al-Mamun tunnel.
Photo by Jon Bodsworth.

inside advanced 0.1 inch per revolution. This is, according to C. Dunn, an incredible rate, even for the best of modern drills when working with granite. Today, 0.0002 inch per turn is average—five hundred times slower than the speeds the Egyptians apparently attained four thousand five hundred years ago."[10]

If the granite trough was indeed used as a sarcophagus, no pharaoh was ever laid to rest in a more miserable funerary box, contrary to its unparalleled internment in the world's grandest monument. Anomalous for a kingly coffin, it was rough-hewn despite the high-tech power drills that fashioned it, unpainted, unadorned, and missing a lid. If this, too, was made of granite, removing it from the small King's Chamber would have been impossible unless robbers broke the slab into several pieces for no apparent purpose. If carved of wood, such a cover was worthless. There is no indication that the stone basin ever had a lid, further tending to debunk the container's characterization as a sarcophagus.

Sections above the King's Chamber are divided into five additional chambers separated by several feet of airspace with alternating layers of nine and eight granite beams. Its gabled roof is pitched with a jeweler's precision, a feat made all the more outstanding when we learn that the cut blocks of this elaborate internal arrangement weigh seventy tons each. Combined, they exert 3,010 tons of pressure on the small King's Chamber below. Additionally, Egyptian granite often comprises more than 55 percent silicon quartz and is therefore a superb material for electrical purposes.

Containing conductive mica and feldspar in addition to silicon dioxide, granite generates a piezoelectric field when submitted to intense pressure. The tonnage of microscopic quartz lining this chamber is in the many hundreds. How much voltage could the 3,010 tons of pressure on the King's Chamber generate? From 10,000 to 100,000 volts per square meter, according to Paul Devereux, a British researcher into the piezoelectric qualities of Western Europe's megalithic sites.[11] In fact, the King's Chamber is a highly charged field in which the alternating layers of granite slabs and airspaces above it are nothing less than a capacitor, a device used for storing an electrical charge. Also, piezoelectricity is similar to the charge created by the subterranean pressure leading to an earthquake.

So-called earthquake lights observed immediately preceding seismic events closely resemble the discharge of pressurized quartz, even to the bluish luminescence that accompanies both. These azure mists or clouds that suddenly appear as pressure builds are aggregations of highly charged ion molecules. Although the King's Chamber is located near the center of the Great Pyramid, it is actually off-center. But beneath it, in a direct line between the apex above and the equally large square excavated into the bedrock, lies the smaller Queen's Chamber. Contrasting with the room's rough, unworked floor, its ceiling was constructed of gigantic, precisely cut limestone slabs pitched at a 30-degree, 26-minute slope, creating another gabled roof identical to that of the King's Chamber, down to the same degree and minute.

The Queen's Chamber is almost square: its north-south wall is seventeen feet, two inches and its east-west wall is eighteen feet. Into this wall was carved a cavity sixteen feet high and three feet, five inches deep. If this niche originally held a vessel of liquid almost in proportion to the cavity, the entire Queen's Chamber would have been similar to the altered wine bottle William Siemens experimented with atop the pyramid—in other words, a kind of Leyden jar or condenser of static electricity.

The Great Pyramid's internal passageways travel directly to its compartments like service corridors through which attendants could reach each chamber in the shortest possible time. The four alleged air shafts leading from the bases of the King's and Queen's Chambers outwardly direct the longitudinal, or shear, waves generated by a piezoelectric transducer. And that is the original identity of the Great Pyramid. It is a high-voltage generator, a device designed and constructed to convert physical energy into electrical energy—to transmute and disfuse seismic energy into an outward electric discharge.

A transducer is the application of piezoelectricity, like the ceramic phonograph needle that made vinyl long-playing records possible. The first radio receivers (crystal sets), television remote controls, some of today's high-end ink-jet printers, and most medical ultrasound scanners are piezoelectric transducers. Likewise, when the button on an electric cigarette lighter or a portable sparker used to light stoves is depressed, it trips a spring-loaded hammer to strike a tiny crystal that consequently generates enough voltage to ignite the stored butane. The transducer identity of the Great Pyramid is restated by its so-called Grand Gallery, the structure's largest internal feature. At 125 feet long and 26 feet high, it is an ascending corridor configured like a parallelogram, rising at a forty-five-degree angle from the end of the Queen's Chamber's horizontal passageway and connecting with a smaller anteroom abutting the King's Chamber.

These days tourists climb through the Grand Gallery to the King's Chamber, but the wooden stairway they use is a modern addition.

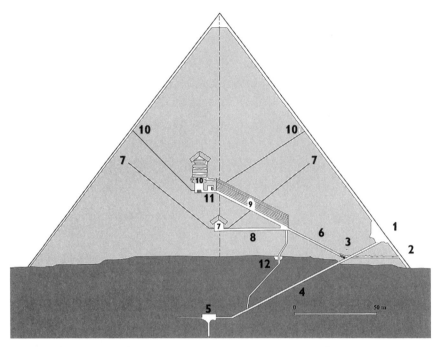

Figure 20.7. Egypt's Great Pyramid as a geotransducer. 1) service entrance
2) service entrance 3) originally closed door for safety precautions
4) descending passageway service tunnel connecting with other corridors
5) subterranean vault (ground) 6) Grand Gallery service corridor
7) Queen's Chamber or Leyden jarlike static charge accumulator with
"air shafts"; actually vents for lateral shear, overloading discharges
8) service corridor to charge accumulator 9) Gallery containing
Heimholtz resonators 10) King's Chamber, i.e., electrical accelerator
and location of the crystal capacitor with "air shaft" lateral shear vents
11) connecting station between Heimholtz resonators and piezoelectric
quartz crystal 12) greaves shaft; purpose unknown.
Original illustration from "Egyptological Curiosities,"
London: Brandywine Publishers, 1848.

Previously the Grand Gallery never provided access between the chambers and defied the ability of mainstream scholars to adequately explain this persistent enigma until Christopher Dunn looked at it through different eyes. After all, the Great Pyramid was not built by Egyptologists but by master construction engineers like himself.

# 21
# Pyramid Power

*It may be said of some very old places, as of some very old books, that they are destined to be forever new. The nearer we approach them, the more remote they seem: the more we study them, the more we have yet to learn. Time augments rather than diminishes their everlasting novelty; and to our descendants of a thousand years hence it may safely be predicted that they will be even more fascinating than to ourselves. This is true of many ancient lands, but of no place is it so true as of Egypt.*

AMELIA BLANFORD EDWARDS,
*A THOUSAND MILES UP THE NILE*

Christopher Dunn recognized the Grand Gallery (see plate 27) as a resonator hall used to reflect sound and direct it into the King's Chamber with its crystal capacitor. The twenty-seven pairs of slots (which have stumped conventional thinkers) in the side ramps contained a framework of wood (an efficient responder to vibration) to hold banks of Heimholtz resonators—spheres of varying sizes used to determine each one's specific resonating frequency.

Their purpose was to step up the vibrational energy from the Queen's Chamber, amplify it into the King's Chamber above, and convert and concentrate the vibrations into airborne sound. This would explain the remarkable acoustics found in the Grand Gallery and the King's Chamber. For the series of different Helmholtz resonating spheres to function as intended, they would have required progressively smaller partitions, thereby preventing any frequency from crossing or bleeding into one another and eliminating distortion of individually generated resonance. As though to perfectly accommodate such an arrangement, the Grand Gallery's walls do indeed step inward from floor to ceiling in seven short, separate partitions. The magnified vibrations accumulating there would have created too much oscillation for such a confined cavity to contain. To prevent it from being broken apart, its thirty-six ceiling stones are, in fact, unattached and removable, allowing them to oscillate in vibrational sympathy while avoiding any structural damage. "As a result," author Edward Malkowsky explains, "the maximization of resonance is achieved, and the entire granite complex becomes a vibrating mass of energy."[1]

While the Grand Gallery's otherwise inexplicably stepped walls and unattached ceiling stones are identifiable features of Dunn's resonator hall, at least one of its Helmholtz resonators has been known since 1872. In that year a granite ball was discovered in the Queen's Chamber, where it appears to have rolled through the horizontal corridor from the base of the Grand Gallery in which it had been originally installed. Among the very few artifacts ever recovered from inside the Great Pyramid, the unadorned sphere weighs one pound, three ounces. Nothing like it has been found in any other ancient Egyptian context, yet this unique object appeared in the same structure that made use of Heimholtz resonators.

Typically, transducers are cone-shaped or pyramidal to force the energy radiated from the core (the King's Chamber) into and through a narrowing area smaller than that of the core itself, thereby increasing its intensity as energy is forced upward. According to Illinois physicist Joseph Farrell, "Professor [Charles] Nelson [physics department, Concordia College, Maryland] suggests that if the coffer in the King's

Chamber was filled with an aqueous solution of natron ($NaHCl_3$, $NaCl$, and $Na_2SO_4$) the salt water itself would act as an effective conductor of electricity for piezo-electric induction from the matt-finished walls of the King's Chamber. This, Professor Nelson affirms, would make it unnecessary to line the coffer with metal; salt is an effective conductor of electricity. In fact, salt deposits have been found throughout the internal features of the Great Pyramid. Professor Nelson correctly points out that such a process would naturally produce poisonous chlorine gas, which, somehow, would have been vented from the Chamber."[2]

"The Queen's Chamber," Dunn writes in *Atlantis Rising* magazine, "served as a reaction chamber, and the shafts leading to this chamber supplied two chemicals (I proposed a combination of dilute hydrochloric acid and hydrated zinc) that, when mixed together, created hydrogen."[3]

In addition to outwardly directing latitudinal shear waves of piezoelectrical discharges, the so-called air shafts may have simultaneously vented poisonous chlorine gases resulting from the coffer's conductive solution. Although a natron solution would have been effective, a large crystal would have been more safe, efficient, stable, and capable of simultaneously collecting and generating greater static discharge. The stone itself would have to have been sufficiently large, approximately three feet long and two feet thick, to accommodate the massive energies focused in it—entirely possible, because crystals can grow up to twenty feet and longer. A specimen displayed at the Chicago Museum of Natural History is some five feet long and weighs nearly one thousand pounds.

Crystals are today vital components in numerous electronic instruments because they magnify, resonate, refine, and direct electrical energy. Thus, the Great Pyramid's crystal would have been of exceptional clarity, a visible expression of its fine internal symmetry and striations, and hence, high conductivity. It was not simply dumped into the granite coffer presently passing as a sarcophagus, but first placed inside a metallic (made ideally of gold) container that enhanced the crystal's function as a capacitor. This is not unfounded assumption.

The renowned French mythologist René Guénon recounts an Arab narrative that described a Stone of Destiny maintained in its own chamber within the Great Pyramid.[4] Indeed, its cross section compares identically with the cut-away of a standard, basic transducer, including its piezeoelectric crystal. That the very configuration of Egypt's pre-eminent monumental structure was predetermined according to the Stone of Destiny it contained is suggested by the termination of natural quartz crystals, which most often slant at 510 degrees, 51 minutes, the same angle of the Great Pyramid. A modern transducer's exponential cone is also present in the Great Pyramid, at the very base of which, literally cut into the bedrock, is a ground that matched in area the gold pyramidian 481 feet directly above.

Precisely in between is located the condenser (the Queen's Chamber), which, from its pitched roof, threw the stored electrical charge to the off-center capacitor (the King's Chamber). There the energy was accelerated and jumped to another crystal at the apex, surrounded in its triangular chamber of high-conductive gold, from whence it was focused and directed upward with a massive spark discharge into the atmosphere. Six million tons of surrounding calcium carbonate limestone blocks acted as insulation necessary to contain such dangerously high accumulations of energy. Focused current would have streamed from the pyramidian in a vertical column of light toward the sky, just as seismic pressures preceding an earthquake build beneath a conical mountain. The most memorable display of this kind was witnessed by hundreds of observers in 1878, when Mount Logelbach in Alsace shot a vertical, radiant pillar, akin to an immense searchlight, from its summit toward the heavens.

Around the turn of the past century, finds made inside the Great Pyramid tended to confirm its original function as a monumental electronic device. In 1995 and again in 2002, robotic investigations of air shafts in the Queen's Chamber discovered two "doors," each with metal "handles." Dunn told *Atlantis Rising* magazine that "the so-called handles are actually electrodes of a circuit, or circuits, which would be closed if electrically conductive fluid were to rise up the shafts to the necessary level." Electrodes are conductors through which electricity enters or leaves an object or substance. More electrodes were found in a pair of pins.

Dunn explained the ingenuity of these ancient designers.

The ancient maintenance crew also left instructions on how to wire the pins! These instructions were painted as symbols onto the floor and represent a simple wiring diagram. The uppermost symbol— depicted as a number 5, with the lower loop almost closed— represents the left connector through which the pin is pushed until the end of the loop meets the limestone. All that has been revealed by the Djedi robot describes an electrical device, which was accessible to workers for maintenance. . . . Gantenbrink's *Apuaut II* [German robotics engineer Rudolf Gantenbrink] also revealed another important feature of the electrodes. After they were positioned in the hole, a sealant was applied, and this can be seen clearly. . . .

The camera-equipped robots also video-recorded signs of ancient electrical wiring. The helical wraps of more flexible conduit can be seen lying on the floor near the bottom of the image just left of the red-painted line, probably left there by the maintenance crew. The metallic appearance of this object and the helical turns of the metal have the same appearance as a length of flexible conduit that has been pulled apart while being disassembled would have.[5]

Above all their other achievements, the ancient builders created the most earthquake-proof structure in history. After unknown millennia of sometimes major seismic disturbances at the Giza Plateau, the Great Pyramid continues to stand fundamentally intact. A few blocks have shifted from their original positions, while others show cracks and fissures from causes other than tectonics, but none have broken or fallen. As the authors of *Earth Facts,* Scarlett Hall and Cally O'Hara, point out, pyramid-shaped structures are built to withstand the stresses of ground tremors, so there may be good reasons for their design. The electromechanical energy produced by even a moderate earthquake is prodigious.[6]

Seismic upheavals are sporadic concentrations of geologic intensity, but the whole Earth is constantly alive with various dynamic energy fields that are only partially understood by geophysicists. Even the easily demonstrable magnetosphere defies universally acceptable explanations for its origins and means of operation. The telluric forces ceaselessly at work within our planet are incessantly generating levels of energy that escape the surface, and the Great Pyramid is strategically placed at the one position on the face of the globe where it can take maximum advantage of those telluric forces: it was originally positioned as close as possible to the absolute center of the world's landmass. This means that the pyramid sits at a unique location where the lines of latitude and longitude pass over more of the Earth's surface than at any other place on the planet.

As prominent Russian mathematician Alexander Braghine explains, "the summit of the Pyramid is situated 290 58' 51.22" of north latitude. This circumference at first sight does not seem significant. The moment, however, we remember that the apparent position of the Polar Star is invariably 1' 8.78" out, owing to the phenomenon of atmospheric refraction, we see what was in the mind of the builder. If we add the value of the refraction, i.e., 1' 8.78" to 290 58' 51.22," we get exactly 300, and we realize that the mysterious builder of the Pyramid, guiding himself by the Polar Star (or by a corresponding point in the constellation of Draconis) wished to center the Pyramid upon the 13th Parallel. This Parallel is remarkable for the fact that it separates a maximum of the land of our planet from the maximum of the ocean surfaces. Apparently, the builder wished to record permanently the distribution of the continents and oceans of those days, and we can see that this distribution has remained almost the same until our own times."[7]

Physicist Michael Csuzdi confirmed Braghine's observations: "The six continents of the Earth markedly form a pentagonal pyramid. Africa is at the apex; lines drawn from its center to the centers of the other continents are evenly spaced at seventy-two degrees. The other five centers are evenly spaced on a common plane to form the pyramid's base line."[8]

As a piezoelectric transducer, the Great Pyramid was purposely built to change geologic energy into electric energy. The entire structure had to work with seismic forces, not against them. If the very energies it was intended to harness could damage or destroy it, the pyramid would have failed the function for which it was designed. Except for the Temple of Artemis at Ephesus and the Statue of Zeus at Olympia (both destroyed by fire), earthquakes toppled the other Seven Wonders of the World, save only the Great Pyramid. It has successfully withstood the seismic violence it was meant to exploit because it is, if not perfectly earthquake-proof, then effectively earthquake-resistant.

For example, an almost imperceptible indentation in each of the four faces dampen structural oscillations that would otherwise shatter them. This subtle feature alone virtually proves that its designers had earthquakes in mind before construction began on the Great Pyramid. Its Grand Gallery's roof slabs are separately jointed, thereby evenly distributing the tonnage along its whole length, while the King's Chamber walls are only loosely attached to the surrounding interior. These features accommodate rather than resist the sharp movement associated with seismic activity. When the Arab builders of Cairo's mosques stripped the Great Pyramid of its limestone casing, they revealed its alternating courses of larger and smaller blocks, a configuration that ameliorates the exponential accumulation of vibrational effects that can tear a structure apart. British historian Ralph Ellis determined that the arrangement of stone courses in the Great Pyramid was identical to the kind of banding automotive engineers discovered for designing their rubber tires to prevent loud resonance when the car is in motion.[9]

Taken altogether, these internal details demonstrate that they were deliberately incorporated into the Great Pyramid as seismic safeguards to enable its perpetual survival by riding earthquakes or moving with them instead of rigidly resisting them and breaking into pieces.

Somewhat less than one hundred pyramids from Giza in the north down to the Nubian border in the south stand on either side of the River Nile. No original burial was ever found in any of them, and most feature variations of essentially the same internal configuration found inside the Great Pyramid. Its commonly accepted characterization as a tomb has always been a source of amusement for anyone who has wriggled and crouched through its cramped, airless spaces—not exactly the most accommodating passageways for the kind of ornate, well-attended funeral cortège expected of a mighty pharaoh's internment. Imagine dynastic pallbearers trying to manage a bulky sarcophagus through such tight corners! Impossible!

As for that dingy, confined space labeled the King's Chamber, no more than a dozen persons at a time would have had enough elbow room for what could have only been the most modest of ceremonies, hardly befitting a ruler of Egypt. And no self-respecting female sovereign would have allowed her remains to have been deposited in something as inglorious as the misnamed Queen's Chamber. How peculiar, too, that none of the magnificent temple art, no lengthy quotations from the Book of the Dead, no written homage or prayers on behalf of the deceased, not a single authentic hieroglyph—all of which profusely decorate the walls and ceilings of every other royal burial site throughout Egypt—are present inside Giza's foremost structure and its pyramidal counterparts!

Such a glaring contrast is apparent in the true identity of these structures as power plants (to cite Christopher Dunn's convincing representation of them), the internal spaces of which are unadorned because they were not tombs but service corridors for regular maintenance, just as the interior of today's nuclear generating stations do not resemble a mortuary. Perhaps all one hundred or so pyramids were tectonic transducers intentionally positioned along the seismically active Nile valley to diffuse the worst of the potentially destructive earthquakes that threatened the new civilization being built in early dynastic, or even predynastic, times, contrary to official archaeological chronologies that are themselves far from precisely accurate.

The northeast region of Africa today appears geologically quiescent, but it has a long history of violent upheaval. On August 8, 1303, exceptionally powerful tremors destroyed most of the famous Pharos Lighthouse. "The walls of the Great Mosque of Alexandria and a large part of the Pharos of Alexandria sunk" during a prolonged earthquake forty-two years earlier, as described in *Les Seismes a Alenandrie et la Destruction du Phare*.[10] Previous earthquakes in 1258, 1211, 1202, 1196, 1191, 1198, and 365 BCE left their enduring scars on strata throughout the Nile delta. On December 28, 955, a "swarm" or series of catastrophic aftershocks rolled across Egypt and Syria for half an hour according to Al-Mas'udi, a renowned Arab historian who lived through the terrifying experience.[11] Ancient Egyptian geotransducers minimized earthquake activity in the seismically unstable Nile valley by discharging seismic energy into electricity.

As a small-scale example, many modern watches and small travelers' clocks feature a built-in quartz tuning fork that produces a regularly timed series of electrical pulses to accurately count hours, minutes, and seconds. These quartz components, as do all piezoelectric crystals, have their own precisely defined natural frequency determined by shape and size. They oscillate at a specific rate, thereby stabilizing the frequency of a periodic voltage applied to the crystal. Similarly, a sufficiently large, appropriately configured, and symmetrical piezoelectric quartz installed in Giza's transducer would have had an ameliorating effect on seismic energy by dampening it to the crystal's lower stabilizing frequency.

The bluish earthquake lights serve similar purposes. Some geologists believe these illuminated discharges not only warn of imminent tremors but also may tend to dissipate them. Indeed, early representations of the pyramids, such as the mastaba temple art circa 2800 BCE at Thebes, depict the apex not in gold but blue pigment, indicating that the electrostatic corona of the pyramidian was known to the ancients. All evidence suggests that the Great Pyramid was envisioned, designed, and constructed as a tremendously powerful geotransducer for the transformation of telluric energies into electrical energies. It was primarily a device for dispersing seismic stress to minimize the destructiveness of earthquakes, specifically in Nile valley population centers.

Remarkably, the same electrical components utilized in the Great Pyramid were independently rediscovered by Nikola Tesla, an impoverished Serbian who migrated to the United States in 1884. Seven years later he invented the Tesla impulse coil (see plate 28), still used in television sets and numerous other electronics today. Farrell was the first to notice a comparison with the Great Pyramid, which is "an electrical coil that is segmented—exactly in accordance with the principles discovered by Tesla—not only into separate 'windings' in the stone courses, but each of these 'windings' in turn is segmented into a discrete number of stones. The pyramidal form itself gives the distinctive geometry and properties of a Tesla impulse coil."[12]

Fundamental resemblance of this early electrical device to the Great Pyramid helps confirm its ancient function as a geotransducer. The most vital single component of this Earth-powered machine was a Stone of Destiny—according to thirteenth-century Arab accounts, an exceptionally large, clear quartz crystal. It long ago magnified and focused telluric energies channeled through the pyramid but later disappeared during any one of Egypt's several civil upheavals that imperiled dynastic civilization.

New discoveries tend to support Christopher Dunn's late twentieth-century Giza Power Plant revelation. In 2018, members of a research team from ITMO University in Saint Petersburg, Russia, and Hannover, Germany's Laser Zentrum that were investigating the monumental structure were surprised by what they uncovered. "We wanted to find out what peculiarities of electro-magnetic energy distributions can be obtained in the Great Pyramid and environment under the condition of its strong interaction with electromagnetic waves," said ITMO's Andrey Evlyukhin. He and his colleagues found that the pyramid focuses electromagnetic energy in its internal chambers and under its base, creating pockets of higher energy (see plate 29). When subjected to wavelengths between 656 and 1968 feet, the pyramid resonated, scattering and absorbing much more energy from electromagnetic waves than other bandwidths and revealing its unsuspected and unusual electromagnetic properties.[13]

"The results will help scientists in the fields of optics," reported the *New York Post*. "Having tested wave distribution and magnetic energies at such a large scale will assist in our understanding of how particles and waves interact at a nano level. The remarkable electromagnetic properties of the Great Pyramid of Giza could soon inspire nanoparticle designs for highly efficient sensors and solar cells." The pyramid's electromagnetic qualities, Evlyukhin claimed, "can apply to design nanoparticles capable of reproducing similar focusing effects in the optical range. Such nanoparticles can be used as building blocks for construction of different optical devices for management of light energy at nanoscale."[14]

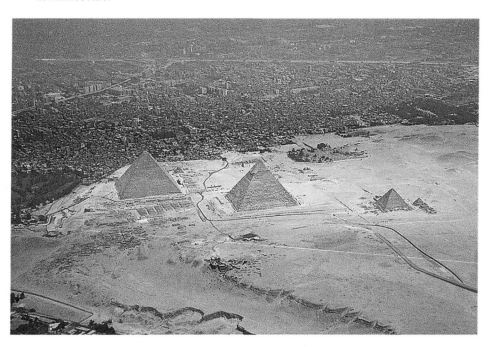

Figure 21.1. Modern Cairo's urban sprawl stops just short of the Giza Plateau pyramids.

274   ⫷ Pyramid Power

Thus, dynastic Egypt's foremost structure is advancing the development of twenty-first-century science. For that contribution alone, it is the ancient world's most remarkable specimen of high technology. Yet the Great Pyramid is greater still: it is a machine beyond anything of the kind we know today, an anti-earthquake device that made pharaonic civilization possible for three thousand years. Because modern construction engineers are currently beginning to approach certain levels of ancient achievement, they are now able to recognize the Great Pyramid's original function and replicate it for our time.

It is something we need as much today as the Egyptians urgently required more than forty-five hundred years ago. Only such a dire purpose could have effectively summoned the participation of every man, woman, and child at the Nile delta, mostly as a labor force, skilled and unskilled, but also for the genius of their intellectual elite. As such, it was the supreme public works project of all time. Class distinctions and social divisions dissolved in the shared construction of their common task. When it was finished and began to successfully undertake its historic mission, the Great Pyramid concretized that national unity and self-respect, standing forever after as the embodiment of Egypt herself.

# Antiquity Reborn

*Study the past if you would define the future.*
Confucius, *The Analects*, circa 485 BCE

Figure A.1. Detroit's abandoned schoolbook repository.
Photo by Shane Gorski.

The innovative creations described in the foregoing chapters—and so many more, known and unknown—were obliterated by the Western world's late fifth-century collapse, followed 430 years later with the East's own dark ages, hard on the heels of China's Tang Dynasty demise. In the wake of such a catastrophic fall, human progress likewise fell backward, much to the cultural impoverishment of all subsequent generations, blind to their ruined heritage, down to the present day.

It is truly impossible for us to imagine how far humanity might have risen by now, had all our early high achievements in advanced science escaped destruction and have been allowed instead to consistently develop and continually improve over time since their invention so long ago.

While we are beginning to pick up some scattered pieces of the high technology devised by Zhang Heng, Heron, and their genuinely avant-garde colleagues, one might do better to first understand how and why they lost their civilizations, thereby avoiding the same lethal mistakes we are seeing repeated by our own modern society.

# Notes

## INTRODUCTION.
## AHEAD OF THEIR TIME . . . AND OURS

1. Barnett, *Explosives.*
2. Taylor, "Carving of Modern Bicycle Found on Wall of 2,000-Year-Old Temple."
3. Watson, "Archaeologists Digging Up Pre-Columbian Sounds."
4. Watson, "Archaeologists Digging Up Pre-Columbian Sounds."
5. The College of Optometrists, "Eskimo Goggles: The First Eyewear?" The College of Optometrists website online exhibitions, spectacle gallery, accessed February 10, 2020.
6. Kenyon, "Debunking the Myth of 'Primitive' Ancestors."

## CHAPTER 1.
## AUTOMATION

1. Schmidt, *Herons von Alexandria Druckwerke und Automatentheater.*
2. Drachmann, *The Mechanical Technology of Greek Antiquity.*
3. Qureshi, "Ten Ancient Robots that Were Built without Modern Technology."
4. Qureshi, "Ten Ancient Robots that Were Built without Modern Technology."
5. Tomas, *We Are Not the First.*
6. Balchin, *100 Scientists Who Changed the World.*
7. Mayor, *Gods and Robots.*
8. Qureshi, "Ten Ancient Robots that Were Built without Modern Technology."
9. Mayor, *Gods and Robots.*

10. Mayor, *Gods and Robots*.

11. Polybius. *The Histories*.

12. Wikipedia, s.v. "Apega of Nabis," accessed February 10, 2020.

13. Hyginus, *Fabulae*.

14. Balchin, *100 Scientists Who Changed the World*.

15. Mayor, *Gods and Robots*.

16. Wilson, "Machines, Power and the Ancient Economy."

17. Qureshi, "Ten Ancient Robots that Were Built without Modern Technology."

18. Alter, *The Hebrew Bible: A Translation with Commentary*.

19. David Reigle, "Robots in Atlantis," January 31, 2017, *The Book of Dyzan: The Quest for an Original Text of the Book of Dyzan* (blog).

20. Tenn, "There Are Robots Among Us."

21. Robert Lamb, "Meet Talos, the Killer Robot from Ancient Greek Mythology," January 9, 2018, How Stuff Works website.

22. Lamb, "Meet Talos, the Killer Robot from Ancient Greek Mythology."

23. Qureshi, "Ten Ancient Robots that Were Built without Modern Technology."

## CHAPTER 2.
## HUMAN FLIGHT

1. Woodman, *Nazca*.

2. Woodman, *Nazca*.

3. Woodman, *Nazca*.

4. Woodman, *Nazca*.

5. *The Classic of Mountains and Seas*, trans. Anne Birrell.

6. Jigen, *Yinxu yu Shang wen hua*.

7. Lewis, *China's Cosmopolitan Empire*.

8. Steiger, *Worlds Before Our Own*.

## CHAPTER 3.
## ANCIENT AVIATION

1. Jochmans, "Ancient Wings Over the Nile."

2. Jochmans, "Ancient Wings Over the Nile."

3. Jochmans, "Ancient Wings Over the Nile."

4. Childress, *Technology of the Gods*.

5. Jochmans, "Ancient Wings Over the Nile."

6. *Ancient Discoveries,* "Ancient Cars and Planes," the History Channel, aired January 30, 2007. Available as "Ancient Egyptian Planes." Posted by Sparkleystitch on October 26, 2008, YouTube, accessed March 6, 2020.
7. Jochmans, "Ancient Wings Over the Nile."
8. Jochmans, "Ancient Wings Over the Nile."
9. Jochmans, "Ancient Wings Over the Nile."
10. Tara MacIsaac, "First Robotic Drone Created in 350 BC?" October 14, 2014, the Epoch Times website.

## CHAPTER 4.
## PREVENTIVE MEDICINE

1. Julie Edgar, "Medicinal Uses of Honey: What Researchers Are Learning about Honey's Possible Health Benefits," WebMD, last revised December 20, 2011.
2. Varro, *Rerum Rusticarum Libri Tres.*
3. James and Thorpe, *Ancient Inventions.*
4. American Chemical Society, "Ancient Egyptian Cosmetics: 'Magical' Makeup May Have Been Medicine for Eye Disease," January 11, 2010, American Chemical Society website.
5. Vallery-Radot, *Louis Pasteur.*
6. Giuliani, *An Alternative View of the Distant Past.*
7. Pormann, *The Oriental Tradition of Paul of Aegina's Pragmateia.*
8. Stephen Levy, "The Hypodermic Syringe: Greatest Medical Device of All Time?," April 11, 2014, Informa website.
9. Morison, *Samuel de Champlain.*
10. Steiger, *Worlds Before Our Own.*
11. Reproduced by Corliss, *Ancient Man.*
12. Childress, *Technology of the Gods.*

## CHAPTER 5.
## SURGICAL WONDERS

1. Breasted, *The Edwin Smith Surgical Papyrus.*
2. Bhishagratna, *Susruta Samhita.*
3. "Remarkable Skill of Ancient Peru's Cranial Surgeons," June 8, 2018, Science Daily website.

4. Steiger, *Worlds Before Our Own.*

5. Kenyon, "Ancient Healing Procedures."

6. Kenyon, "Ancient Healing Procedures."

7. Corliss, *Archaeological Anomalies.*

8. Kellar, "The C.L. Lewis Mound and the Stone Mound Problem."

9. Corliss, *Archaeological Anomalies.*

10. Holloway, "From Jewel-Capped Teeth to Golden Bridges."

11. Bernardini et al., "Beeswax as Dental Filling on a Neolithic Human Tooth."

12. von Klein, *The Medical Features of the Papyrus Ebers.*

13. Killgrove, "Archaeologists Discover A New Profession In An Ancient Egyptian Woman's Teeth."

14. James and Thorpe, *Ancient Inventions.*

15. James and Thorpe, *Ancient Inventions.*

16. James and Thorpe, *Ancient Inventions.*

17. Julius, "They Came for the Cocaine," in *Discovering the Mysteries of Ancient America,* ed. Frank Joseph.

18. Howell, "Frankincense: Could It Be a Cure for Cancer?"

19. Moussaieff, "Boswellia Resin."

20. Kenyon, "Mysterious Frankincense."

21. Mingren, "Frankincense."

22. Hosseini-Sharifabad et al., "Beneficial Effect of *Boswellia serrata* Gum Resin on Spatial Learning and the Dendritic Tree of *Dentate gyrus granule* Cells in Aged Rats."

23. Jochmans, in *Lost Powers.*

24. Mingren, "Frankincense."

25. Miller, "Frankincense May Infuse Users with Mild Euphoria."

26. "Ancient Amber," Nammu website.

27. Cartwright, "Amber in Antiquity."

28. "Benefits of Amber," Amber by Amanda website.

29. Snyder, "Amber Waves of Woo."

## CHAPTER 6.
## THERAPEUTIC ACHIEVEMENTS

1. "Electron," Amber Goods website.

2. Tanya Newman, "What's with Watts?," *Tanya Newman Rowing* (blog), January 28, 2019.

3. Kenyon, "Cancer among the Ancients."

4. Kenyon, "Electro-Magnetic Therapy."

5. Wogan, "Magnetic Nanoparticles Fry Tumors."

6. Wogan, "Magnetic Nanoparticles Fry Tumors."

7. Solecki, *The Proto-Neolithic Cemetery in Shanidar Cave.*

8. Zukerman, "Chinese Medicine Offers New Parkinson's Treatments."

9. Wright, "Silphium Rediscovered."

10. Hippocrates, *Ancient Medicine.*

11. Theophrastus, *Enquiry into Plants.*

12. Wright, "Silphium Rediscovered."

13. Gorvett, "The Mystery of the Lost Roman Herb."

14. Fage, s.v. "The Libyans," *The Cambridge History of Africa,* 141.

15. Williams, Henry Smith, *The Historians' History of the World.*

16. L. Prakash, "Biomechanics and Pathophysiology of Fracture Healing with a Special Reference to Noninvasive Biological Methods," Slideshare, accessed January 8, 2020.

17. Snow, "BYU Professor Finds Evidence of Advanced Surgery in Ancient Mummy."

18. University of Basel, "A Wooden Toe: Swiss Egyptologists Study 3,000-Year-Old Prosthesis."

19. James and Thorpe, *Ancient Inventions.*

20. James and Thorpe, *Ancient Inventions.*

21. James and Thorpe, *Ancient Inventions.*

# CHAPTER 7.
## OPTICS

1. *Hrafnkel's Saga and Other Icelandic Stories*, trans. Hermann Palsson.

2. Crystal, "Viking Sunstones."

3. Koenig, "Did a Sunstone Guide the Vikings to America?," in *Unearthing Ancient America.*

4. Koenig, "Did a Sunstone Guide the Vikings to America?," in *Unearthing Ancient America.*

5. Koenig, "Did a Sunstone Guide the Vikings to America?," in *Unearthing Ancient America.*

6. Temple, *The Crystal Sun.*

7. Temple, *The Crystal Sun.*

8. Hart, "Science around 2,000 BC."

9. Temple, "Advanced Lens-crafting in Ancient Egypt."

10. Temple, "Advanced Lens-crafting in Ancient Egypt."

11. Temple, *The Crystal Sun.*

12. Temple, *The Crystal Sun.*

13. Cicero, *The Republic and The Laws.*

14. Pliny, *Natural History.*

15. Aelian, *On the Characteristics of Animals.*

16. Silva, "Avebury's Mysterious Rectangle."

17. Temple, *The Crystal Sun.*

18. Bacon, *Opus Majus.*

19. Pliny, *Natural History.*

20. Stonehill, "From Alexandria to Yereven."

21. Radka, *The Electric Mirror on the Pharos Lighthouse and Other Ancient Lighting.*

22. Shaw and Shaw, *Theurgy and the Soul.*

# CHAPTER 8.
## MODERN MARVELS FROM LONG AGO

1. Austin AC Express, "The History of Home Heating."

2. Steiger, *Worlds Before Our Own.*

3. The Local Switzerland, "Ancient Roman Fridge Discovered Near Basel Keeps Beer Cool for Months."

4. Curious History, "Ancient Egyptian Air Conditioner over 4,000 Years Old."

5. Castleden, *Minoans.*

6. Castleden, *Minoans.*

7. Childress, *Technology of the Gods.*

8. Corliss, *Archaeological Anomalies.*

9. James and Thorpe, *Ancient Inventions.*

10. Baldwin, "There's a 1,200-Year-Old Phone in the Smithsonian Collections."

11. Booksfact, "Ancient Alarm Clock Invented by Plato (4th Century BCE)."

12. Seneca, *Letters from a Stoic.*

13. Childress, *Technology of the Gods.*

14. Price, "An Ancient Greek Computer."

15. Cicero, *The Republic and The Laws.*

16. Needham, *Science and Civilisation in China.*

17. Corliss, *Archaeological Anomalies*.

18. Pine, *The Diamond Sutra*.

19. Colleen Anne Coyle, "Do Archaeologists Have Any Idea Who Made the Phaistos Disk?" Quora discussion board. November 10, 2019, accessed January 8, 2020. Coyle quotes from Herbert Brekle's "The Typographic Principle," from the *Gutenberg-Jahrbuch*.

20. Schwartz, "The Phaistos Disk."

21. Haury, *The Hohokam*.

22. Corliss, *Archaeological Anomalies*.

23. Steiger, *Worlds Before Our Own*.

# CHAPTER 9.
## WEAPONS OF MASS DESTRUCTION

1. Wikipedia, s.v. "Fritz Haber," accessed February 10, 2020.

2. Mayor, *Greek Fire, Poison Arrows, and Scorpion Bombs*.

3. Temple, *The Genius of China*.

4. Mayor, *Greek Fire, Poison Arrows, and Scorpion Bombs*.

5. Herodian, *History of the Empire*.

6. Ison, "War Elephants: From Ancient India to Vietnam."

7. Wikipedia, s.v. "Battle of Heraclea," accessed February 10, 2020.

8. Ball, "The Truth about Hannibal's Route across the Alps."

9. James Howard Williams, *Elephant Bill*.

10. Plato, *Timaeus and Critias*.

11. Donnelly, *Atlantis, the Antediluvian World*.

12. Italicus, *Punica*.

13. Strabo, *The Geography of Strabo*.

14. Childress, *Technology of the Gods*.

15. Noorbergen, *Secrets of the Lost Race*.

# CHAPTER 10.
## WONDER WEAPONS

1. Noorbergen, *Secrets of the Lost Race*.

2. Mayor, *Greek Fire*.

3. Partington, *A History of Greek Fire and Gunpowder*.

4. Choniates, *City of Byzantium*.

5. Kenyon, *Forbidden Science*.

6. Herodotus, *The Histories*; Pliny, *Natural History*.

7. Needham, *Science and Civilisation in China*.

8. PBS, "Secrets of the Viking Sword."

9. PBS, "Secrets of the Viking Sword."

10. PBS, "Secrets of the Viking Sword."

11. "Welding BC," *New Scientist* (May 12, 1960), p. 1216.

12. Plutarch, *Lives of the noble Grecians and Romans*.

13. Qureshi, "Ten Ancient Robots that Were Built without Modern Technology."

14. Tzetzae, *Historiarum Variarum Chiliades*.

15. Diocles, *On Burning Mirrors*.

16. Boyer, *A History of Mathematics*.

17. "Revisited and Re-Busted: An Array of Bronze Mirrors Can Set a Wooden Ship on Fire." "Archimedes' Death Ray," *MythBusters*, episode 46. MythBusters Results website.

18. Temple, *The Crystal Sun*.

19. Temple, *The Crystal Sun*.

20. Temple, *The Crystal Sun*.

21. Plutarch, *Lives of the Noble Grecians and Romans*.

22. Farnell, *The Cults of the Greek States*.

23. Aristophanes, *The Clouds*.

24. Theophrastus, *Characters*.

25. Temple, *The Crystal Sun*.

26. Godwin, *Athanasius Kircher's Theatre of the World*.

27. Banchich, *The History of Zonaras*.

28. Whittaker, *Macrobius*.

# CHAPTER 11.
## CHILDREN OF THE SUN

1. Plutarch, *Lives of the Noble Grecians and Romans*.

2. Perlin, "Burning Mirrors."

3. Perlin, "Burning Mirrors."

4. Perlin, "Burning Mirrors."

5. Lloyd, "Giant Solar Mirrors and Sophisticated Lenses: Advanced Ancient Technology Used by Our Ancestors."

6. Diehl, *The Olmecs.*

7. Carlson, "Olmec Concave Iron-Ore Mirrors."

8. Joyce, *Scientific Dialogues.*

9. Temple, *The Crystal Sun.*

10. Hsu, "Engineers Upgrade Ancient, Sun-Powered Tech to Purify Water with Near-Perfect Efficiency."

## CHAPTER 12.
## STONE INTO GLASS

1. Foerster, *Lost Ancient Technology Of Peru And Bolivia.*

2. Dunning, "The Mystery of Vitrified Forts," Skeptoid website.

3. Redfern, *Weapons of the Gods.*

4. Maxwell, *Proceedings of the Society of Antiquaries of Scotland.*

5. *Arthur C. Clarke's Mysterious World,* Yorkshire Television 1980, episode 3: "Ancient Wisdom" (Network DVD 7952792).

6. Ralston, *Celtic Fortifications.*

7. Ralston, *Celtic Fortifications.*

8. Parker, *Bronze Age Britain.*

9. Squier and Davis, *The American Antiquarian and Oriental Journal.*

10. Squier and Davis, *The American Antiquarian and Oriental Journal.*

11. Wilson, *From Atlantis to the Sphinx.*

12. Bricker, *Supplement to the Handbook of Middle American Indians.*

13. Brinton, *Ancient Nahuatl Poetry, Containing the Nahuatl Text of XXVII Ancient Mexican Poems.*

14. George Savage, "American Indian Pottery," Britannica online, accessed January 8, 2020.

15. Childress, *Ancient Technology in Peru & Bolivia.*

16. Foerster, *Lost Ancient Technology Of Peru And Bolivia.*

## CHAPTER 13.
## ELECTRIC POWER

1. König, *Im Verlorenen Paradies-Neun Jahre Irak.*

2. Steiger, *Worlds Before Our Own.*

3. Ley, "An Electric Battery 2,000 Years Ago."

4. König, *Im Verlorenen Paradies-Neun Jahre Irak.*

5. Winton, "Baghdad Batteries B.C."
6. "Riddle of Baghdad's Batteries," February 27, 2003, BBC.
7. Jochmans, "The Baghdad Battery Mystery."
8. Radka, *The Electric Mirror on the Pharos Lighthouse and Other Ancient Lighting.*
9. Keyser, "The Purpose of the Parthian Galvanic Cells."
10. *Arthur C. Clarke's Mysterious World,* Yorkshire Television 1980, episode 3: "Ancient Wisdom" (Network DVD 7952792).
11. Stone, "Archaeologists Revisit Iraq."
12. Frood, "Riddle of 'Baghdad's Batteries.'"
13. Ley, "An Electric Battery 2,000 Years Ago."
14. König, *Im Verlorenen Paradies-Neun Jahre Irak.*
15. Noorbergen, *Secrets of the Lost Race.*
16. Radka, "A Short History of Ancient Electricity."
17. Jochmans, "The Baghdad Battery Mystery."
18. Corliss, *Ancient Man.*
19. Giuliani, *An Alternative View of the Distant Past.*
20. Sneiderman, "Gilding Technique Inspired by Ancient Egyptians May Spark Better Fuel Cells for Tomorrow's Electric Cars."
21. Jochmans, "India's Magical Ancient Pillar."
22. Jochmans, "India's Magical Ancient Pillar."
23. Jochmans, "India's Magical Ancient Pillar."
24. Mohan, "Iron Pillar that Never Rusts—Ancient Secret Revealed?"

# CHAPTER 14.
## ORGANIZED LIGHTNING

1. Jochmans, "The Baghdad Battery Mystery."
2. Lucan, *Pharsalia.*
3. Radka, *The Electric Mirror on the Pharos Lighthouse and Other Ancient Lighting.*
4. Radka, *The Electric Mirror on the Pharos Lighthouse and Other Ancient Lighting.*
5. Radka, *The Electric Mirror on the Pharos Lighthouse and Other Ancient Lighting.*
6. Radka, *The Electric Mirror on the Pharos Lighthouse and Other Ancient Lighting.*

7. "Levitating Temple Statues of Antiquity," November 12, 2012, Above Top Secret website.

8. Hodgkin, *Letters Of Cassiodorus.*

9. Treadgold, *The Middle Byzantine Historians.*

10. Manetho, *History of Egypt and Other Works.*

11. Pliny, *Natural History.*

12. Libanius, *Selected Orations.*

13. Radka, *The Electric Mirror on the Pharos Lighthouse and Other Ancient Lighting.*

14. Harley, *The History of Cartography.*

15. Adams, *Lighthouses and Lightships.*

16. Lockyer, *The Dawn of Astronomy.*

17. Kenyon, "Sparks from the Gods."

18. ACS News Service, "Ancient Technology for Metal Coatings 2,000 Years Ago Can't Be Matched Even Today."

19. Radka, *The Electric Mirror on the Pharos Lighthouse and Other Ancient Lighting.*

## CHAPTER 15.
## INNER AND OUTER ENLIGHTENMENT

1. Richter, *The Theology of Hathor of Dendera,* 56.

2. Manetho, *History of Egypt and Other Works.*

3. Dörnenburg, "Lights of the Pharaos."

4. Corliss, *Ancient Infrastructure.*

5. Mercatante, *Who's Who in Egyptian Mythology.*

6. Dörnenburg, "Lights of the Pharaos."

7. Habeck and Krassa, *Das Licht der Pharaonen.*

8. Dunn, *Lost Technologies of Ancient Egypt.*

9. Habeck and Krassa, *Das Licht der Pharaonen.*

10. Jochmans, "Did Ancient Egypt Really Have Electricity?"

11. Jochmans, "Did Ancient Egypt Really Have Electricity?"

12. Dunn, *Lost Technologies of Ancient Egypt.*

13. Kreisberg, Glenn (ed.), *Lost Knowledge of the Ancients.*

14. Dunn, *Lost Technologies of Ancient Egypt.*

15. Prophessor ACE, "Egyptian Light Bulb—Plausible."

16. Wikipedia, s.v. "William Crookes," accessed February 19, 2020.

## CHAPTER 16.
## MEGA STRUCTURES

1. Beard, *The Parthenon.*
2. Corliss, *Ancient Infrastructure.*
3. Michell, *The View Over Atlantis.*
4. Alberge, "Lucky Strike?"
5. Foerster, "Very Strange Ancient 'Out of Place Artifacts' in Museums in Mexico."
6. Dunn, *Lost Technologies of Ancient Egypt.*
7. Dunn, *Lost Technologies of Ancient Egypt.*
8. Dunn, *Lost Technologies of Ancient Egypt.*
9. Dunn, *Lost Technologies of Ancient Egypt.*
10. Fergusson, *History of Indian and Eastern Architecture.*
11. Mohan, "Hoysaleswara Temple, India—Built with Ancient Machining Technology?"
12. Mohan, "Hoysaleswara Temple, India—Built with Ancient Machining Technology?"


## CHAPTER 17.
## ANCIENT ENGINEERING

1. Personal conversation with the author at the Cuzco Hotel, Peru, October 10, 1994.
2. Clough, "The Earliest and Greatest Engineers Were the Incas."
3. O'Kon, *The Lost Secrets of Maya Technology.*
4. De Camp, *The Ancient Engineers.*
5. Vālmīki, *The Ramayana.*
6. Prakriti Mata, "Rama Setu (Adam's Bridge) Scientific Explanation with Proof."
7. Prakriti Mata, "Rama Setu (Adam's Bridge) Scientific Explanation with Proof."
8. Rediff News, "Adam's Bridge a Man-Made Structure."
9. The Science Channel, "Could This Be The Legendary 'Magic Bridge' Connecting India And Sri Lanka?"
10. The Science Channel, "Could This Be The Legendary 'Magic Bridge' Connecting India And Sri Lanka?"
11. Prakriti Mata, "Rama Setu (Adam's Bridge) Scientific Explanation with Proof."
12. O'Kon, *The Lost Secrets of Maya Technology.*
13. O'Kon, *The Lost Secrets of Maya Technology.*

14. Patrick, "By 25 BC Ancient Romans Developed a Recipe for Concrete."

15. Preuss, "Roman Concrete Holds a Secret to Cutting Carbon Emissions."

16. McGrath, "Scientists Explain Ancient Rome's Long-Lasting Concrete."

17. Bennett, "The Ancient Romans' Concrete Recipe Could Help Us Beat Back Rising Seas."

18. Bennett, "The Ancient Romans' Concrete Recipe Could Help Us Beat Back Rising Seas."

19. De Camp, *The Ancient Engineers.*

20. Newman, "The Titans of Baalbek."

21. Newman, "The Titans of Baalbek."

22. Newman, "The Titans of Baalbek."

23. Foerster, "Baalbek In Lebanon: Megaliths Of The Gods Full Lecture."

## CHAPTER 18.
## SUBTERRANEAN CITIES

1. Xenophon, *Anabasis.*

2. Duckeck, "Cave Dwellings of Cappadocia."

3. Hicks, *The Empire Builders.*

4. Harrison, *The Great Empires of the Ancient World.*

5. Hicks, *The Empire Builders.*

6. Hicks, *The Empire Builders.*

7. Drews, *The End of the Bronze Age.*

8. Franzen and Larsson, in *Natural Catastrophes During Bronze Age Civilizations.*

9. Baillie, in *Natural Catastrophes During Bronze Age Civilizations.*

10. Samuel Birch (ed.), *Facsimile of an Egyptian Hieratic Papyrus of the Reign of Ramses III,* now in the British Museum. Available at Universitätsbibliothek Heidelberg digitized literature.

11. Wright, "Empires in the Dust."

## CHAPTER 19.
## TUNNELING INTO ANTIQUITY

1. Kusch and Kusch, *Tore zur Unterwelt.*

2. Kusch and Kusch, *Tore zur Unterwelt.*

3. Dunn, *Lost Technologies of Ancient Egypt.*

4. Dunn, *Lost Technologies of Ancient Egypt.*

5. Dunn, *Lost Technologies of Ancient Egypt.*
6. Borisov, "Lighting Up Saqqara."
7. Dunn, *Lost Technologies of Ancient Egypt.*
8. Jones, *The Emperor Titus.*
9. Winchester, *The Man Who Loved China.*
10. Childress, *Technology of the Gods.*
11. Corliss, *Ancient Infrastructure.*
12. Kenyon, "Advanced Ancient Water Technology in Nazca, Peru."

## CHAPTER 20.
## THE GREAT HIGH-TECH MYSTERY

Selected material excerpted from *Opening the Ark of the Covenant* © 2007 by Frank Joseph and Laura Beaudoin, used with permission from New Page Books, an imprint of Red Wheel Weiser, LLC, Newburyport, Mass., www.redwheelweiser.com.

1. Jon Adams Jerde interview, KSTP-TV (Minneapolis, Minn.), telecast 9 November 2000.
2. Petrie, *Seventy Years in Archaeology.*
3. Dunn, *The Giza Power Plant.*
4. Davidovits, *Alchemy and the Pyramids.*
5. Petrie, *Seventy Years in Archaeology.*
6. Kenyon, *Forbidden Science.*
7. Fix, *Pyramid Odyssey.*
8. Andrews, "Hydraulics and the Ancients."
9. Kirkham, "Egyptian Pyramid Shock."
10. Corliss, *Ancient Infrastructure.*
11. Devereux, *Places of Power.*

## CHAPTER 21.
## PYRAMID POWER

Selected material excerpted from *Opening the Ark of the Covenant* © 2007 by Frank Joseph and Laura Beaudoin, used with permission from New Page Books, an imprint of Red Wheel Weiser, LLC, Newburyport, Mass., www.redwheelweiser.com.

1. Malkowski, *Before the Pharaohs.*

2. Farrell, *The Giza Death Star.*

3. Dunn, "The Pyramid Electric."

4. Guénon, *Insights into Islamic Esoterism and Taoism.*

5. Dunn, "The Pyramid Electric."

6. Hall and O'Hara, *Earth Facts.*

7. Braghine, *The Shadow of Atlantis.*

8. Csuzdi, *Breakthrough in Energy.*

9. Ellis, *Thoth, Architect of the Universe.*

10. *Les Seismes a Alenandrie et la Destruction du Phare,* cited in Radka, *The Electric Mirror on the Pharos Lighthouse and Other Ancient Lighting.*

11. Shboul, *Al-Mas'udi and His World.*

12. Farrell, *The Giza Death Star.*

13. Geogiou, "Ancient Egypt."

14. Geogiou, "Ancient Egypt."

# Bibliography

ACS News Service, "Ancient Technology for Metal Coatings 2,000 Years Ago Can't Be Matched Even Today." July 24, 2013. American Chemical Society website.

Adams, W. H. Davenport. *Lighthouses and Lightships. A Descriptive and Historical Account of Their Mode of Construction and Organization.* New York: Palala Press, 2015.

Aelian, Claudius. *On the Characteristics of Animals.* Vol. I, Book I. Cambridge, Mass.: Harvard University Press & William Heinemann, 1958.

Alberge, Dalya. "Lucky Strike? How Lightning Inspired Builders of Callanish." *The Guardian,* December 21, 2019.

Alter, Robert. *The Hebrew Bible: A Translation with Commentary.* New York: W. W. Norton & Company, 2018.

Andrews, Arlan. "Hydraulics and the Ancients." *Atlantis Rising.* Vol. 9, no. 58, July/August 2006.

Aristophanes. *The Clouds.* Cambridge, Mass.: Harvard University Press, 1998.

*Arthur C. Clarke's Mysterious World.* Yorkshire Television 1980; episode 3: "Ancient Wisdom" (Network DVD 7952792).

Austin AC Express. "The History of Home Heating." Austin AC Express "Tip of the Day" page on their website.

Bacon, Roger. *Opus Majus.* Mont.: Kessinger Publishing, LLC, 2002.

Baillie, Michael. In *Natural Catastrophes During Bronze Age Civilizations: Archaeological, Geological, Astronomical and Cultural Perspectives.* Edited by Trevor Palmer and Mark E. Bailey, Oxford: Archaeo Press, 1998.

Balchin, Jon. *100 Scientists Who Changed the World.* Brooklyn: Enchanted Lion Books, 2003.

Baldwin, Neil. "There's a 1,200-Year-Old Phone in the Smithsonian Collections." December 13, 2013. Smithsonian Magazine online.

Ball, Philip. "The Truth about Hannibal's Route across the Alps." April 3, 2016. The Guardian online.

Banchich, Thomas. *The History of Zonaras*. London: Routledge Classical Translations, 2011.

Barnett, E. (Edward) de Barry. *Explosives*. New York: D. Van Nostrand Co., 1919.

Beard, Mary. *The Parthenon*. Cambridge, Mass.: Harvard University Press, 2010.

Bennett, Jay. "The Ancient Romans' Concrete Recipe Could Help Us Beat Back Rising Seas." *Popular Mechanics,* July 5, 2017.

Bernardini, Federico, Claudio Tuniz, Alfredo Coppa, Lucia Mancini, Diego Dreossi, Diane Eichert, Gianluca Turco, Matteo Biasotto, Filippo Terrasi, Nicola De Cesare, Quan Hua, and Vladimir Levchenko. "Beeswax as Dental Filling on a Neolithic Human Tooth." *PLOS One,* September 19, 2012.

Bhishagratna, Kaviraj Kunjalal. *Susruta Samhita: Text in Sanskrit with English Translation*. Delhi, India: Sanskrit Series Office, 1998.

BooksFact, "Ancient Alarm Clock Invented by Plato (4th Century BCE)." BooksFact website. Accessed January 8, 2020.

Borisov, Konstantin. "Lighting Up Saqqara: An Electrifying Alternative Theory for the Oversized Serapeum Sarcophagi." Ancient Origins website. July 27, 2018.

Boyer, Carl Benjamin. *A History of Mathematics*. Hoboken, N.J.: John Wiley & Sons, 1991.

Braghine, Alexander. *The Shadow of Atlantis*. New York: Aquarian Press reprint of the 1940 original, 1980.

Breasted, James Henry. *The Edwin Smith Surgical Papyrus: Hieroglyphic Transliteration, Translation And Commentary*. Mont.: Kessinger Publishing, 2010.

Bricker, Victoria. *Supplement to the Handbook of Middle American Indians*. Knoxville: University of Texas Press, 2013.

Brinton, Daniel Garrison. *Ancient Nahuatl Poetry, Containing the Nahuatl Text of XXVII Ancient Mexican Poems*. London: Forgotten Books (Classic Reprint), 2012.

Carlson, John B. "Olmec Concave Iron-Ore Mirrors: The Aesthetics of a Lithic Technology and the Lord of the Mirror." In *The Olmec & Their Neighbors*. Washington, D.C.: Dumbarton Oaks Research Library and Collections and Trustees of Harvard University, 1981.

Cartwright, Mark. "Amber in Antiquity." Ancient History Encyclopedia website. September 11, 2017.

Castleden, Rodney. *Minoans: Life in Bronze Age Crete.* U.K.: Routledge, 1993.

Childress, David Hatcher. *Ancient Technology in Peru & Bolivia.* Kenyon, Ill.: Adventures Unlimited Press, 2012.

———. *Technology of the Gods: The Incredible Sciences of the Ancients.* Kenyon, Ill.: Adventures Unlimited Press, 2000.

Choniates, Niketas. *City of Byzantium.* Translated by Harry J. Magoulias. Detroit, Mich.: Wayne State University Press, 1984.

Cicero. *The Republic and The Laws.* Oxford: Oxford University Press, 2009.

Clough, G. Wayne. "The Earliest and Greatest Engineers Were the Incas." Smithsonian Magazine online. January 2014.

Corliss, William R. *Ancient Infrastructure: Remarkable Roads, Mines, Walls, Mounds, Stone Circles.* Glen Arm, Md.: Sourcebook Project, 2006.

———. *Ancient Man: A Handbook of Puzzling Artifacts.* Glen Arm, Md.: Sourcebook Project, 1977.

———. *Archaeological Anomalies: Small Artifacts: Bone, Stone, Metal Artifacts, Footprints, High Technology.* Glen Arm, Md.: Sourcebook Project, 2003.

*The Classic of Mountains and Seas.* Translated by Anne Birrell. New York: Penguin, 2014.

Crystal, Ellie. "Viking Sunstones." Crystalinks website. Accessed January 8, 2020.

Csuzdi, Michael. *Breakthrough in Energy.* Kingston, Ontario: Core Publishing, 1980.

Curious History, "Ancient Egyptian Air Conditioner over 4,000 Years Old." Curious History website. May 28, 2016.

Davidovits, Joseph. *Alchemy and the Pyramids.* Saint Quentin, France: Geopolymer Institute, 1983.

De Camp, L. Sprague. *The Ancient Engineers: An Astonishing Look Back at the Ancient Wonders of the World and Their Creators.* New York: Ballantine Books, 1995.

Devereux, Paul. *Places of Power: Secret Energies at Ancient Sites: A Guide to Observed or Measured Phenomena.* New York: Sterling Publishing, 1990.

Diehl, Richard. *The Olmecs: America's First Civilization.* London: Thames & Hudson, 2004.

Diocles. *On Burning Mirrors.* New York: Springer, 2012.

Donnelly, Ignatius. *Atlantis, the Antediluvian World.* New York: Harpers, 1882.

Dornenburg, Frank. "Lights of the Pharaos: The Translation." Pyramid Mysteries website.

Drachmann, Aage Gerhardt. *The Mechanical Technology of Greek Antiquity: A Study of the Literary Sources.* Madison: University of Wisconsin Press, 1963.

Drews, Robert. *The End of the Bronze Age: Changes in Warfare and the Catastrophe ca. 1200 B.C.* Princeton, N.J.: Princeton University Press, 1993.

Duckeck, Jochen. "Cave Dwellings of Cappadocia." Showcaves.com.

Dunn, Christopher. *The Giza Power Plant: Technologies of Ancient Egypt.* Rochester, Vt.: Bear & Co., 1998.

———. *Lost Technologies of Ancient Egypt: Advanced Engineering in the Temples of the Pharaohs.* Rochester, Vt.: Bear & Co., 2010.

———. "The Pyramid Electric." *Atlantis Rising* 15, no. 90. Nov/Dec, 2011.

Dunning, Brian. "The Mystery of Vitrified Forts." September 4, 2012. Skeptoid website.

Ellis, Ralph. *Thoth, Architect of the Universe.* U.K.: Edfu Publishing, 1998.

Fage, J. D., ed. *The Cambridge History of Africa: From c. 500 BC to AD 1050.* volume II s.v. "The Libyans." U.K.: Cambridge University Press, 1967.

Farrell, Joseph P. *The Giza Death Star.* Kenyon, Ill.: Adventures Unlimited Press, 2002.

Farnell, Lewis Richard. *The Cults of the Greek States.* Vol. 2. Boston: Adamant Media Corporation, 2002.

Fergusson, James. *History of Indian and Eastern Architecture.* Vol. I. London: Milward Press, 2007.

Fix, William. *Pyramid Odyssey.* New York: Smithmark Publishing, 1978.

Foerster, Brien. "Baalbek In Lebanon: Megaliths Of The Gods Full Lecture." November 11, 2018. YouTube.

———. *Lost Ancient Technology Of Peru And Bolivia.* Vol. 2. Independently published, 2018.

———. "Very Strange Ancient 'Out of Place Artifacts' in Museums in Mexico." Hidden Inca Tours website.

Franzen, Lars, and Thomas B. Larsson. In *Natural Catastrophes During Bronze Age Civilizations:Archaeological, Geological, Astronomical and Cultural Perspectives,* edited by Trevor Palmer and Mark E. Bailey, Oxford, England: Archaeo Press, 1998.

Frood, Arran. "Riddle of 'Baghdad's Batteries.'" BBC News. February 27, 2003.

Gaius, Plinius Secundus. *Natural History.* New York: Penguin Classics, 1991.

Geogiou, Aristos. "Ancient Egypt: Incredible Electromagnetic Discovery in

Great Pyramid of Giza's Hidden Chambers." July 31, 2018. *Newsweek* online.

Giuliani, Charles. *An Alternative View of the Distant Past*. New York: Lulu, 2008.

Godwin, Joscelyn. *Athanasius Kircher's Theatre of the World: His Life, Work, and the Search for Universal Knowledge*. Rochester, Vt.: Inner Traditions, 2015.

Gorvett, Zaria. "The Mystery of the Lost Roman Herb." September 7, 2017. BBC.

Guénon, René. *Insights into Islamic Esoterism and Taoism*. Hillsdale, NY: Sophia Perennis, 2004.

Habeck, Reinhard, and Peter Krassa. *Das Licht der Pharaonen. Hochtechnologie und elektrischer Strom im alten Ägypten*. Berlin: Herbig, 1996.

Hall, Cally, and Scarlett O'Hara. *Earth Facts*. London: Dorling Kindersley, 1995.

Harley, J. B. *The History of Cartography*. Vol. 2. Chicago: University of Chicago Press, 1992.

Harrison, Thomas. *The Great Empires of the Ancient World*. New York: J. Paul Getty Museum, 2009.

Hart, Kelly. "Science around 2,000 BC." Humanpast.net. Accessed January 8, 2020.

Haury, Emil W. *The Hohokam: Desert Farmers and Craftsmen, Excavations at Snaketown, 1964–1965*. Tuscon: University of Arizona Press, 2016.

Herodian. *History of the Empire*. Vol. 2, Books 5–8. Translated by C. R. Whittaker. Cambridge, Mass.: Loeb Classical Library No. 455; Harvard University Press, 1970.

Herodotus. *The Histories*. Translated by Tom Holland. New York: Penguin Classics, 2015.

*Hrafnkel's Saga and Other Icelandic Stories*. Translated by Hermann Palsson. New York: Penguin Classics, 1971.

Hicks, Jim. *The Empire Builders*. New York: Little Brown & Company, 1974.

Hippocrates. *Ancient Medicine*. Vol. I. Cambridge, Mass.: Harvard University Press, 1923.

Hodgkin, Thomas. *Letters of Cassiodorus*. Oxford: Oxford House, 1886.

Holloway, April. "From Jewel-Capped Teeth to Golden Bridges: 9,000 Years of Dentistry." March 8, 2014. Ancient Origins website.

Hosseini-Sharifabad, Mohammad, Razieh Kamali-Ardakani, and Ali Hosseini-Sharifabad. "Beneficial Effect of *Boswellia serrata* Gum Resin on Spatial Learning and the Dendritic Tree of *Dentate gyrus granule* Cells in Aged Rats." *Avicenna Journal of Phytomedicine* 6, no. 2 (March–April 2016): 189–97.

Howell, Jeremy. "Frankincense: Could It Be a Cure for Cancer?" Tuesday, February 9, 2010, BBC online.

Hsu, Charlotte. "Engineers Upgrade Ancient, Sun-Powered Tech to Purify Water with Near-Perfect Efficiency." May 3, 2018. University at Buffalo website.

Hyginus. *Fabulae*. Munich, Germany: Saur, 1993.

Ison, David. "War Elephants: From Ancient India to Vietnam." Warfare History Network website. Accessed January 8, 2020.

Italicus, Silius. *Punica*. Vol. 1, Books 1–8. Loeb Classical Library No. 277. Translated by J. D. Duff. Cambridge, Mass.: Harvard University Press, 1934.

James, Peter J., and Nick Thorpe. *Ancient Inventions*. New York: Ballantine Books, 1994.

Jigen, Tang. *Yinxu yu Shang wen hua: Yinxu ke xue fa jue 80 zhou nian ji nian wen ji*. Beijing: Ke xue chu ban she, 2011.

Jochmans, Joseph Robert. "Ancient Wings Over the Nile." *Atlantis Rising,* no. 74, March/April, 2009.

———. "The Baghdad Battery Mystery." *Time-Capsule Report*, vol. 4, issue 11. March/April 2008.

———. "Did Ancient Egypt Really Have Electricity?" May 22, 2015. Bewust Worden website.

———. "India's Magical Ancient Pillar." *Atlantis Rising,* 12, no. 75. May/June 2009.

———. In *Lost Powers: Reclaiming Our Inner Connection*. Mont.: Atlantis Rising, 2016.

Jones, Brian W. *The Emperor Titus*. New York: Palgrave Macmillan, 1984.

Joseph, Frank. *Opening the Ark of the Covenant*. Newburyport, Mass.: Red Wheel/Weiser, 2008.

Joyce, Jeremiah. *Scientific Dialogues*. London: Forgotten Books, 2018.

Julius, A. J. "They Came for the Cocaine." In *Discovering the Mysteries of Ancient America*. Edited by Frank Joseph. Wayne, N.J.: New Page Books, 2006.

Kellar, James H. "The C. L. Lewis Mound and the Stone Mound Problem." *Prehistory Regular Series* 3, no. 4. Indianapolis: Indiana Historical Society, June 1960.

Kenyon, J. Douglas. "Advanced Ancient Water Technology in Nazca, Peru." *Atlantis Rising* 16, no. 118. July/August 2016.

———. "Ancient Healing Proceducres." *Atlantis Rising* no. 125. September/October, 2017.

———. "Cancer among the Ancients." *Atlantis Rising* no. 102. July/August, 2009.

———. "Debunking the Myth of 'Primitive' Ancestors." *Atlantis Rising* 19, no. 126, November/December, 2017.

———. "Electro-Magnetic Therapy." *Atlantis Rising* no. 122. March/April, 2017.

———. *Forbidden Science: From Ancient Technologies to Free Energy.* Rochester, Vt.: Bear & Company, 2008.

———. "Mysterious Frankincense." *Atlantis Rising* no. 126. January/February, 2018.

———. "Sparks from the Gods." *Atlantis Rising* no. 126. November/December 2017.

Keyser, Paul T. "The Purpose of the Parthian Galvanic Cells: A First-Century A. D. Electric Battery Used for Analgesia." *Journal of Near Eastern Studies* 52, no. 2 (April 1993): 81–98.

Killgrove, Kristina. "Archaeologists Discover A New Profession In An Ancient Egyptian Woman's Teeth." *Forbes,* April 11, 2019.

Kirkham, Matthew. "Egypt Pyramid Shock: How 'Energy Source from Giza Pyramid Was Used for Incredible Reason." *Daily Express* online, December 4, 2018.

Koenig, Earl. "Did a Sunstone Guide the Vikings to America?" In *Unearthing Ancient America.* Edited by Frank Joseph. N.J.: New Page Books, 2009.

König, Wilhelm. *Im Verlorenen Paradies-Neun Jahre Irak.* Munich: Heise Verlag, 1939.

Kreisberg, Glenn (ed.). *Lost Knowledge of the Ancients: A Graham Hancock Reader.* Rochester, Vt.: Bear & Company, 2010.

Kusch, Heinrich, and Ingrid Kusch. *Tore zur Unterwelt: Das Geheimnis der unterirdischen Gänge aus uralter Zeit.* Vienna: Sammler Verlag, 2009.

Lewis, Mark Edward. *China's Cosmopolitan Empire: the Tang Dynasty,* Vol. 4. Cambridge, Mass.: Harvard University Press, 2009.

Ley, Willy. "An Electric Battery 2,000 Years Ago." *Astounding* magazine. March 1954.

Libanius. *Selected Orations.* Vol. I. Cambridge, Mass.: Harvard University Press, 1969.

Lloyd, Ellen. "Giant Solar Mirrors and Sophisticated Lenses: Advanced Ancient Technology Used by Our Ancestors." Ancient Pages website. June 17, 2017.

Local Switzerland, The, "Ancient Roman Fridge Discovered Near Basel Keeps

Beer Cool for Months." July 6, 2018. The Local Switzerland website.

Lockyer, J. Norman. *The Dawn of Astronomy: A Study of Temple Worship and Mythology of the Ancient Egyptians.* New York: Dover Books reprint, 2006.

Lucan. *Pharsalia.* Translated by Jane Wilson Joyce. Ithaca, N.Y.: Cornell University Press, 1993.

Lucian. *The Works of Lucian of Samosata.* Vol. 1. Translated by Henry Watson Fowler and Francis George Fowler. London: Forgotten Books, 2007.

Malkowski, Edward F. *Before the Pharaohs: Egypt's Mysterious Prehistory.* Rochester, Vt.: Bear & Company, 2005.

Manetho. *History of Egypt and Other Works.* Translated by W. G. Waddell. Cambridge, Mass.: Harvard University Press, 1940.

Maxwell, Gordon. *Proceedings of the Society of Antiquaries of Scotland*: Session 1966–1967: Vol. XCIX. Glasgow: Raleigh Publishing, 1968.

Mayor, Adrienne. *Greek Fire, Poison Arrows, and Scorpion Bombs: Biological and Chemical Warfare in the Ancient World.* New York: Harry N. Abrams, 2008.

———. *Gods and Robots: Myths, Machines, and Ancient Dreams of Technology.* Princeton, N.J.: Princeton University Press, 2018.

Mercatante, Anthony S. *Who's Who in Egyptian Mythology.* New York: Clarkson N. Potter, Inc., 1978.

McGrath, Matt. "Scientists Explain Ancient Rome's Long-Lasting Concrete." July 4, 2017. BBC online.

Michell, John. *The View Over Atlantis.* London: Abacus, 1975.

Miller, Mark. "Frankincense May Infuse Users with Mild Euphoria." Ancient Origins website. August 17, 2018.

Mingren, Wu. "Frankincense: How to Use Ancient Wonder Cure for Healing." October 15, 2011. Ancient Origins website.

Mohan, Praveen. "Hoysaleswara Temple, India—Built with Ancient Machining Technology?" August 9, 2017. YouTube.

———. "Iron Pillar that Never Rusts—Ancient Secret Revealed?" November 7, 2017. YouTube.

Morison, Samuel Eliot. *Samuel de Champlain: Father of New France.* New York: Little, Brown and Company, 1972.

Moussaieff, Mechoulam. "Boswellia Resin: from Religious Ceremonies to Medical Uses; A Review of In-Vitro, In-Vivo and Clinical Trials." *J. Pharm. Pharmacol.* 1 no. 10, October 6, 2009.

Needham, Joseph. *Science and Civilisation in China*. Vol. 1. Cambridge: Cambridge University Press, 1954.

Newman, Hugh. "The Titans of Baalbek." *Atlantis Rising* 13, no. 111. May/June 2015.

Noorbergen, Rene. *Secrets of the Lost Race*. New York: Barnes & Noble, 1978.

O'Kon, James A. *The Lost Secrets of Maya Technology*. Pompton Plains, N.J.: Weiser, 2012.

Parker, Michael. *Bronze Age Britain*. London: Pearson Batsford, 1993.

Partington, James Riddick. *A History of Greek Fire and Gunpowder*. Baltimore, Md.: Johns Hopkins University Press, 1999.

Patrick, Neil. "By 25 BC Ancient Romans Developed a Recipe for Concrete Specifically Used for Underwater Work Which Is Essentially the Same Formula Used Today." September 6, 2016. The Vintage News website.

PBS. "Secrets of the Viking Sword." Nova. October 10, 2012.

Perlin, James. "Burning Mirrors." *Whole Earth* no. 99. Winter 1999.

Petrie, William Matthew Flinders. *Seventy Years in Archaeology*. Cambridge: Cambridge University Press, 2013.

Pine, Red. *The Diamond Sutra*. Berkeley, Calif.: Counterpoint Press, 2002.

Plato. *Timaeus and Critias*. Translated by Desmond Lee. New York: Penguin Classics, 2008.

Pliny. *Natural History*. Cambridge, Mass.: Loeb Classical Library, 1916.

Plutarch. *Lives of the Noble Grecians and Romans*. Oxford: Benediction Classics, 2015.

Polybius. *The Histories*. Translated by Robin Waterfield. U.K.: Oxford University Press, 2010.

Pormann, Peter. *The Oriental Tradition of Paul of Aegina's Pragmateia*. The Netherlands: Brill, 2004.

Prakriti Mata. "Rama Setu (Adam's Bridge) Scientific Explanation with Proof." April 29, 2013. YouTube.

Preuss, Paul. "Roman Concrete Holds a Secret to Cutting Carbon Emissions." August 31, 2013. Solar Today Magazine online.

Price, Derek J. de Solla, "An Ancient Greek Computer." *Scientific American* 200, no. 6. June 1959.

Prophessor ACE, "Egyptian Light Bulb—Plausible." November 12, 2015. African Creation Energy website.

Qureshi, Asim. "Ten Ancient Robots that Were Built without Modern Technology." Wonderful Engineering website. October 5, 2017.

Radka, Larry Brian. *The Electric Mirror on the Pharos Lighthouse and Other Ancient Lighting.* Parkersburg, W.V.: The Einhorn Press, 2006.

———. "A Short History of Ancient Electricity." Bibliotecapleyades website.

Ralston, I. *Celtic Fortifications.* U.K.: Tempus, 2006.

Redfern, Nick. *Weapons of the Gods.* Newburyport, Mass.: Weiser, 2016.

Rediff News. "Adam's Bridge a Man-Made Structure." July 31, 2007. Rediff News online.

Richter, Barbara A. *The Theology of Hathor of Dendera: Aural and Visual Scribal Techniques in the Per-Wer Sanctuary.* Conn.: Lockwood Press, 2016, page 56.

"Riddle of Baghdad's Batteries." February 27, 2003. BBC online.

Schmidt, Wilhelm. *Herons von Alexandria Druckwerke und Automatentheater.* Madampatti, India: Isha Books, 2013.

Schwartz, Benjamin. "The Phaistos Disk." *Journal of Near Eastern Studies* 18, no. 2 (April 1959): 105–12.

Science Channel, The, "Could This Be The Legendary 'Magic Bridge' Connecting India And Sri Lanka?" January 9, 2018. YouTube.

Seneca, Lucius Annaeus. *Letters from a Stoic.* New York: Penguin Books, 1969.

Shaw, George, and Gregory Shaw. *Theurgy and the Soul: The Neoplatonism of Iamblichus.* University Park: Penn State Press, 1971.

Silva, Freddy. "Avebury's Mysterious Rectangle." Invisible Temple website. 2017.

Sneiderman, Phil. "Gilding Technique Inspired by Ancient Egyptians May Spark Better Fuel Cells for Tomorrow's Electric Cars." December 19, 2017. Johns Hopkins University Office of Communications Hub.

Snow, Karen. "BYU Professor Finds Evidence of Advanced Surgery in Ancient Mummy," BYU Magazine online. Accessed January 8, 2020.

Snyder, John. "Amber Waves of Woo." April 11, 2014. Science-Based Medicine website.

Solecki, Ralph S. *The Proto-Neolithic Cemetery in Shanidar Cave.* College Station, Tex.: Texas A&M University Press, 2004.

Squier, E. G., and Edwin Davis. *The American Antiquarian and Oriental Journal.* Vol. 13. Cambridge, Mass.: Ulan Press, 2012.

Steiger, Brad. *Worlds Before Our Own.* San Antonio, Tex.: Anomalist Books, 2015.

Stonehill, Paul. "From Alexandria to Yereven." *Fate Magazine* 56, no. 3. March 2003.

Strabo. *The Geography of Strabo.* Translated by Duane W. Roller. Cambridge: Cambridge University Press, 2014.

Stone, Elizabeth. "Archaeologists Revisit Iraq." *Science Friday*. National Public Radio. March 23, 2012.

Taylor, Joshua. "Carving of Modern Bicycle Found on Wall of 2,000-Year-Old Temple." Mirror. July 24, 2018.

Temple, Robert. "Advanced Lens-Crafting in Ancient Egypt." *New Dawn* 12, no. 24. July/August 2013.

———. *The Crystal Sun*. London: Century, 2000.

———. *The Genius of China: 3000 Years of Science, Discovery & Invention*. London: Andre Deutsch, 2013.

Tenn, William. "There Are Robots among Us." *Popular Electronics*. December 1958.

Theophrastus. *Characters*. Abingdon, U.K.: Routledge, 2018.

———. *Enquiry into Plants*. Translated by A. F. Hort, Cambridge, Mass.: Loeb Classical Library, 1926 [1916].

Tomas, Andrew. *We Are Not the First: Riddles of Ancient Science*. London: Souvenir Press, 1971.

Treadgold, Warren. *The Middle Byzantine Historians*. New York: Palgrave Macmillan, 2013.

Tzetzae, Ioannis. *Historiarum Variarum Chiliades*. London: Forgotten Books, 2017.

University of Basel. "A Wooden Toe: Swiss Egyptologists Study 3,000-Year-Old Prosthesis." EurekAlert website. June 20, 2017.

Vallery-Radot, René. *Louis Pasteur, His Life and Labours*. London: Andesite Press, 2015.

Vālmīki. *The Ramayana: Translated Into English Prose From the Original Sanskrit; Āranya Kāndam* (Classic Reprint). London: Forgotten Books, 2018.

Varro, Marcus Terentius. *Rerum Rusticarum Libri Tres*. Translated by Lloyd Storr-Best, 1912. Ithica, N.Y.: Cornell University Library, 2009.

von Klein, Carl H. *The Medical Features of the Papyrus Ebers*. London: Forgotten Books, 2018.

Watson, Julie. "Archaeologists Digging Up Pre-Columbian Sounds." *LA Times*. July 6, 2008.

Whittaker, Thomas. *Macrobius: Or Philosophy, Science and Letters in the Year 400*. Cambridge: Cambridge University Press, 2014.

Williams, Henry Smith. *The Historians' History of the World: A Comprehensive Narrative of the Rise and Development of Nations As Recorded By Over*

*Two Thousand of the Great Writers of All Ages.* Vol. 25. London: Forgotten Books, 2012.

Williams, James Howard. *Elephant Bill.* London: Rupert Hart-Davis, 1954.

Wilson, Colin. *From Atlantis to the Sphinx.* New York: Fromm International, 1997.

Wilson, Andrew. "Machines, Power and the Ancient Economy." *The Journal of Roman Studies* 92, pp. 1–32 (7f.), 2002.

Winchester, Simon. *The Man Who Loved China: The Fantastic Story of the Eccentric Scientist Who Unlocked the Mysteries of the Middle Kingdom.* San Francisco, Calif.: HarperCollins Publishers, 2008.

Winton, Walter. "Baghdad Batteries B.C." *Sumer.* Vol. 18, 1962.

Wogan, Tim. "Magnetic Nanoparticles Fry Tumors." July 1, 2011. *Science.*

Woodman, James. *Nazca: The Flight of Condor I.* London: John Murray, 1980.

Wright, Karen. "Empires in the Dust, Collapse of Bronze Age Cultures in 2000 B.C." *Discover Magazine* 12, no. 59. March, 1998.

Wright, W. S. "Silphium Rediscovered." *Celator* 15, no. 2, 2001.

Xenophon. *Anabasis.* Cambridge, Mass.: Harvard University Press, 1998.

Zukerman, Wendy. "Chinese Medicine Offers New Parkinson's Treatments." June 17, 2011. New Scientist website.

# Index

Numbers in *italics* preceded by *pl.* indicate color insert plate numbers.

*About Surgery,* 41
aerial drone, 35–36
African Creation Energy website, 184
Agathodaemon, 78–79
al-Idrisi, Muhammad, 171
Amatore, Christian, 39–40
amber
    about, 53–54
    Baltic, 54–55
    defined, 53
    in Egyptian medical practice, 56–57
    succinic acid, 54–55
Amun-Ra, 34
Andrews, Arlan, 255
antibiotics, 39
Antikythera Device, 90–91
aquifers, Peruvian, 247–48, *pl. 25*
Archimedes
    array of mirrors, 124–25
    death of, 135
    as military inventor, 121–28
    Siege of Syracuse and, 121–24, 135
    solar weapon, 124–25, 136
Archytas of Tarentum, 35–36
arc light, 168–69, 170
*Argonautica,* 13–15

Aristotle, 116, 127, 135
*Arthashastra,* 98
artificial intelligence, 7, 13, 15–17
artificial light, 172, 176–77
Arutunyan, Viktor, 79
Ashoka Pillar, 157–62. *See also* Delhi
    Iron Pillar
Athenian Parthenon doors, 186, 187
Atlanteans, 12–13, 105, 129
aurochs, 108, 109
Austrian tunnels, 233–34
automation
    Atlantean origins of, 12–13
    cam-operated, 8
    Chinese, 8–9
    Ctesibius, 8
    Dafeng Ma, 9
    Han Zhile, 8, 16
    Heron of Alexandria, 7, 11
    King Nabis, 9–10
    Lan Ling, 11, 12
    Laodamia, 10–11
    Ling Zhao, 11, 18
    man vs. machine and, 15–18
    Philon of Byzantium (Mechanicus),
        11–12, 18

robotic warriors, 13–15
Talos, 13–15, *pl. 3*
Yin Wenliang, 9
Avebury monument, 77–78
aviation, ancient, 28–36
Aztec death whistle, 3–4
Aztec obsidian mirror, 132–33, 134, *pl. 9*

Baalbek's Temple of Jupiter. *See also* engineering
about, 217
blocks, lifting and, 220
illustrated, 218
monoliths, 218–19
bacterial infection, treating, 39–40
badgir, 83, 84–85
Baghdad battery. *See also* electric power
battery interest, 152–53
discovery, 148–49
Eggebrecht experiments, 151–52
General Electric Company replica, 149–50
illustrated, 150
König's theory and, 148–49
*MythBusters* demonstration, 151
Pierczynski replica, 150
Baltic amber, 54–55
batteries
Baghdad, 148–53
galvanic, 153
mass-produced, 163
one-to-four-volt galvanic, 163
Bennett, Jay, 216
bicycle, Panchavarnaswamy Temple, 2
bioelectrical fields, 57
biological warfare, 98–105
biomagnetism, 58

birefringence, 69
Bi Sheng, 93–94
blood poisoning, 58
Boeotian flamethrower, 113–14
*Boswellia,* genus, 52, 53
Bourneville, 142–43
brain surgery, 46–48
bridges. *See also* engineering
Incan, 205–6, *pl. 20*
Mayan, 206–7
"old bridge," 206
Persian, 207–9
Rama's Bridge, 209–11
Broken Menhir of Er Grah, 188–89, 191
Bronze Age wheels, 141–42
Building C (Burnt Palace), 145
burning glasses, 125

cam-operated automation, 8
cancer cures, 5, 52, 58–59
Cappadocia. *See also* subterranean cities
about, 221
Derinkuyu, 224–25, 226, *pl. 22*
first discovery in, 222–23
Kaymakli, 224, 225
light source, 225
population, 225
reason for construction, 231
cement
carbon dioxide and, 214
marine, 216–17
Mayan, 212–13
modern, 215
Roman, 5, 214–16
with volcanic ash, 213
volcanic tufa, 215
Chalchiuhtlicue myth, 133

chambers, 258–61
Chan Chan, 86–87
chemical warfare, 97–98
Chi-Kung people, 26
Children of the Sun, 130
Childress, David Hatcher, 28
Chinese
  burning mirrors, 131
  chemical warfare, 98
  cybernetics, 8–9
  falarica, 107
  health care, 5, 67
  herbal remedies, 60–61
Clamond thermopile, 167–68
Claw, the, 122–23
cocaine, 51
"Cody War Kite," 21
communication, 86–87
computer, mechanical, 90–91
Condor I, 24–25, pl. 4
cooling and heating, 82–85
cordierite, 69–70
cosmetic surgery, 46
cosmic activity, 230–31
Craig Phadrig, 137–38, 139–40
Crookes, William, 182, 184
Crookes tubes, 182–84, pl. 15
Ctesibius, 8
Ctesibius clepsydra, 88–89
Cuzco's granite walls, 147
cybernetics, 7–9

Dafeng Ma, 9
death whistles, Aztec, 3–4
Delhi Iron Pillar
  about, 156
  breakthrough, 159
  "Chandra," 160–62
  composition, 157

  dating of, 160
  illustrated, 156, 161
  iron hydrogen phosphate hydrate
    and, 159–60
  misawite and, 159
  phosphorus and, 159, 160
  proximity to Qutub Minar, 161, 162
  riddle of, 158–59
  self-preservation, 157
  tests on, 157–58
Dendera
  about, 173
  academic consensus opinion about
    images, 179–80
  baboons and, 176–77
  djed column, 175–76, 178, 181
  frogs and, 176–77
  Hall 5 reliefs, 177–78
  monuments, 174
  panels, 176
  photograph of, pl. 14
  schematic discovery, 174–75
  Temple of Hathor, 175–76
  tubes, 178, 180
  Van de Graaff generator, 182–83
Denisova Cave artifacts, pl. 1
dentistry
  Egyptian, 50
  father of modern, 51
  Indiana skull, 49
  Mayan, 48–49
  Pakistan sites, 49–50
  Peruvian, 50
  Phoenician, 50
Derinkuyu, 224–25, 226, pl. 22
dog and fox, 23–24
Dunn, Christopher, 192–94, 235–36,
    240, 249, 262, 263–65, 266, 272
Dunning, Brian, 138

dust storm illusion, 99–100
Dvorsky, George, 65

earthquake-proof Andean stonework, 205
earthquakes
　Incan construction and, 203–5
　Menhir of Er Grah and, 189
　Pharos Lighthouse and, 171
　seismometer in detection of, 91–93
　Sigiriya (Lion Rock) and, 202
　subterranean cities and, 225
Eggebrecht, Arne, 151–52
Egyptians. *See also* Great Pyramid
　antibacterial eyeliner, 39–40, *pl. 2*
　artificial light, 172, 178–85
　cancer cures, 5, 52
　Crookes tube, 182–84, *pl. 15*
　dentistry, 50
　electrochemical exchange, 154–55
　electromagnetic therapies, 56–57, 58
　herbal remedies, 59–60, 61–63
　"Khufu's barge," 85
　machining, 192–94
　optics, 71–73
　pain killers, 51–53
　Pharos Lighthouse, 164–74
　prosthetic innovations, 64
　Sakkara Bird, 33–34
　tooling, 193–94
　tunnels, 234–41
electric power
　Baghdad battery, 148–53
　Delphi Iron Pillar, 156–62
　Egyptian statues, 154–55
electrochemical exchange, 154–55
electromagnetic fields, 169
electromagnetic therapies, 56–59

elephants
　Atlanteans and, 105
　Battle of Heraclea and, 102–3
　Battle of Ipsus and, 102
　first European sighting of, 102
　in fording rivers, 101–2
　Hannibal and, 103–4
　ivory hunting and, 104
　massed formations of, 101
　militarized, 100–105
　in transport convoys, 102
engineering
　Baalbek's Temple of Jupiter, 217–20
　bridges, 205–11
　cement, 212–17
Enoch, Jay, 71
environmental cataclysms, 230
etching, 95
eyeglasses, 71
eyeliner, antibacterial, 39–40, *pl. 2*
eyes, quartz crystal, 71–72

falarica, 106–7
Fauchard, Pierre, 51
Fink, Colin G., 154–55
firearms, 109–10
"Fish Mouth Levee" (Yuzui), 243–46
flamethrowers, 113–16
"flight of the shaman," 23
floating bridge, Persian, 5–6, 207–9
Foerster, Brien, 192
frankincense, 51–53
furnace technology, 95–96

Garn, Walter, 179–80, 181–82
Giza Plateau, 155, 241, 252–53, 255, 273, *pl. 29*
golden ratio, 253
Golden Triangle, 254–55

Grand Gallery (Great Pyramid),
261–62, 263–64, 269, *pl. 27*
Great Pyramid
about, 249–51
accuracy of build, 251
Al-Mamun tunnel, 259
condenser and capacitor, 266
crystal, 265
design ingenuity, 267
electrical components, 271–72
electromagnetic properties, 273
as electronic device, 266–67
as geotransducer, 262, 269,
271–72
golden section and, 253
Grand Gallery, 261–62, 263–64,
269, *pl. 27*
height and volume, 249
high-tech purpose, 256
interior of, 257–62
King's Chamber, 258–60, 263–65,
266, 270
limestone, 251–52
photographs of, 250, 254, *pl. 28*
piezoelectricity and, 256–57, 261,
265
Queen's Chamber, 260–61, 265,
266, 270
ramps and, 255–56
sarcophagus, 258–59
seismic safeguards, 269
size of, 250
Stone of Destiny, 266
stones, 251, 253
strategic placement of, 268–69
Greeks
Greek fire, 114–16
lathe, 191
optics, 73–75

pregnancy prevention, 43
pregnancy tests, 42–43
Greville Chester Great Toe, 64–65
Gull, William Withey, 37
gunpowder, 107
gynecology, 44

Hadfield, Abbott, 157
Halas, Naomi, 59
Han Zhile, 8, 16
Hattusa, 228–30
health care systems/facilities,
advanced, 66–67
Healy, Paul, 3
heating and cooling, 82–85
heat ray, 125, *pl. 8*
Heliopolis Syriaca, 217, 220
Hellespont bridge, 207–9
herbal remedies. *See also* therapeutic
achievements
Chinese, 60–61
Egyptian, 59–60, 61–63
kuzbarah, 59–60
medicinal plants, 60
silphium, 61–63
Heron of Alexandria, 7, 11, 90
Hicks, Jim, 228, 229–30
high-tech gadgets and gizmos, 88–93
Hittites, 227–30
Hohokam, 94–95
holy water dispenser, 90
honey, in healing, 38–39
Hoysaleswara Temple, 75–76, 194–97,
*pl. 16, pl. 17*
human flight
Archytas of Tarentum, 22
dog and fox, 23–24
"flight of the shaman," 23
historical records, 26–27

Nazca Lines and, 19–20, 22–23, 24
    twentieth century re-creation, 24–26

Incas
    earthquake-proof architecture, 5,
        203–5
    suspension bridges, 205–6, *pl. 20*
    vitrification, 147
incendiary mirrors, 126–28
incendiary missiles, 105–8
India
    Hoysaleswara Temple, 75–76
    optics, 75–77
    Rama's Bridge, 209–11, *pl. 21*
    rust-free iron pillar, 5, 156–62
    tooling, 194–97
infection, halting, 38–40
inoculation, ancient, 41–42
Inuit goggles, 4–5
iron, rust-defying, 5, 156–62
iron hydrogen phosphate hydrate, 159–60

Jackson, Dr. Richard T., 64
James, Nick, 66–67
Jochmans, Joseph Robert, 29–32, 33–34,
    53, 151, 157–58, 162, 163, 183
Joyce, Rev. J., 134

Kaymakli, 224, 225
Kenyon, Douglas, 47, 57, 58, 172
khawai-shuh, 8
"Khufu's barge," 85
Khujut Rabu, 148–52. *See also*
    Baghdad battery
Koenig, Earl, 69–70
König, Wilhelm, 148–49, 153
Kon-Tiki-Viracocha, 22
Ko-Shau-King, 26–27
Kunkel's cofferdam theory, 255

Kusch, Heinrich, 232–33
Kushner, David S., 46–47
kuzbarah, 59–60

Lakshminarayanan, Vasudevan, 71
Lamb, Robert, 13–14
Lan Ling, 11, 12
Laodamia, 10–11
lathe, 191
Layard lens, 73–74
Le Grand Menhir Brise, 188–89
Li Bing, 243–46
Lighthouse of Alexandria. *See* Pharos
    Lighthouse
lightning, attracting, 190
Ling Zhao, 11, 18
Lockyer, Sir J. Norman, 171–72

machining
    for colossal construction, 197–202
    Egyptians, 192–93
    Indian, 194–97
Machu Picchu, 203–5, *pl. 19*
Magnifying glasses, 74–75
manikin war bonnets, 99
man vs. machine, 15–18
Marcellus, Claudius, 121–22,
    123–24, 135
marine cement, 216–17
Martian surface map, 79
Mayans
    bridges, 206–7
    cement, 212–13
    dentistry, 48–49
mechanical analog computer, 90–91
mechanical birds, 8
medical instruments, 43–44
medicinal plants, 60
medicine, preventive, 37–44

mega structures
  Athenian Parthenon doors, 186, 187
  Broken Menhir of Er Grah, 188–89, 191
  machining and, 197–202
  Site XI, 189–90
  tooling and, 191–97
Messiha, Dowoud Khalil, 29–30, 31, 32, 33, 34
military surgery, 45–46
Mingren, Wu, 52, 53
mirrors
  array of, 124–25
  Aztec obsidian, 132–33, 134, *pl. 9*
  bronze, 131
  burning, 131
  incendiary, 126–28
  metallic, 126
  militarized speculum, 124
  Olmecs, 131–32
  silver, 130
  smoking, 133
  thermal, 130
  Xiuhtecuhtli, 133
  Ying-Yang, 131
Mitchell, John, 189
modern marvels
  communication, 86–87
  cooling and heating, 82–85
  high-tech gadgets and gizmos, 88–93
  printed word, 93–96
  toilets, 85–86
Mohar, Praveen, 2
movable-type printing, 93–94

Nabis, King, 9–10
naptha, 166
nautilus shells, 253–54

Nazca
  drawings, 22
  hot-air balloons, 24–26
  Lines, 19–20, 22–23, 24
  tapestries, 24
Newman, Hugh, 218–19, 220
Noorbergen, Rene, 108, 109–10
Norse sunstones, 69, 71

O'Kon, James A., 206–7, 212–13
olibanum, 51–53
Olmecs, 131–32
optical calcite, 70
optics
  about, 68–69
  Avebury monument and, 77–78
  cordierite and, 69–70
  Indian, 75–77
  Italian eyeglasses and, 71
  Layard lens and, 73–74
  magnifying glasses and, 74–75
  Norse sunstones and, 69, 71
  quartz crystal eyes and, 71–72
  telescopes and, 78–80
opus caementicium, 213, 217
Orichan, 20–21

Padi-Imen's burial tomb, 34
pain killers
  amber, 53–55
  cocaine, 51
  frankincense, 51–53
Pakistan dentistry sites, 49–50
Parker, Samuel, 134
Parthenon, 186, 187
Pathariecolorn, 246–47
Persians
  aqueducts, 246
  badgir, 83, 84–85

biological warfare, 99
chemical warfare, 98
floating bridge, 5–6, 207–9
one-to-four-volt galvanic batteries, 163
refrigerators, 6, 83
yakhchal, 83–85
Peruvians
dentistry, 49
infection treatment, 46–47
puquios, 247–48, *pl. 25*
Phaistos artifact, 94
Pharos Lighthouse
about, 164
arc light, 168–69, 170
artist's conception, *pl. 12*
carbon vapor in arc, 168
contorted theories, 173
damage, 171
dimensions, 164
flame magnitude, 166–67
fuel for beacon, 165–66
height advantage, 165
magnetism, 169
thermoelectric generator, 168
undersea discovery, *pl. 13*
Pharos of Abusir, 165
Philon of Byzantium (Mechanicus),
    11–12, 18
Phoenician dentistry, 50
Phrygians, 226–27
Pierczynski, John B., 150
piezoelectricity, 239–41, 256, 261, 265
*Pigeon,* self-propelled device, 35–36
Plato, 88, 105, 107, 129, 133
Pliny the Elder, 63, 75, 78, 117, 129,
    170
plumbate pottery, 146, *pl. 10*
polarization, 70
polishing, 196–97

polybolos
about, 110–11
ballista reconstruction, 112
re-creation, 111
Romans' improvement on, 112–13
use of, 111–12
Pons Subiacus, 213
Portland cement, 214
poterns, 227
pre-Aztec heat ray, 143–47
pregnancy tests and prevention,
    42–44
preventive medicine
about, 37–38
halting infection and, 38–41
inoculation and, 41–42
sex ed and, 42–44
printing, 93–96
Proclus, 128
prosthetic innovations, 64–66
proto-telephone, 87
puquios, 247–48, *pl. 25*
Pyramid of Khafre, 254
pyramids, 270–71, 273, *pl. 29. See
    also* Great Pyramid

Radka, Larry Brian, 151, 164, 165–67,
    170, 173
Ralston, Ian, 140, 141
Rama's Bridge, 209–11, *pl. 21*
*Ramayana,* 160, 195, 201, 209–10
Ramskov, Thorkild, 69, 70
refrigerators, Persian, 6, 83
Reigle, David, 12–13
rifling, 83–84
robotic warriors, 13–15
Romans
Baalbek's Temple of Jupiter, 217–20
cement, 5, 214–16

cool storage, 83

crane, 220

health care systems/facilities, 66–67

heating, 82

incendiary missiles, 105

optics and, 75

polybolos, 112–13

Portland, 214

sambucas, 122, 123

water management, 241–43

Sacsayhuamán, 147

*Sactya Grantham,* 41

Sakas, Ioannis G., 125–26

Sakkara Bird

about, 29

aerodynamic properties, 33

bird beak, 30

composition and appearance, 29–30

function in ancient Egypt, 33–34

as glider craft, 29–30

illustrated, *pl. 5*

as Item 33109, 29, 32

replicas, 32, 35

scientific testing of, 32–33

virtual reality flight simulator, 33

wind tunnel experiments, 33

wings and tail, 32

sambucas, 122, 123

sanitation, 86

Schneiderman, Phil, 155

seismometer, 91–93

Seleucia Pieria, 241–43

self-propelled cart, 7–8

Seneca, 42

sepsis, 58

Serapeum, 234–41, *pl. 24*

Serapeum boxes

about, 234–35

extra-weighted, illustrated, 239

fermentation, 238, 239

illustrated, 236, *pl. 25*

Khaemweset mummy, 238

piezoelectricity and, 239–41

precision of construction, 235–36

pressures inside, 238, 239

replication attempt, 236

*Shan Hai Jing,* 26

Siberian bracelet, 5

Siddiqui, M. Z., 52, 53

Siege of Syracuse, 121–24, 135

Siemens, William, 256–57

Sigiriya (Lion Rock)

about, 197

illustrated, 198, *pl. 18*

machining, 199

marble, 200

Mirror Wall, 198

reaching summit of, 197–98

site selection, 200–201

square shafts, 202

steps, 199, 202

as World Heritage Site, 201

silphium, 61–63

Site XI, 189–90

Skar, 45

sky compass, 69–70

"sky globe," 93

"Smoking Mirror," 133

snow goggles, Inuit, 4–5

solar power, 125, 126, 134–35

solar stills, 135–36

"Sorcerer's Apprentice, The," 17

"soul-hunting frog," 98

Spartan steel, 118

Spohrer, William, 25

Sri Lanka, 197–201, 209

stinging insects, 99

stone into glass
  Bourneville, 142–43
  Building C (Burnt Palace), 145
  Craig Phadrig and, 137–38,
    139–40
  Cuzco's granite walls, 147
  erosion and, 141
  German forts, 142
  Irish forts, 141–42
  pre-Aztec heat ray, 143–47
  Scottish forts, 138–41
  Tula vitrified pottery, 146
  vitrification, 138, 141
  vitrified forts and, 138–42
submarines, 116–17
"submersible chambers," 116
subterranean cities
  about, 221–22
  Cappadocia, 221–27
  configuration of, 223–24
  cruciform alcove, 226
  Derinkuyu, 224–25, 226, *pl. 22*
  first discovery of, 222–23
  floors, 223
  Hattusa, 228–30
  Hittites and, 227–30
  illustrated, *pl. 23*
  Kaymakli, 224, 225
  light source, 225
  Phrygians and, 226–27
  size of, 223–24
succinic acid, 54–55
sunlight. *See also* mirrors
  Children of the Sun and, 130
  focusing, onto cotton wool, 130
  solar power, 125, 126, 134–35
  solar stills, 135–36
  water sanitation, 136
sunstones, 69, 71, *pl. 6*

surgery
  brain, 46–48
  cosmetic, 46
  dentistry, 48–51
  military, manual of, 45–46
  pain killers and, 51–55
surgical instruments, 43–44
*Sushruta Samhita,* 46
suspension bridges, 205–7, *pl. 20*
Svebølle sword, 120–21
swords, 117–21
syringes, 41–42

"Tale of Say-Ausar, The" 16
Talos, 13–15, *pl. 3*
telescopes, 78–80
Temple, Robert, 70, 72, 74, 77, 124,
    125–26, 134–35, 183
Temple of Hathor. *See also* Dendera
  artificial light, 178, 181–82
  chamber walls, 175–76
  model, 181
  potential lightbulbs, 180
  tubes, 179
Temple of Jupiter. *See* Baalbek's
    Temple of Jupiter
Tesla, Nikola, 272
Theophrastus, 127
therapeutic achievements
  electromagnetic therapies, 56–59
  health care systems/facilities, 66–67
  herbal remedies, 59–63
  prosthetic innovations, 64–66
Thom, Alexander, 78
Thorpe, Peter, 66–67
tobermorite, 215
toilet paper, 86
toilets, 85–86
Toltecs, 144, 146

tooling, advanced, 191–97
trench mortar, *pl. 7*
trepanation, 46–47
trepanned skulls, 47–48
tufa, 222
Tula
    abandonment of, 144–45
    about, 143–44
    Atlantean columns, *pl. 11*
    bas relief, 144
    vitrified pottery, 146
tunnels
    Al-Mamun, 259
    Austrian, 233–34
    Egyptian, 234–41
    in Europe, 232
    Hittite, 227
    Vespasianus Titus Tunnel, 241–43
    Yuzui, 243–46
Turkey. *See* subterranean cities

Ulfberht sword, 118–19

Van de Graaff generator, 182–83
Varro, Marcus Terentius, 39
Vespasian, 241–43
Viking Age, 118
vitrification, 138, 139–40, 141,
    145–47
vitrified forts, 138–43

water clocks, 88–89
water management, 241–43, 247

weapons
    Archimedes and, 121–28
    array of mirrors, 124–25
    Boeotian flamethrower, 113–14
    the Claw, 122–23
    firearms, 109–10
    Greek fire, 114–16
    heat ray, 125, *pl. 8*
    naptha, 166
    pneumatics and, 114–15
    polybolos, 110–13
    sambuca, 122, 123
    submarines, 116–17
    swords, 117–19
weapons of mass destruction, 97–108
Wilson, Colin, 143
wine servant, 11
Winton, Walter, 150–51
Wogan, Tim, 58–59
Woodman, James, 19–21, 24–25
world map, 78–79

Xiuhtecuhtli, 132–33

yakhchal, 83–85
Yaxchilan suspension bridge, 206–7
Ying-Yang mirror, 131
Yin Wenliang, 9
Yuzui ("Fish Mouth Levee"), 243–46

Zhang Heng, 9, 92–93
zodiac, 94
Zukerman, Wendy, 60